100% Beef!! **BISON** ☆ **BURGER** Hunting your heart

Un déjeuner
sublime pour moins
00 yens,
isson incluse !

BISON BUR

V

★ ★ ★ ★ ★ ★ ★ ★ ★ ★ ★ ★ ★ ★ ★ ★ ★ ★ ★

QUI N'A JAMAIS RÊVÉ DE DEVENIR UN SUPER-HÉROS?

RATMAN

Sekihiko Inui
犬威赤彦

QUI N'A JAMAIS RÊVÉ DE DEVENIR UN SUPER-HÉROS?

RATMAN

05

SEKIHIKO INUI PRÉSENTE

OUAH !! T'AS VU LA QUEUE ??!

GRANDE OUVERTURE
B
BISON BURG

Elle est trop sexy !

ON FAIT QUOI, KANTA ?

BEN, MAINTENANT QU'ON EST LÀ, AUTANT FAIRE LA QUEUE...

PizzaFat
ピザファット

ÇA ? EUH... LE PROPRIO DE BISON BURGER ME L'A OFFERT QUAND IL EST PASSÉ DIRE BONJOUR.

UN BON GARS, D'AILLEURS...

IL A SUFFI D'UN MENU BURGER POUR T'ACHETER ?

HÉ, PAPA ! TU MANGES QUOI, LÀ ?

c'est bon !

MAZETTE... ÇA, C'EST DE LA FILE D'ATTENTE...

LES PIZZAS NE JOUENT PAS SUR LE MÊME TERRAIN QUE LE FAST-FOOD, MAIS ÇA NE ME DIT QUAND MÊME RIEN QUI VAILLE...

QUOI ? ILS FONT AUSSI DES LIVRAISONS ! PERSONNE NE ME L'AVAIT DIT, ÇA !

C'EST L'INVASION AMÉRICAINE !! FAUT DIRE QUE LEUR SPECTACLE EST BIEN RODÉ... ILS LIVRENT MÊME LEURS HAMBURGERS !

BON SANG... CES COW-BOYS M'ÉNERVENT DÉJÀ...

ALORS, ARRÊTE DE MANGER LEUR HAMBURGER, PAPA...

BEN, À CAUSE D'EUX, ON N'A EU QUE 5 COMMANDES AUJOUR- D'HUI.

QUOI !!?

7

TIENS, C'EST VRAI.

T'AS VU LÀ-BAS ? ON DIRAIT UNE SCÈNE.

TARATATA ♪♪♪♩♫

... WELCOME TO BISON BURGER!

LADIES AND GENTLE-MEN...

HA HA HA

LE SUPER-HÉROS OFFICIEL DE LA CHAÎNE DE FAST-FOOD AMÉRICAINE BISON BURGER
MISTER BIG HORN

EH BEN... ILS ONT SORTI LE GRAND JEU...

OUAH ! C'EST LEUR SUPER-HÉROS OFFICIEL !

HI GUYS ! MERCI À TOUS D'ÊTRE VENUS.

JE SUIS MISTER BIG HORN, JE SUIS UN VRAI SUPER-HÉROS ET J'ARRIVE TOUT DROIT DES U.S.A. !

JE ME SUIS MÊME ENREGISTRÉ COMME SUPER-HÉROS PUBLICITAIRE AUPRÈS DE L'ASSOCIATION DES SUPER-HÉROS.

JE SUIS VENU CAR ON M'A DIT QU'IL Y AVAIT UNE MODE DES SUPER-HÉROS AU JAPON.

CROYEZ-MOI, L'HISTOIRE DES SUPER-HÉROS ET DES FAST-FOODS DE CE PAYS VA CHANGER À TOUT JAMAIS !!!

VOILÀ LA VRAIE PUISSANCE ! LES VRAIS MUSCLES !

L'AVALUNCH DU PRINCE

GOOD!!

LEUR STRATÉGIE PUBLICITAIRE BASÉE SUR UN SUPER-HÉROS FORT ET PERCUTANT, DES UNIFORMES SOIGNEUSEMENT ÉTUDIÉS ET L'AUTHENTICITÉ A PORTÉ SES FRUITS.

IL N'A FALLU QUE QUELQUES JOURS À BISON BURGER POUR CONNAÎTRE UN GRAND SUCCÈS.

SI ÇA CONTINUE COMME ÇA, MES BÉNÉFICES VONT S'EFFON-DRER...

JE NE VOIS QU'UNE CHOSE : ILS ONT UN TRUC QUE NOUS N'AVONS PAS.

RÉUNION FAMILIALE CHEZ PIZZA FAT

JE NE VOIS QU'UNE CHOSE...

POUR CE QUI EST DU SUPER-HÉROS PUBLICITAIRE, MÊME SI LE NÔTRE N'EST PAS AU TOP, AU MOINS, ON EN A UN AUSSI...

PAS AU TOP !!?

BON, MÊME SI ÇA NE RIME À RIEN DE COMPARER UNE PIZZA ET UN HAMBURGER, NIVEAU GOÛT ET VOLUME, ON LES BAT À PLATE COUTURE.

... LES UNIFORMES SEXY DE LEURS SERVEUSES !!

ATTENDS... C'ÉTAIT QUOI, CE SOUPIR ? TU ME DÉGOÛTES !

BON, D'ACCORD... DE TOUTE FAÇON, TU ES ENCORE AU COLLÈGE. PAS QUESTION DE TE FAIRE SERVIR...

Euh...

PFFF.

JE VOIS... ET TU M'AS FAIT VENIR POUR LE GOÛTER...

... QUE JE SUIS EN TRAIN DE RÉFLÉCHIR À UN NOUVEAU MENU QU'ILS NE POURRONT JAMAIS SURPASSER !!

ET C'EST POUR ÇA...

ALLEZ, MANGE ET DONNE-MOI TON AVIS.

O.K...

C'EST ÇA !

CA DES PIZZAS ?

...

ON COMMENCE AVEC UNE PIZZA BOEUF ET OIGNONS, ON ENCHAÎNE AVEC UNE PIZZA AU TOFU ÉPICÉ FAÇON SHISEN, ET ON TERMINE AVEC UNE PIZZA AU CURRY INDIEN À PRÉPARER SOI-MÊME.

ET CE N'EST PAS TOUT !

VOICI LE COMBO LE PLUS CALORIQUE AU MONDE !! PLUS DE 6000 CALORIES, 5 ÉPAISSEURS, JE TE PRÉSENTE LA "GIGA FOOD" !!

QUI VOUDRAIT MANGER UN TRUC PAREIL ?

C'EST N'IMPORTE QUOI !!

HMMM... LE GOÛT, ÇA VA, MAIS POUR CE QUI EST DE L'IMPACT...

ALORS, SHÛTO ?

PARDON... J'AI PEUT-ÊTRE ÉTÉ UN PEU TROP FRANC.

NON, NON, ÇA VA... SI JE T'AI DEMANDÉ DE LES GOÛTER, C'EST JUSTEMENT PARCE QUE JE RESPECTE TON OPINION.

...

COMMENT DIRE...? À TROP VOULOIR FAIRE DANS L'ORIGINALITÉ, AU FINAL, AUCUNE DES PIZZAS N'EST VRAIMENT INTÉRESSANTE...

QUELLE CLASSE, FATMAN !!

JE NE SUIS QU'UN HUMBLE PIZZAÏOLO.

JE PEUX ENCAISSER LES CRITIQUES !!

MERCI, NOS CŒURS SONT À L'UNISSON !!

CLAP

JE TE COMPRENDS ! DONNE-MOI UN PEU DE TON ENTHOUSIASME !!

EUH...

GRAND FRÈRE ! C'EST TERRIBLE !!

C'EST UNE ATTAQUE DIRECTE CONTRE NOUS.

T'AS RIEN COMPRIS !

QUE VOIS-JE ? ILS VONT BIENTÔT LANCER UN SANDWICH GARNI DE FROMAGE, DE SALAMI ET DE SAUCE À PIZZA, ET ILS ONT APPELÉ ÇA, LE BISON PIZZA BURGER ?

ET ALORS ? ÇA NE M'A PAS L'AIR MAUVAIS DU TOUT...

IL EST LONG À LA DÉTENTE...

GRRRR !!

QUOI !!? ET POURQUOI ILS FONT ÇA ?

Hi Hi Hi...

JE NE VAIS PAS ME LAISSER FAIRE !! AU BOULOT, ON CONTINUE À BOSSER SUR LE NOUVEAU MENU !!

LA FERMETURE DE CE RESTAURANT N'EST QU'UNE QUESTION DE TEMPS.

TOUJOURS ÉCRASER SANS PITIÉ LA CONCURRENCE LOCALE... C'EST COMME ÇA QUE BISON BURGER S'EST RÉPANDU PARTOUT EN AMÉRIQUE.

QUE LES GAMINS JAPONAIS SONT LAIDS...

HÉ, MONSIEUR LA VACHE, TU ME LE DONNES MON BALLON ?

BURP !

OUI, MÊME MOI, JE NE PEUX PLUS VOIR UNE PIZZA EN PEINTURE.

O.K... STOP, JE NE PEUX PAS AVALER UNE MIETTE DE PLUS...

UN DESSERT !!?

BON, MOI, JE MANGERAIS BIEN UN DESSERT...

SÉRIEUX !!?

NON, JE TE REMERCIE...

TU VEUX ALLER MANGER UNE SOUPE DE NOUILLES, HISTOIRE DE CHANGER UN PEU D'AIR ?

PFFF... ÇA Y EST, TU AS L'AIR CALMÉ...

CLAC

QU'EST-CE QUE C'EST ?

HEIN ?

CELA DIT, MON PROBLÈME N'EST PAS RÉSOLU. JE N'AI RIEN TROUVÉ POUR CONTRER BISON BURGER.

UN TEST. J'AI FAIT CUIRE UNE PIZZA À L'ABRICOT.

TU VEUX BIEN LA GOÛTER ?

IL PARAÎT QUE PAPA A EU L'IDÉE DE CETTE PIZZA LE JOUR DE MA NAISSANCE.

AH ?

ABRICOT ? C'EST UNE DES SIGNIFICATIONS DE TON PRÉNOM, NON ?

OUI !!

GROUNCH

AAAH...

Enfin...

C'EST DÉLI-CIEUX !

C'EST VRAIMENT SUPER-BON, ANZU !

OUF...

OH... C'EST...!!

LE GOÛT LÉGER EXPLOSE EN BOUCHE, COMME LA SENSATION DIVINE DES PREMIERS PAS SUR LA PREMIÈRE NEIGE... ET IL Y A L'HARMONIE EXQUISE DE L'ACIDITÉ D'ABRICOTS ET DE L'ARÔME DES AMANDES... ENFIN BREF... EN GROS, C'EST TOUT ÇA...

TU NE T'EN SOUVIENS PAS ? QUAND ON ÉTAIT PETITS, PAPA NOUS LA FAISAIT SOUVENT.

MAIS CETTE PIZZA N'EST PAS SUR NOTRE MENU, N'EST-CE PAS ?

COMME LA PÂTE EST FINE, CE N'EST PAS LOURD DU TOUT.

HMM... ON N'A PAS L'HABITUDE DES PIZZAS AUX FRUITS, MAIS À BIEN Y RÉFLÉCHIR, C'EST UN PEU COMME UNE TARTE.

...

J'ADORAIS CETTE PIZZA MAIS QUAND PAPA A VU QUE ÇA ME FAISAIT GROSSIR, IL A DÉCRÉTÉ QU'IL ARRÊTAIT DE LA PRÉPARER.

ET IL A TENU PAROLE. DEPUIS CE JOUR-LÀ, IL NE L'A PLUS JAMAIS FAITE.

... ET VOUS POURRIEZ ATTIRER LA CLIENTÈLE FÉMININE EN LA VENDANT COMME DESSERT.

VOUS N'AVIEZ PAS DE PIZZA AUX FRUITS SUR VOTRE MENU...

C'EST ÇA !!

C'EST CE QU'IL VOUS FAUT !

C'EST JUSTEMENT POUR ÇA QUE PIZZA FAT A BESOIN DE RENOUVELER SON MENU !!

ON A ESSAYÉ D'ALLER DANS CE SENS SANS SUCCÈS, TU T'EN SOUVIENS ?

JE VEUX BIEN, MAIS IL Y A DES GENS POUR QUI UNE PIZZA DOIT DÉBORDER DE VIANDE ET DE FROMAGE...

OH, TU M'ÉNERVES !!!!

MAIS SI CE N'EST PAS CALORIQUE, CE N'EST PAS BON...

NON, NON !
IL FAUT
APLATIR LA
PÂTE AVEC
LE ROULEAU
AVANT DE
METTRE LA
SAUCE !

N'OUBLIE
PAS QU'IL
FAUT QUE
LA PÂTE SOIT
FINE SI TU
VEUX QUE
LA PIZZA
LAISSE UNE
IMPRESSION
DE LÉGÈRETÉ.

HMM !!
ÇA ME
PARAÎT
BIEN,
ON VA
LA FAIRE
CUIRE.

キャーリ
SLURP

ALORS
?

ET SI ON
AJOUTAIT
UN PEU DE
GLACE À LA
VANILLE, ÇA
SERAIT BON,
NON ?

OH,
BONNE IDÉE !!
J'AIME BIEN !

ON NE LES A PAS VUS POUSSER, CES DEUX-LÀ...

Hi Hi Hi... OUI, LES ENFANTS GRANDISSENT TOUT SEULS...

http://www.pizzafat.xx.jp

Apricot sweet
DOUCEUR D'ABRICOT

CETTE PIZZA ÉLABORÉE À QUATRE MAINS A ÉTÉ BAPTISÉE "DOUCEUR D'ABRICOT".

ELLE EST DEVENUE POPULAIRE GRÂCE AU BOUCHE-À-OREILLE, PARTICU-LIÈREMENT AUPRÈS DES JEUNES FEMMES ET DES EMPLOYÉES DE BUREAU.

UNE PIZZA D'UNE DÉLICIEUSE SIMPLICITÉ
NOUVEAUTÉ !!

女性情報誌
PenPen

女性情報誌
PenPen

* MAGAZINE FÉMININ PENPEN.

EN CE MOMENT, DEUX RESTAURANTS FONT FUREUR CHEZ LES JEUNES. IL Y A DE QUOI EN FAIRE UN DOSSIER SPÉCIAL.

QU'EN PENSEZ-VOUS, MADAME LA RÉDAC-TRICE EN CHEF ?

IL S'AGIT DE BISON BURGER ET DE PIZZA FAT. ON POURRAIT CRITIQUER LES PLATS LES PLUS POPULAIRES.

POUR-QUOI PAS...?

FAISONS GOÛTER TOUT ÇA À MUCHULIN, LE GOURMET SUPER-HÉROS 3 ÉTOILES.

MAIS CE N'EST PAS SUFFISANT.

Les pâtes fraîches sautées de Fujinomiya, c'est 3 étoiles !

MUCHULIN, LE GOURMET SUPER-HÉROS ? VRAIMENT ?

AH...

SI ON SE CONTENTE DE FAIRE ÇA, CE QU'ILS NOUS LIVRERONT SERA FORCÉMENT BON.

DONC... ON PASSE UNE COMMANDE AUX DEUX ET ON LEUR DEMANDE DE NOUS LIVRER ICI ?

ET SI NOUS ORGANISIONS AUSSI UN MATCH EN PRENANT EN COMPTE D'AUTRES ÉLÉMENTS, TELS QUE LA VITESSE DE LIVRAISON OU LE SERVICE ?

...ET MAR- QUE LE COUP D'ENVOI DE CETTE TER- RIBLE BATAILLE !!!

C'EST AINSI QUE TEL UN GONG, LE TÉLÉ- PHONE A RETEN- TI...

ANZU ! C'EST PAS LE MOMENT DE RÊVASSER !!!

IL ME FAUT UNE DOUCEUR D'ABRICOT !! C'EST UNE URGENCE ABSOLUE !!

C'EST NOTRE CHANCE ! AVEC ÇA, ON VA REPRENDRE L'AVANTAGE SUR BISON BURGER !

QUOI ! UNE COMMANDE DE LA RÉDACTRICE EN CHEF DE PENPEN EN PERSONNE ! JE PARIE QUE C'EST POUR FAIRE UN ARTICLE SUR NOTRE PIZZA À L'ABRICOT !

EH BEN... C'EST SUPER, ÇA...

QUOI ? SÉRIEUX ?

PizzaFat
ピザファット

QU'EST-CE QUE TU RACONTES ?!!

Pizzaf
ピザファット

O.K. !!! C'EST PARTI POUR UNE LIVRAISON EN GRANDE POMPE !

CATACLOP CATACLOP

SUR UN TAU-REAU ?

EUH...

NON, NE ME DITES PAS QU'IL A AUSSI EU UNE COMMANDE DE PENPEN ?!

QUOI !!

JE L'AI FABRIQUÉE EN ME DISANT QU'UN JOUR FATMAN EN AURAIT BESOIN POUR SAUVER PIZZA FAT D'UNE SITUATION DÉSESPÉRÉE.

JE TE PRÉSENTE LA FATMOBILE !!!

PAPA, C'EST...

Et ne le dis pas non plus...

- à D.C. ou à Warner.

NE LE RÉPÈTE PAS À TA MÈRE.

T'as sûr ? On a le droit ?

LA FAT-MOBILE...

ALLEZ, EN AVANT, FATMAN !

JE ME CHARGE D'ARRONDIR LES ANGLES DERRIÈRE TOI AVEC L'ASSOCIATION DES SUPER-HÉROS ET LES AUTRES.

VUAP

QUOI!!?

BEN, COMME D'HABITUDE IL LIVRE EN SCOOTER, IL SAIT À PEINE CONDUIRE UNE VOITURE...

J'ESPÈRE QU'IL NE VA RIEN LUI ARRIVER...

EN PLUS, IL VA DEVOIR CONDUIRE COMME UN FOU...

VIENS,
ON VA LE
SUIVRE.

SHÛTO ?

NE ME
DIS PAS
QUE...?

IL EST LÀ !!

PizzaFat

C'EST PAS VRAI ! LE MAGAZINE LEUR A AUSSI COMMANDÉ QUELQUE CHOSE ?

PizzaFat

PIZZA FAT !!?

UTILISER UNE TECHNIQUE MORTELLE EN PLEINE RUE... C'EST UN MALADE, CE TYPE...

TOUT VA BIEN, LA PIZZA EST INTACTE.

COMMENT TU AS FAIT POUR ENCAISSER BULL HORN SPIRAL ET T'EN SORTIR SANS UNE ÉGRATI-GNURE ?

HÉ, FAT-BOY !

LA SOLIDITÉ, C'EST LE POINT FORT D'UN VRAI SUPER-HÉROS !

FATMAN, ÇA VA ?

GRAND FRÈRE !

RATMAN ET ANZU ?

DÉ-SO-LÉ...

NE T'EXCUSE PAS. TU N'ES PAS BLESSÉ, C'EST LE PRINCIPAL.

LA PIZZA ET MOI, ÇA VA, ON EST EN UN SEUL MORCEAU. MAIS LA VOITURE A ÉTÉ PULVÉRISÉE...

ON PEUT OUBLIER LA LIVRAISON.

SHÛT...

RATMAN ?

TIENS, ANZU.

PRENDS-EN SOIN.

TANT QU'IL Y AURA QUELQU'UN POUR TENIR CETTE PIZZA, IL FAUDRA LA LIVRER !

HE, RATMAN ! ATTENDS UN PEU !

LA LIVRAI-SON DE BISON BURGER ?

TU ES SÛR ?

IL Y A AUSSI ÇA.

TU VEUX BIEN LE LIVRER ?

FATBOY...

...

ÇA NE SERAIT PAS JUSTE.

JE NE VEUX PAS GAGNER FAUTE D'ADVERSAIRE.

BIENVENUE CHEZ PENPEN. QUE PUIS-JE POUR VOUS ?

DING DONG

TU N'AS PAS D'INQUIÉTUDE À AVOIR. C'EST IMPOSSIBLE DE NE PAS AIMER CETTE PIZZA !

ET PUIS, SOUVIENS-TOI...

... QUE TON PÈRE A INVENTÉ CETTE RECETTE POUR TE FAIRE SOURIRE.

BONJOUR, JE VIENS DE LA PART DE PIZZA FAT ET DE BISON BURGER.

JE VOUS AI APPORTÉ...

... DES PLATS DÉLICIEUX ET LE SOURIRE !!

À SUIVRE DANS LE PROCHAIN ÉPISODE...

TROUBLE ★ SISTERS

c'est
pour une
livraison.

ANA, YUNA, IL EST L'HEURE DE RENTRER !

D'ACCORD !

J'ALLAIS PARTIR SANS PANCHÛ.

Attends !!

AH !!

VOUS N'AVEZ RIEN OUBLIÉ D'AUTRE ?

NON !!

ÉPISODE 21

PANCHÛ !

CLIC !!

SACRE-
BLEU...
JE VAIS
M'Y
CASSER
LES
DENTS !

UNE JOURNÉE ★ AVEC ★ PANCHÛ

M.H.K

UNE
JOURNÉE
AVEC
PANCHÛ !

ÇA
COMMENCE !

HEIN ?!!

TAP TAP

YUNA, PANCHÛ VIENT DE COMMENCER !

NON, ATTENDEZ-MOI !

C'EST PARTI POUR LA CHANSON DU DESSIN DE PANCHÛ ! LES AMIS, DESSINEZ AVEC NOUS !

DESSINONS TOUS ENSEMBLE !

C'EST PAS PARFAIT DU TOUT !!!

ça sera parfait !

DELIX BRIOCHES SUCRÉES FOURRÉES S'IL VOUS PLAÎT ! AVEC UNE GROSSE BRIOCHE À LA VIANDE, ÇA SERA PARFAIT !

Tu veux te battre ?

Ça te pose un problème ?

JE TROUVE ÇA COMPLÈTEMENT NUL !

EN PLUS, LES SUPER-HÉROS, C'EST DEVENU FRANCHEMENT RINGARD !

JE T'INTERDIS DE TE MOQUER D'ARSARMAN ! IL EST DIFFÉRENT DES SUPER-HÉROS À EFFETS SPÉCIAUX HABITUELS, C'EST UNE RELECTURE ORIGINALE DU MYTHE DES 12 CHEVALIERS DE LA TABLE RONDE ET...

OH, TU NOUS SOÛLES, PAUVRE OTAKU DES SUPER-HÉROS !

TAP

HA HA HA !

JE TROUVE ÇA COMPLÈTEMENT NUL !

QUOI ? RÉPÈTE UN PEU POUR VOIR !

TAP

TU N'AS PAS LE DROIT DE RENTRER DANS MA CHAMBRE SANS PERMISSION !

HE !

OÙ TU VAS ?

BONG !!!

OH ?!!

CRASH BLANG SCHLONK

AÏE...

QU'EST-CE QU'IL FAIT LÀ, CE CARTON...?

ELLE EST INTROUVABLE !

TU RÉALISES CE QUE TU AS FAIT ?

NON !!!

LE BRAS DE MA FIGURINE !!!!

ANA...

DONC TU T'ES DISPUTÉE AVEC UNE DE TES SŒURS...

VOILÀ, TU SAIS TOUT.

COMME JE SUIS UNE FILLE, JE COMPRENDS POURQUOI TA SŒUR A BESOIN QU'ON S'INQUIÈTE POUR ELLE, MAIS JE COMPRENDS AUSSI TES SENTIMENTS DE FAN DE SUPER-HÉROS...

POUR ÊTRE HONNÊTE, JE COMPRENDS VOS DEUX POINTS DE VUE.

JE VOIS...

JE CROIS QU'UNE PETITE FILLE NE PEUT PAS COMPRENDRE CE QU'UN SUPER-HÉROS A DE REMARQUABLE.

CELA DIT, ÇA M'A FAIT UN CHOC D'APPRENDRE QUE TA FIGURINE ÉDITION LIMITÉE DE MISTER BLAST ÉTAIT CASSÉE.

C'EST AFFREUX, N'EST-CE PAS !

En plus, elle n'est plus disponible.

AH ?

MOI, JE NE LA COMPRENDS PAS. J'ADORE LES SUPER-HÉROS DEPUIS QUE JE SUIS TOUTE PETITE.

IL FAUDRAIT PEUT-ÊTRE QU'UN SUPER-HÉROS LA SAUVE D'UN ENLÈVEMENT OU D'UNE AGRESSION POUR QU'ELLE COMPRENNE LEUR INTÉRÊT...

STOP ! QU'EST-CE QUE TU DIS ? TU ME FAIS PEUR !

MAIS TU SAIS, MOI, J'AURAIS BIEN AIMÉ AVOIR UNE PETITE SŒUR. JE T'ENVIE UN PEU.

OUI, C'EST VRAI QU'ELLE A DE LA RESSOURCE, CETTE PETITE.

DE TOUTE FAÇON, C'EST UNE TELLE TÊTE DE MULE QU'ELLE FERAIT PLEURER SES RAVISSEURS...

DU CALME, JE RIGOLE.

PAR CHANCE, APPAREMMENT, CE NE SONT ENCORE QUE DES SOUS-FIFRES.

CA NE CHANGE PAS GRAND-CHOSE. LES DROGUES, C'EST TRÈS DANGEREUX.

AU FAIT, TU ES AU COURANT ?

IL PARAIT QUE DES TRAFIQUANTS DE DROGUE SÉVISSENT DANS LES ENVIRONS.

OUI, MAIS DU COUP, NE PARLE PAS D'ENLÈVEMENT NI D'AGRESSION À LA LÉGÈRE, D'ACCORD ?

VA VITE TE RÉCONCILIER AVEC TA PETITE SŒUR.

HMM... O.K.

AH ! LA VOILÀ, ELLE EST SORTIE, BOSS !

ET ELLE A LA PELUCHE AVEC ELLE !

REGARDEZ, LA VOICI.

URAP

OUI... PAR-DON.

PARFAIT, C'EST LA BONNE, PAS DE DOUTE.

BOSS ! J'AI RÉCUPÉRÉ LA PELUCHE !

O.K, C'EST BIEN... MAIS NE LE CRIE PAS SI FORT, PAUVRE CRÉTIN !

C'EST POUR ÇA !

ELLE A DÛ PRENDRE LA PELUCHE AVEC LA MARCHANDISE EN PENSANT QUE C'ÉTAIT LA SIENNE.

ELLE A LA MÊME PELUCHE QUE CELLE QUE TU AS RAMENÉE...

AH OUAIS, SÉRIEUX ?

OUI... MON NEVEU EN EST FAN. DU COUP, JE LUI EN AI OFFERT UNE.

C'EST NORMAL. C'EST UNE PELUCHE DE PANCHÛ, TOUS LES MÔMES L'ADORENT.

C'EST PAS VRAI !!!!

BEN OUI... À MON AVIS, TOUS LES GAMINS DE SON ÂGE CONNAISSENT CE PERSONNAGE.

HEIN ? COMMENT TU SAIS ÇA ? CETTE SOURIS, LÀ ?

ARGH !!!

IL FALLAIT LE DIRE PLUS TÔT !

VOUS AVIEZ L'AIR TELLEMENT CERTAIN D'AVOIR TROUVÉ L'IDÉE DU SIÈCLE QUE JE N'AI PAS VOULU VOUS REFROIDIR.

AH OUI... BIEN SÛR !!

BON, C'EST PAS TOUT ÇA, ON LES SUIT ?

C'EST PAS UN PEU DANGEREUX POUR DES PETITES FILLES D'ALLER DANS UN GRAND MAGASIN TOUTES SEULES ?

C'EST PAS À NOUS DE NOUS INQUIÉTER POUR ÇA...

MERCI BEAUCOUP !

AH... ON VA LE RECOL- LER...

ALLEZ, JE VOUS FAIS UNE FLEUR. JE VOUS DONNE ÇA.

ÇA PERMET- TRA AU MOINS DE RECOLLER LE BRAS.

SPLAT

* AROSO ALPHA.

HMM ?

5 ▾ ▴ 6

OUI.

ÇA N'EST PAS LA MÊME CHOSE, MAIS C'EST QUAND MÊME GENTIL DE LA PART DU VENDEUR.

OUF...

ANA AUSSI VEUT SE RÉCONCILIER AVEC SHÛTO, ÇA ME FAIT PLAISIR.

BLINK

OH!

PANCHÛ !

VOUS ÊTES SÛR QU'ELLES VONT TOMBER DANS LE PANNEAU ?

MAIS OUI, CONTINUE.

JE RÊVE ! ELLES FONCENT TÊTE BAISSÉE !!!

PANCHÛ, JE T'ADORE !

IL EST TROP MIGNON !

BADA BADA BADAM

VLAM !

HEIN ?!!

JE NE ME SUIS PAS VRAIMENT CONDUIT EN ADULTE. ET ELLE, CE N'EST ENCORE QU'UNE ENFANT...

NOUS RÉCONCILIER...

TIENS, MAMAN ?

JE VAIS M'EXCUSER EN RENTRANT.

ALLÔ, SHÛTO ?!! C'EST UNE CATASTROPHE !!

JE ME SUIS ABSENTÉE LE TEMPS DE FAIRE UNE COURSE EN LAISSANT ANA ET YUNA À LA MAISON...

... ET ELLES ONT DISPARU !!

EN PLUS, COMME ELLES VENAIENT DE RENTRER DE L'ÉCOLE, ELLES ONT LAISSÉ LEURS PORTABLES AVEC LEURS AFFAIRES...

TU NE SAIS PAS OÙ ELLES SONT ALLÉES ?

BIP.

JE NE SAIS PAS OÙ ELLES SONT ALLÉES, MAIS J'AI MA PETITE IDÉE SUR CE QU'ELLES ONT VOULU FAIRE.

OÙ ELLES SONT ALLÉES ?!!

NON, MAIS JE VAIS ALLER VÉRIFIER LEURS ENDROITS HABITUELS.

...UN MAUVAIS PRESSENTI-MENT...

J'AI COMME...

VRAP

OÙ SOMMES-NOUS ?

J'AI PEUR.

ÇA VA ALLER, YUNA. N'AIE PAS PEUR.

J'AI OUBLIÉ MON PORTABLE À LA MAISON !

C'EST MALIN...

JE N'AI QUE LA FIGURINE DE SUPER-HÉROS, CASSÉE, ET LA COLLE...

UN SUPER-HÉROS, C'EST ÇA QU'IL NOUS FAUDRAIT...

 ... C'EST À CET INSTANT QUE TU DEVIENDRAS UN SUPER-HÉROS.

 UN JOUR, IL FAUDRA QUE TU PROTÈGES QUELQU'UN...

MAINTENANT JE COMMENCE À COMPRENDRE...

... CE QU'IL VOULAIT DIRE.

 ALI SECOURS...

... GRAND FRÈRE !!

 ALI SE-COURS ...

PAPA, MAMAN...

BON, MESDEMOI-SELLES, VOUS VOULEZ BIEN ME DONNER VOTRE PELUCHE ?

PARDON ?

VOUS VOULEZ PANCHÛ ?

AÏE !

VLAN

OUAIS, C'EST ÇA, PANCHÛ...

BIEN SÛR, ON NE PEUT PAS VOUS EN VOULOIR POUR ÇA.

MES PETITES... NOUS AVIONS LAISSÉ LA MÊME PELUCHE QUE LA VÔTRE DANS LE PARC ET VOUS L'AVEZ EMPORTÉE PAR ERREUR.

EN REVANCHE, JE SUIS DÉSOLÉ...

BOSS, C'EST LA BONNE, C'EST CONFIRMÉ PAR LE GPS.

PAR-FAIT !!

...JE N'AIME PAS LES TÉMOINS GÊNANTS.

BOSS, ARRÊTEZ. VOUS N'ÊTES PAS SÉRIEUX ?

votre main tremble...

LA FERME ! TU CROIS QUE ÇA ME PLAÎT ?

HEIN
?!!

JE
SUIS
RAT-
MAN.

ENCHANTÉ !!

BLAM
!!!

VROUGH

TECHNIQUE ULTIME...

SI ELLES AVAIENT EU LA MOINDRE ÉGRATIGNURE...

... JE NE SAIS PAS SI J'AURAIS PU ME RETENIR...

JE...

JE SUIS DÉSOLÉ...

GLOUPS... !!

AH...

L'ARRESTATION DE CES DEUX CRIMINELS A PERMIS DE METTRE SOUS LES VERROUS UN GRAND NOMBRE DE TRAFIQUANTS DE CE RÉSEAU. MAIS LE CHEF DE L'ORGANISATION COURT TOUJOURS.

J'AI LAISSÉ LA POLICE S'OCCUPER DE L'AFFAIRE D'ENLÈVEMENT. J'AI RACCOMPAGNÉ MES PETITES SŒURS EN RATMAN, ET JE SUIS ENSUITE RENTRÉ À LA MAISON SOUS MA FORME NORMALE COMME SI DE RIEN N'ÉTAIT.

VOUS N'AVEZ RIEN ?

ARRÊTE. VOUS ÊTES REVENUES SAINES ET SAUVES, C'EST TOUT CE QUI M'IMPORTE.

PAR-DON DE T'AVOIR INQUIÉ-TÉE...

ANA... YUNA...

ANA, JE SUIS
DÉSOLÉ POUR
HIER. ÇA NE SERAIT
PAS ARRIVÉ SI
JE NE M'ÉTAIS
PAS FÂCHÉ.

NON,
TOUT VA
BIEN.

ET ELIH...
PARDON
DE M'ÊTRE
MOQUÉE
DES SUPER-
HÉROS...

NON, NON,
C'EST MOI,
PARDON
D'AVOIR
CASSÉ TON
JOUET...

!! GLOUPS

HEIN ?
ELIH,
NON...
ÇA NE ME
DIT RIEN...

TU
CONNAIS
RATMAN ?

AH !!
TU LUI AS
DIT QU'ON
AVAIT ÉTÉ
SAUVÉES PAR
UN SUPER-
HÉROS ?

C'EST
VRAI,
ÇA !!

AH BON...
ÇA M'ÉTONNE
DE LA PART
D'UN OTAKU
DES SUPER-
HÉROS
COMME TOI.

À TA PLACE, JE ME RENSEIGNERAIS SUR LUI !! JE CROIS QU'IL VA VITE DEVENIR TRÈS CÉLÈBRE !!

VIVE RATMAN !!!

TIENS, LE BRAS DE MISTER BLAST A ÉTÉ RECOLLÉ.

L'ANGLE EST UN PEU BIZAR-RE...

Hi Hi...

J'AI RECOLLÉ LE BRAS POUR ME FAIRE PARDONNER !! YUNA

À SUIVRE DANS LE PROCHAIN ÉPISODE...

ROIKO EST DEVENUE FOLLE !

La chanson du dessin de Panchû

①
Deux brioches sucrées fourrées s'il vous plaît ♪
(Chante avec entrain.)

②
Avec une grosse brioche à la viande, ça sera parfait ♪
(Les brioches de chez Horai sont un régal ♪)

③
Ensuite un pain à hot-dog coupé en deux !
(L'abus d'aliments gras est mauvais pour la santé ♪)

④
On ajoute deux baguettes pour allonger un peu ?
(Pensez à prendre vos propres baguettes pour pique-niquer.)

⑤
Le pantalon Uniqlo, par lot de 3, pour économiser ! ♪
(Ce sont mes préférés.)

⑥
Quelqu'un a dit que les pieds, c'était pour décorer !
(Pour quelqu'un de bien, ça, c'est incompréhensible.)

⑦
Deux petits coups de pistolet ! ♪
(On se livre à la police ?)

⑧
Le sigle de McDonald's inversé ? ?
(C'est juste un W.)

⑨
Oh ! Et hop, voilà Panchû ! ☆
(Ça devrait vous prendre 40 secondes environ.)

J'AI FINI !!

ENFIN NON, ON NE PEUT PAS VRAIMENT QUALIFIER ÇA DE COMBAT. ELLE ATTAQUAIT, ET MOI, JE M'ENFUYAIS.

JE ME SUIS BATTU CONTRE UNE FEMME.

ET QUANT AU FAIT QU'ELLE SOIT UNE FEMME, J'AI ENCORE COMME UN DOUTE...

ÉPISODE 22

DATE INDÉTER-MINÉE.

QUELQUES ÉCLAIRCIES À PRÉVOIR, PLUIE DE MISSILES INTERMITTENTE.

RATMAN : ÉPISODE 22
ROIKO EST DEVENUE FOLLE !

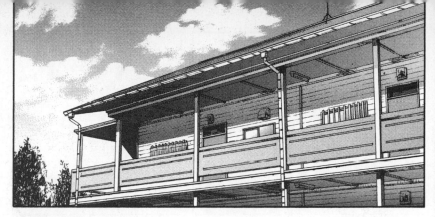

ANDÔ

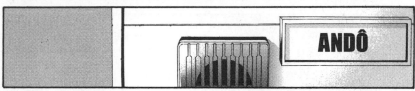

タタ タタ TAP タタ TAP TAP

Ah !

ZUT !!

J'AI OUBLIÉ D'ÉTEINDRE LE FEU SOUS LA CASSEROLE !

IL FAIT BEAU AUJOURD'HUI, PROFESSEUR.

OUF... VOILÀ, C'EST ÉTEINT.

JE GRILLERAI LE POISSON PLUS TARD.

...

HIRONOBU ANDÔ

OLAC

HEIN ?

AH...

BAM

HE, ÇA NE VA PAS ?!!

ROIKO, QU'EST-CE QUI T'ARRIVE ?

AH, C'EST JUSTE ÇA... SA BATTERIE EST VIDE, COMME D'HABITUDE.

VIDE

MALHEU-
REUSEMENT,
COMME JE L'AI
FABRIQUÉE
MOI-MÊME,
JE N'AI PAS DE
QUOI RÉSOUDRE
CE PROBLÈME
DE COUPURES
DE COURANT
IMPRÉVUES.

...

PAS
AVEC UNE
CONSOM-
MATION
D'ÉLECTRICITÉ
PAREILLE !!!

ON NE
PEUT PAS
DIRE QUE
TU SOIS TRÈS
ÉCOLOGIQUE...

... ROÏKO.

10 FOIS LA
PUISSANCE
D'UN
CLIMATISEUR
ET 4 HEURES
DE RE-
CHARGE...

LA
FACTURE
D'ÉLECTRICITÉ
DE CE
MOIS-CI
VA ÊTRE
EFFROYABLE.

HMM
...

OH NON !
NE ME DITES
PAS QUE JE
SUIS ENCORE
TOMBÉE À
CAUSE DE MES
BATTERIES ?

OH,
BONJOUR,
PROFES-
SEUR.

C'EST
DÉJÀ
LE
SOIR...

ROIKO,
IL FAUT
QU'ON
PARLE.

VOUS VOULEZ QUE J'AILLE TRAVAILLER COMME DOMESTIQUE CHEZ UN MULTIMIL-LIONNAIRE ?!!

HEIN ?!!

ROIKO, ALLONS, CALME-TOI...

JE SAIS ! VOUS EN AVEZ TROUVÉ UNE AUTRE !!!

NON !! JE NE VEUX PAS DU TOUT !! VOUS VOULEZ ME VENDRE, C'EST ÇA ? VOUS ÊTES LASSÉ DE MOI ?

VOUS VOUS APPELEZ ANDÔ ET MOI AUSSI ! JE SUIS VOTRE ANDROÏDE !!! C'EST TROP FACILE DE M'ABAN-DONNER !!!

VOUS AVEZ OUBLIÉ MON NOM ?

NON, JE NE ME CALME-RAI PAS !!!

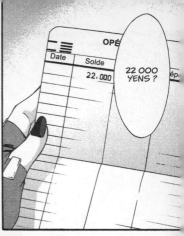

J'AI ÉTÉ RAVI DE CE MIRACLE...

... MAIS JE N'AI RIEN INVENTÉ DE BIEN FABULEUX DEPUIS...

D'ACCORD, TU ES UN ANDROÏDE CAPABLE DE RESSENTIR ET D'EXPRIMER DES SENTIMENTS. MAIS TU SAIS, TA CONCEPTION DOIT PLUS AU HASARD QU'À MES COMPÉTENCES SCIENTIFIQUES...

OH... む

JE SAIS !!

EN PLUS, LES MATÉRIAUX ET LE GARAGE DONT JE ME SERVAIS POUR MES RECHERCHES ONT ÉTÉ SAISIS.

ET JE NE PEUX PAS VRAIMENT TRAVAILLER DANS CE STUDIO MINUSCULE...

JE VAIS DEVENIR UNE SUPER-HÉROÏNE !!!

VRAI-MENT ?

EUH...

ON POURRAIT APPELER ÇA "ANDÔ ELECTRONICS" OU UN TRUC DANS LE GENRE !!

ET ON DEMANDERAIT À DES SPONSORS DE NOUS DONNER DE L'ARGENT !!

MAIS OUI ! LES SUPER-HÉROS, C'EST LA MODE DU MOMENT ! ILS ONT MÊME UNE ASSOCIATION OFFICIELLE !!

VOUS N'AVEZ QU'À LEUR DEMANDER UN PERMIS ET MONTER UNE ENTREPRISE !

ELLE REGARDE TROP LA TÉLÉ...

ET MOI, JE ME BATTRAI ! C'EST ÇA, JE VEUX ÊTRE UNE SUPER-HÉROÏNE COMBATTANTE !!

HMM...

IL EN FAUT PLUS QUE ÇA POUR ME DÉCOURAGER !!

JE NE CROIS PAS QU'ON PUISSE OBTENIR UN PERMIS DE SUPER-HÉROS SI RAPIDEMENT QUE ÇA.

ET PUIS LES FRAIS DE DOSSIER DOIVENT COÛTER UNE FORTUNE.

ET PUIS SINON IL PARAÎT QU'ON PEUT OBTENIR DES BOURSES OU DES AIDES POUR INTÉGRER L'ASSOCIATION DES SUPER-HÉROS.

JE VAIS ATTRAPER UN CRIMINEL RECHERCHÉ AVANT LES SUPER-HÉROS !!

ENFIN, C'EST CE QUE DIT LA RUMEUR ...

LE PROFESSEUR S'INQUIÈTE POUR MOI !!

NE VOUS EN FAITES PAS.

DU CALME. SI TU TE BATS CONTRE DES CRIMINELS QUE MÊME LES SUPER-HÉROS N'ARRIVENT PAS À ARRÊTER, ÇA RISQUE DE MAL FINIR...

... ET MOI, JE N'AI NI L'ARGENT NI LES PIÈCES DE RECHANGE POUR TE RÉPARER.

SLURP

J'AI TOUTES LES ARMES NÉCESSAIRES.

PRFFFF

C'ÉTAIT POUR QUE TU PUISSES TE DÉFENDRE EN CAS D'URGENCE, PAS POUR QUE TU PARTES EN GUERRE !!!

AH BON ? POURTANT C'EST BIEN VOUS QUI M'EN AVEZ ÉQUIPÉE, NON ?

ARRÊTE !! C'EST INDÉCENT !!!

ET ALORS, LÀ, JE LUI DIS...

IL ÉTAIT TENDU ET RENFERMÉ DEPUIS L'INCIDENT DE L'AUTRE JOUR...

JE N'AI PAS RÉUSSI À RÉCUPÉRER LA PHOTO...

SHÛTO A RETROUVÉ SA BONNE HUMEUR.

C'EST PEUT-ÊTRE LE MOMENT.

D'AILLEURS, JE NE L'AI TOUJOURS PAS REMERCIÉ.

JE VAIS ATTENDRE QU'IL AIT FINI DE PARLER...

TU AURAIS VU ÇA !! LE DERNIER ÉPISODE D'ARSAR-MAN ÉTAIT VRAIMENT ÉPIQUE !

LES CRIMINELS RECHERCHÉS NE SONT PAS FACILES À TROUVER.

LE PROFES-SEUR AVAIT RAISON.

... IL FAUT BIEN QUE JE TROUVE UN TRAVAIL D'APPOINT OU UN MOYEN DE FAIRE DES ÉCONOMIES.

MAIS COMME LE PROFES-SEUR N'A VRAIMENT PAS L'AIR D'AVOIR ENVIE DE TRAVAIL-LER...

JE N'AURAI QU'À REMPLACER LA VIANDE PAR LES SAUCISSES QUI SONT DANS LE FRIGO.

HI HI HI... ÇA Y EST, JE FAIS DES ÉCONOMIES, COMME UNE VRAIE PETITE MAÎTRESSE DE MAISON.

POMMES DE TERRE

OH, LES OIGNONS ET LES POMMES DE TERRE NE SONT PAS CHERS DU TOUT...

ET SI JE FAISAIS UN CURRY CE SOIR ?

BON-JOUR, MON-SIEUR JACKY. OH, VOUS FAITES UN POT-AU-FEU AUJOUR-D'HUI ?

JE VOUS AI RAJOUTÉ UN DAÏKON EN CADEAU.

VOILÀ, EN VOUS REMER-CIANT.

ET EN PLUS, IL OFFRE DES LÉGUMES ? C'EST BIEN ÇA...

HMM...

107

MAIS OUI, J'AI VU CET HOMME EN COMBINAISON DE SQUELETTE SUR INTERNET !!! C'EST LUI, PAS DE DOUTE !!

GRRR

ON RECHERC POUR INTRUSIO

C'EST UN CRIMI- NEL JACK RE- CHER- CHE !!!

RE- COMPENS

CLANG

TU NE M'ÉCHAP- PERAS PAS !

HE !

A'! VL'OUCH !!

VRRRR

BOUM

SHÛTO...

TU SAIS
POUR CETTE
HISTOIRE
DE PHOTO...

JE TE TIENS !!

DZOUM

CLAC

LA FÊTE ~

... EST FINIE !!

FROUCH FROUCH

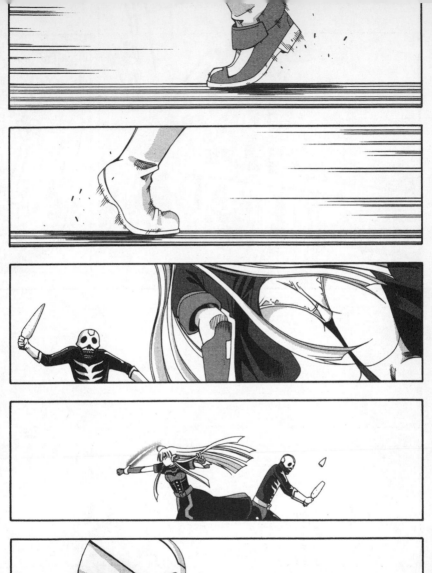

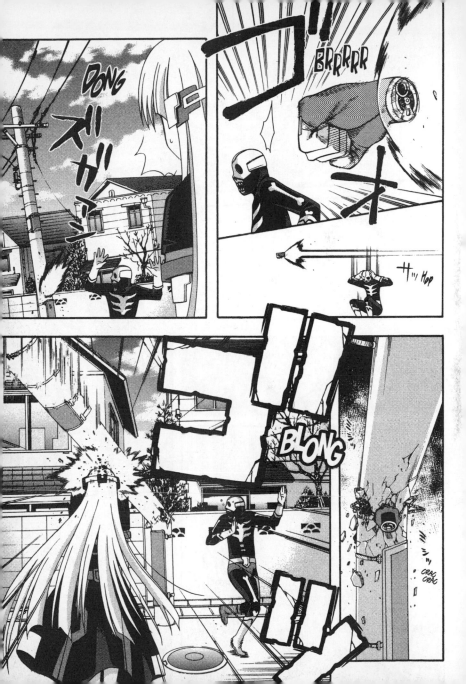

DZZZZ
ZAP

HEIN
...?

JACKY
A TUE
CETTE
FILLE ?!!

JE SAIS QU'ON EST DANS UNE ORGANISATION CRIMINELLE, MAIS LÀ, C'EST TROP GRAVE !

SCRIIITCH

VA TE DÉNONCER À LA POLICE, ALLEZ !!

NON NON NON

ブン ブン ブン

VRRRR スゥー

MODE STANDARD COMPROMIS, DÉMARRAGE DU MODE AUTOMATIQUE...

HEIN ?

HE !

BANG

BANG

BANG

BANG

BANG

BANG

PAN PAN PAN PAN PAN

ZAP

TRANSFOR-MATION !!

OUI

CA EXISTE VRAIMENT ?!

JE RÊVE ? C'EST UN ANDROÏDE ?

BON, DANS CES CONDITIONS... PAS LE CHOIX, IL FAUT QUE J'INTER-VIENNE.

TIENS ? UNE COUPURE DE COURANT ?

DZUN

ET ROIKO QUI N'EST TOUJOURS PAS RENTRÉE...

...

JE NE SAIS PAS POURQUOI, MAIS JE N'AIME PAS ÇA...

C'EST DE LA FOLIE DE TIRER DES MISSILES EN VILLE !!

ELLE EST CINGLÉE !!!

JE DOIS
LA FORCER
À SE BATTRE
AU CORPS À
CORPS AVANT
QU'ELLE NE
BLESSE
QUELQU'UN.

TAP

BAM

BAM

LA
VACHE !!

BAM

ELLE EST SUPER-FORTE AU CORPS À CORPS !!

MAIS ANDROÏDE OU PAS, JE NE PEUX PAS FRAPPER UNE FEMME...

BAM BAM BAM

BAM BAM

?!!

CLAC

DZOUM

VRAP

ROIKO,
ARRÊTÉ.

...

TU
N'ES PAS
COMME
ÇA.

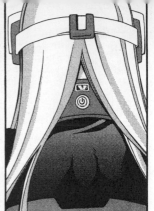

CLIC

ポチッ

ZAP

EXTINCTION FORCÉE DU SYSTÈME...

JE VAIS TRAVAIL-LER.

JE TE LE PRO-METS.

JE N'AVAIS PAS RÉALISÉ À QUEL POINT TA PRÉSENCE ÉTAIT IMPORTANTE POUR MOI.

ET TANT PIS SI ON VIT DANS LA PAUVRETÉ ET QUE JE N'INVENTE PLUS RIEN.

JE M'EN FICHE.

ÊTRE AVEC TOI EST TOUT CE QUI COMPTE POUR MOI...

COMME ÇA, JE POURRAI PAYER TES FRAIS D'ENTRETIEN.

À PARTIR DE MAINTENANT, JE VAIS ÊTRE RESPONSABLE ET GAGNER DE L'ARGENT.

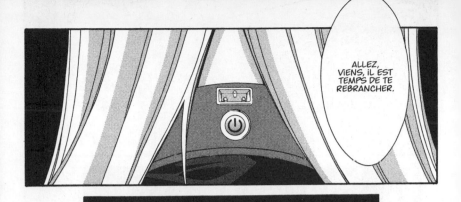

ALLEZ, VIENS, IL EST TEMPS DE TE REBRANCHER.

TOUT EST BIEN QUI FINIT BIEN.

NOUS AUTRES, LES SCIENTIFIQUES, NOUS AVONS TENDANCE À ÊTRE INDISCIPLINÉS ET OBSTINÉS... JE NOUS VOIS MAL OCCUPER DES EMPLOIS NORMAUX...

HI HI HI

LE PROFESSEUR ANDÔ NOUS A PRÉSENTÉ SES EXCUSES, À JACKY ET À MOI. L'INCIDENT EST CLOS.

TU PARLES D'UNE MÉSAVENTURE...

HEIN ?

GRAND-PÈRE, TU AS QUAND MÊME UNE SACRÉE OPINION DE TOI-MÊME...

HMM... VOILÀ DES PAROLES PLEINES DE SAGESSE...

OUI... JE CROIS QUE JE VOUS COMPRENDS...

MINCE, IL EST DÉJÀ SI TARD QUE ÇA ?

JE NE SAURAIS PAS DIRE POUR-QUOI...

J'Y VAIS, ROIKO. PASSE UNE BONNE JOURNÉE.

... MAIS JE PENSE QU'ILS VONT S'EN SORTIR.

À SUIVRE DANS LE PROCHAIN ÉPISODE...

LE GARÇON INSENSIBLE ET LA JEUNE FILLE

キラッ

BLink

QUI N'A JAMAIS RÊVÉ DE DEVENIR UN SUPER-HÉROS ?

RATMAN

HMM...

"PLOF"

UNE VRAIE PRINCESSE... ELLE N'ARRIVE PAS À SE DÉCIDER.

ÉPISODE 23

BONG

EUH... JE... JE VOULAIS JUSTE AIDER MA PETITE SŒUR ADORÉE À CHOISIR SES VÊTEMENTS POUR SON PREMIER RENDEZ-VOUS AMOUREUX.

CREA, SI TOI AUSSI, TU T'Y METS, ÇA NE VA PAS ÊTRE POS- SIBLE...

UNE DE TES TENUES ?

ÉCOUTE-MOI UNE SECONDE. VU QUE TU NE TROUVES PAS TON BONHEUR DANS TA PENDERIE, JE PEUX PEUT-ÊTRE TE PRÊTER QUELQUE CHOSE ?

M'AI- DER ?

NON MERCI.

EH BEN !

T'AS DE LA RÉPAR- TIE !

137

JE VOULAIS À TOUT PRIX VOIR CE FILM DE SUPER-HÉROS.

CREA EST VRAIMENT GENTILLE DES FOIS.

ELLE M'A OFFERT CES PLACES DE CINÉMA, ALORS QUE J'ESSAYAIS D'EN DÉNICHER DEPUIS DES JOURS.

AH BON... C'EST VRAIMENT DIFFÉRENT DE MES FILMS D'ACTION OU DE SUPER-HÉROS.

MOUAIS... J'AURAIS PRÉFÉRÉ L'ENTENDRE DIRE AUTRE CHOSE...

JE M'INQUIÈTE POUR CES DEUX-LÀ. AU MOINS EN LES ESPIONNANT, JE SAURAI À QUOI M'EN TENIR !!

MAIS CE N'EST PAS LE MOMENT POUR ÇA. SUIVONS-LES.

En avant, les Jacky.

GLAC GLAC

AH BON ? DANS CE CAS, ALLONS PLUTÔT VOIR UN FILM MIGNON !

QUEL EST TON NOM ?

C'EST PAS UN FILM PAREIL QUI VA LES METTRE D'HUMEUR ROMANTIQUE, IL NE VA RIEN SE PASSER.

DIRE QUE C'EST MOI QUI AI ACHETÉ LES BILLETS...

... CE FILM EST D'UN RASOIR...

EN PLUS DE ÇA...

HMM チラッ

ET AU MEILLEUR MOMENT DU FILM, HOP, TU LUI ATTRAPES LA MAIN !!

...

TIENS... JE VOUS DONNE DES BILLETS, TU N'AS QU'À ALLER AU CINÉMA AVEC SHÛTO.

C'EST GÉNIAL !! IL N'Y A PAS À DIRE, LES FILMS D'ACTION, C'EST PLUS IMPRESSIONNANT AU CINÉMA.

JE N'AI PAS RÉUSSI À M'Y INTÉRESSER UNE SEULE SECONDE...

D'ACCORD...

JE MEURS DE FAIM, SI ON ALLAIT MANGER QUELQUE CHOSE ?

ÇA M'A COMPLÈTEMENT ASSOMMÉE...

TU N'AS PAS À T'EXCUSER. C'EST TOUJOURS TOI QUI FAIS À MANGER, ALORS AUJOURD'HUI, C'EST À MOI DE T'INVITER.

J'AURAIS DÛ NOUS PRÉPARER UN BENTÔ CE MATIN, MAIS J'ÉTAIS COMPLÈTEMENT DÉBORDÉE. JE N'AI PAS EU LE TEMPS...

SHÛTO... C'EST GENTIL...

JE SUIS DÉSOLÉE.

HMM

ON LUI A COÛTÉ DES POINTS !!!

-30

SI SEULEMENT JE NE L'AVAIS PAS EMPÊCHÉE DE PRÉPARER UN BENTO EN PERTURBANT SES ESSAYAGES !!!

LE COURANT PASSE BIEN ENTRE EUX AUJOUR-D'HUI...

LÀ, C'EST PAS MAL.

BISON BURGER

Hunting your heart

JE NE SAIS PAS... JE N'Y AI JAMAIS MANGÉ.

QUOI ?!!

TU N'AIMES PAS LES FAST-FOODS ?

BISON BURGER ?

NON.

ALORS TU N'AS JAMAIS MANGÉ DE HAMBURGER ?

TU SAIS COMMENT ÇA SE MANGE ?

ÇA ALORS ! IL Y A ENCORE DES GENS QUI N'ONT JAMAIS MANGÉ DE HAMBURGER !

AH BON, C'EST VRAI ? JE NE LE SAVAIS PAS.

EN FAIT... COMME J'AI GRANDI DANS LA CAMPAGNE ANGLAISE...

JE LE TIENS À DEUX MAINS... ET JE MORDS DEDANS ?

HMM, JE NE VOIS PAS DE COUTEAU NI DE FOURCHETTE...

NE ME DIS PAS QU'IL FAUT DES BAGUETTES ?

JE T'EXPLIQUE, C'EST TOUT BÊTE... COMMENCE PAR RETIRER LA MOITIÉ DU PAPIER, PUIS PRENDS LE HAMBURGER À DEUX MAINS ET MORDS DEDANS À PLEINES DENTS !

ALORS
?

HMMM...

C'EST
BON.

HÉ, MAIS C'EST SHÛTO ET MIREA !

OH, OH, IL Y A DU ROMANTISME DANS L'AIR...

OH ? OUI, BIEN SÛR !!

AH BON ? ON PEUT S'ASSEOIR À CÔTÉ DE VOUS ALORS ? TOUTES LES AUTRES TABLES SONT PRISES.

AU FAST-FOOD ? TU PARLES D'UN RENDEZ-VOUS...

ON VOUS DÉRANGE EN PLEIN RENDEZ-VOUS EN AMOU-REUX ?

NON, PAS DU TOUT !! ON A EU DES PLACES DE CINÉMA EN CADEAU. DU COUP, ON Y EST ALLÉS ENSEMBLE, ET LÀ, ON MANGEAIT JUSTE UN TRUC APRÈS LA SÉANCE...

"BIEN SÛR", JE RÊVE ? QUEL CRÉTIN ! IL VEUT CASSER L'AMBIANCE OU QUOI ?

MINCE !

OUAIS !! C'ÉTAIT GÉNIAL ! JE SUIS SÛR QUE ÇA TE PLAIRAIT !!

TU PARLES, C'EST LE RÉALISATEUR DE 400 QUI L'A FAIT. J'AI HÂTE DE LE VOIR !

CES DEUX-LÀ SONT D'UNE NAÏVETÉ HALLUCINANTE...

VOUS AVEZ VU WATCHAMEN ? C'EST PAS MAL...

HOLÀ, DU CALME ! PAS DE SPOILER !

IL Y A DES RÉPLIQUES QUI TUENT !

GNIP
キく

GNIP
キく

HMM...

JE SAIS. SHÛTO EST COMME ÇA.

PARDON, MIREA. ON FILE DÈS QU'ON A FINI DE MANGER.

CES DEUX BENÊTS N'ONT PAS COMPRIS LA SITUATION, ON DIRAIT...

SHÛTO EST UN GROS BÊTA PAS TRÈS DÉGOURDI, MAIS IL EST GENTIL.

TOI AUSSI, YANO...

... TU ES QUEL- QU'UN DE BIEN.

VOUS PARLEREZ DE TOUT ÇA DEMAIN AU LYCÉE !

HEIN ? MAIS ON EST EN TRAIN DE DISCUTER !

ALLEZ, KANTA !! ARRÊTE DE BAVARDER, FINIS DE MANGER QU'ON PUISSE RENTRER !

ÇA ALORS, JE LA CROYAIS BIEN PLUS FROIDE QUE ÇA... MAIS LÀ, EN LA VOYANT SOURIRE...

OUI.

IL Y A UN DERNIER ENDROIT OÙ JE VOUDRAIS ALLER.

IL COMMENCE À FAIRE SOMBRE.

ON FAIT QUOI ? TU VEUX ALLER QUELQUE PART ?

O.K., ON Y VA !!

LES JOURNÉES FILENT À TOUTE VITESSE EN HIVER.

TOUT COMME CES MOMENTS DE BONHEUR...

JE N'AURAIS JAMAIS PU IMAGINER QU'UN TEL JOUR ARRIVERAIT...

PAS COMME J'ÉTAIS AVANT...

LEUR CURIOSITÉ ET LEUR INTÉRÊT SUPERFICIEL...

... ÉTAIENT PÉNIBLES.

SECONDE C

OUI, ELLE NOUS REGARDE DE HAUT !!

VOUS L'AIMEZ BIEN, VOUS, MIREA ?

EN PLUS, COMME ELLE EST UN PEU JOLIE, ELLE SE PREND POUR UNE PRINCESSE.

MOI, J'AI L'IMPRESSION QU'ELLE NOUS MÉPRISE.

LEUR CURIOSITÉ S'EST RAPIDEMENT TRANSFORMÉE EN HOSTILITÉ.

J'AVAIS ÉRIGÉ UNE BARRIÈRE PROTECTRICE TOUT AUTOUR DE MOI.

MAIS, ÇA NE ME TOUCHAIT PAS.

ALLÔ, CREA ?

OUI... J'AI BIEN CHERCHÉ.

JE N'ÉTAIS PAS COMME LES AUTRES.

JE N'AI PAS TROUVÉ DE CANDIDAT CORRESPONDANT À TES BESOINS.

J'ÉTAIS MEMBRE D'UNE ORGANISATION SECRÈTE. J'AVAIS LES MOYENS DE NUIRE À CEUX QUI M'APPROCHAIENT DE TROP PRÈS.

... PLUS MON MUR DE DÉFENSE ÉTAIT SOLIDE, MIEUX JE ME PORTAIS.

ON VA FAIRE UN TOUR AU TEMPLE ?

VOUS AVEZ FINI LE MÉNAGE ?

TU PARLES ! ON EST PARTIES EN LUI LAISSANT TOUT.

NON, MAIS ELLE A DIT QU'ELLE S'EN CHAR- GEAIT.

OUI, C'EST VRAI ! ON NE VOUDRAIT SURTOUT PAS LA DÉRANGER.

DE TOUTE FAÇON, MIREA N'AVAIT PAS L'AIR D'AVOIR ENVIE DE FAIRE LE MÉNAGE AVEC NOUS.

SÉ- RIEUX ? C'EST VRAI- MENT PAS SYMPA.

CE N'ÉTAIT QU'UN BANAL PORTE-CLÉS, MAIS C'ÉTAIT UN CADEAU DE MA SŒUR. C'EST POUR ÇA QUE J'Y TENAIS...

SI ÇA VENAIT DE QUELQU'UN D'AUTRE OU SI ON ME LE RACHETAIT, JE M'EN FICHERAIS COMPLÈTEMENT.

JE DEMANDERAIS PROBABLEMENT CE QUE C'EST QUE CE TRUC, AVANT DE PARTIR EN RIANT.

JE TE JURE...

ÇA VA ALLER.

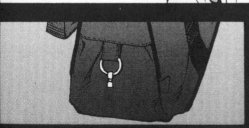

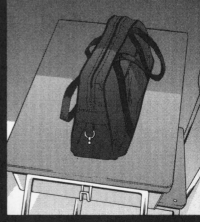

C'EST
BIEN.

LÀ,
JE SUIS
BIEN.

C'EST
LE MONDE
QUE JE
SOUHAITAIS.

C'EST LA
CONSÉQUENCE
DE MES
ACTES.

UNE
SALLE
DE CLASSE
DÉSERTE...

IL ÉTAIT PERDU DANS LES BUISSONS.

SHÛTO A PRIS UNE PLACE DANS MON CŒUR...

... SANS QUE JE M'EN APERÇOIVE.

PAS DU TOUT !

POURQUOI TU TENAIS TANT À LE RETROUVER ? C'EST UN PEU BIZARRE, NON ?

AH ? J'AI REMARQUÉ QU'IL N'ÉTAIT PLUS ACCROCHÉ À TON SAC COMME D'HABITUDE.

COMMENT AS-TU SU QUE C'ÉTAIT ÇA QUE JE CHERCHAIS ?

MOI AUSSI, J'EN AI. ET JE CROIS QUE PERSONNE NE COMPRENDRAIT.

ON A TOUS DES OBJETS AUXQUELS ON TIENT, PAS VRAI ?

DES OBJETS QUE JE NE JETTERAIS POUR RIEN AU MONDE MÊME S'ILS FONT RIRE LES AUTRES ET QU'ON ME DIT QUE C'EST IDIOT.

MOI,
JE NE ME
MOQUERAI
JAMAIS...

...DE
TES
RÊVES.

OUAH !

CE PARC ME RAPPELLE PLEIN DE VIEUX SOUVENIRS !!

BIEN SÛR !!

TU T'EN SOU-VIENS ?

QUE DE CHEMIN PARCOU-RU...

SHÛ-TO...

... DEPUIS CE JOUR.

HMM ?

MERCI.

AH ?

C'EST MOI QUI TE REMERCIE.

J'AI PASSÉ UNE TRÈS BONNE JOURNÉE.

À SUIVRE DANS LE PROCHAIN ÉPISODE...

... DANS LE 6ᵉ VOLUME !!

JE SUIS TORIKO AKUNO, UNE COLLÉGIENNE DE TROISIÈME TOUT CE QU'IL Y A DE PLUS ORDINAIRE.

PARTONS À L'ASSAUT DU MONDE DES MANGAS MIGNONS EN 4 CASES !!

LA GUERRIÈRE MAGIQUE

MAGICAL JACKETTE

J'AI UN RÊVE ! CELUI DE ME BATTRE UN JOUR AU SERVICE D'UNE ORGANISATION DIABOLIQUE !!

JE TE VISE...

...DROIT AU CŒUR !

ZAP

OH ? CETTE BAGUETTE MAGIQUE ME PERMETTRA DE ME TRANS-FORMER EN GUERRIÈRE MAGIQUE ?

HE ! ATTENDEZ !!

ON DIRAIT UN BÂTON DE MAGICAL GIRL !

む ん ず っ SWIP

Authentique

LUIGANO-BIANKI VIRIELL...

~ TOREK-KUPINALEKO SENCHURION !

JE VEUX DEVENIR MEMBRE DE VOTRE ORGANI-SATION DIABO-LIQUE !!

JE...

HEIN ?!!

ZAM

CHEF !!

COMMENCE DONC PAR ÉCRASER CE SUPER-HÉROS !!

C'EST... C'EST MOI, ÇA ?!!

En plus, j'ai des seins énormes !!

HEIN ?

BOUH!

HÉ ! TU VEUX TE BATTRE ?

C'EST FABULEUX !! JE SUIS UNE GUERRIÈRE MAGIQUE ! ÇA DÉPASSE MES RÊVES LES PLUS FOUS !

YOUPI! YOUPI!

EUH... TU FAIS QUOI, LÀ ?

♥ FIN ♥

QUI N'A JAMAIS RÊVÉ DE DEVENIR UN SUPER-HÉROS ?

RATMAN

PRÉSENTÉ PAR
SEKIHIKO INUI

DESIGN DES SUPER-HÉROS ET SUPERVISEUR
RAIYA ☆ ARAHABAKI

ÉQUIPE
AHIRU

NAGI KAZEKAWA

CRÉATION DES COSTUMES
KÔBÔ KAMEARI

TATSUYA KAMISHIMA

NOBUYOSHI TAKAHASHI

KENNOSUKE NAKAMA

GRAPHISTE
TOSHIMITSU NUMA
(D-SHIKI GRAPHICS)

MAKOTO FÛGETSU

Ce manga est publié dans son sens
de lecture originale, de droite à gauche.

Ici, vous êtes donc à la fin.

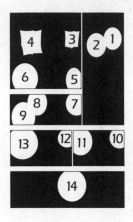

RATMAN

RATMAN vol. 05
© Sekihiko INUI 2009
First published in Japan in 2009 by KADOKAWA SHOTEN Co., Ltd., Tokyo
French translation rights arranged with KADOKAWA SHOTEN Co., Ltd., Tokyo,
Through TOHAN CORPORATION, Tokyo.

© KANA (DARGAUD-LOMBARD s.a.) 2012
7, avenue P-H Spaak - 1060 Bruxelles

Tous droits de traduction, de reproduction et d'adaptation
strictement réservés pour la France, la Belgique,
la Suisse, le Luxembourg et le Québec.

Dépôt légal d/2012/0086/525
ISBN 978-2-5050-1554-3

Conception graphique : Joachim Roussel
Traduit et adapté en français par Julien Delespaul
Adaptation graphique : Eric Montésinos

Imprimé en Italie par L.E.G.O. spa - Lavis (Trento)

Japan, the United States, and Latin America

Japan, the United States, and Latin America

Toward a Trilateral Relationship in the Western Hemisphere

Edited by

Barbara Stallings

and

Gabriel Székely

The Johns Hopkins University Press * Baltimore

First published 1993
in the United States of America by
The Johns Hopkins University Press
2715 North Charles Street
Baltimore, Maryland 21218–4139

Library of Congress Cataloging-in-Publication Data

Japan, the United States, and Latin America: toward a trilateral
  relationship in the Western Hemisphere / edited by Barbara Stallings
  and Gabriel Székely.
     p.   cm.
  Includes bibliographical references and index.
  ISBN 0–8018–4586–6
  1. Latin America—Foreign economic relations—Japan.   2. Japan—
Foreign economic relations—Latin America.   3. Latin America—
Foreign economic relations—United States.   4. United States—
Foreign economic relations—Latin America.   5. Japan—Foreign
economic relations—United States.   6. United States—Foreign
economic relations—Japan.   I. Stallings, Barbara.   II. Székely,
Gabriel, 1953– .
HF1480.55.J3J36   1993
337'.09181'2—dc20   92–30251
                                                               CIP

Contents

v

vi   *Contents*

List of Figures and Tables

Acknowledgments

The papers commissioned for this volume were originally discussed at a meeting at the University of California-San Diego in April 1990.

Support for this meeting and other costs of preparing the manuscript were provided by the the Center for Iberian and Latin American Studies and the Center for US – Mexican Studies (both at UCSD) and the World Peace Foundation. We are pleased to acknowledge their assistance. Barbara Stallings would also like to thank the Global Studies Research Program of the University of Wisconsin-Madison and the Japan Foundation for support; and Gabriel Székely would like to thank the Center for US – Mexican Studies at the University of California – San Diego, the University of California Pacific Rim Program, and the Japan-US Friendship Commission.

For their intellectual input to the book, we would like to acknowledge Manuel Araya, Dario Braun, Leon Hollerman, Chalmers Johnson, Ed Lincoln, Carlos Moneta, Amalia Martínez, Wilson Peres, Frances Rosenbluth, Bill Smith, Peter Smith, Marcelo Suárez, and Ezra Vogel. Administrative assistance was provided by Susanne Wagner.

Finally, for their help in the publication process, we appreciate the support of Tim Farmiloe of Macmillan and Henry Tom of the Johns Hopkins University Press.

BARBARA STALLINGS   GABRIEL SZÉKELY

Notes on the Contributors

Charlotte Elton is a British economist who has lived in Panama for 20 years and is a senior researcher at the Panamanian Center for Research and Social Action (CEASPA). Elton has published extensively on Panamanian economic questions, especially the Panama Canal. She spent the academic year 1988–89 as a fellow of the US–Japan Relations Program at Harvard University and 4 months in 1990–91 as a visiting scholar at the Institute of Developing Economies in Tokyo, where she published *Japan's Natural Resource Strategies and their Environmental Impact in Latin America*.

Pablo de la Flor is a researcher at the Peruvian Center for International Studies (CEPEI) and a former staff member in the Ford Foundation's Lima office. Currently, he is on leave to complete a Ph.D. in Political Science at the University of Chicago. He is the author of *Japón en la escena internacional: sus relaciones con América Latina y el Perú*.

Kotaro Horisaka is Associate Professor of Latin American Studies at Sophia University in Tokyo. Previously, he spent several years in Brazil as the Latin American correspondent for the Japanese financial daily *Nihon Keizai Shimbun*. He is the author of a book (in Japanese) on Japanese finance in Brazil and a large number of articles in English and Spanish on Japan and Latin America. In 1989–90, he spent the year as a visiting fellow at the Latin American Studies Center at Georgetown University. His most recent project has been a survey of the attitudes of the Latin American public toward Japan, carried out with other members of Sophia University's Ibero–American Institute.

Iyo Kunimoto is Professor of Commerce at Chuo University in Tokyo. Her main academic interest is Japanese migration to Latin America. She has published various articles on the subject (in Japanese); she is also co-editor of *La inmigración japonesa en Bolivia: estudios históricos y socio-económicos* and author of *Un pueblo japonés en la Bolivia tropical*. She has frequently travelled to Latin America and has conducted research in Brazil, Argentina, Paraguay, and Mexico in addition to Bolivia.

Hiroshi Matsushita is Professor of History and Director of the Latin American Studies Center at Nanzan University in Nagoya, Japan. An expert on Argentina, he is the author of *Movimiento obrero argentino, 1930–1945* and various articles on Argentina. He is also co-author of a book on Latin America history and co-editor of a volume on democratization in Latin America (both in Japanese).

Neantro Saavedra-Rivano is a Chilean economist who has taught in Brazil at the University of Brasilia and the Getulio Vargas Foundation. Currently, he is a Visiting Professor in the Graduate Program of Area Studies at Tsukuba University in Japan. Saavedra previously spent 6 months as a visiting scholar at the Institute of Developing Economies in Tokyo, where he published *Recent History and Future Prospects of Economic Relations between Japan and Latin America*.

Barbara Stallings is Professor of Political Science and Director of the Global Studies Research Program at the University of Wisconsin-Madison. She has written extensively on international finance and US–Latin American economic relations, including *Banker to the Third World: US Portfolio Investment in Latin America, 1900–1986*. She has recently begun to publish on Japanese trade, investment and financial relations with Latin America. She is chairperson of the Latin American Studies Association's Task Force on Scholarly Relations with Japan. She spent spring 1989 as a fellow of the US–Japan Relations Program at Harvard University and has visited Japan under the auspices of the Japan Foundation, the Ministry of Finance, and the Japanese Association of Latin American Studies.

Gabriel Székely is a Mexican political scientist who is a Senior Fellow at the Center for US–Mexican Studies of the University of California-San Diego; formerly he was Associate Director of the Center. He is also an international consultant. The co-author (with Daniel Levy) of *Mexico: Paradoxes of Stability and Change*, he has also written many articles on the Mexican political economy. Over the last few years, he has been directing a project on US and Japanese investment in Mexico and is the editor of *Manufacturing across Borders and Oceans: Japan, the United States, and Mexico*, a book resulting from the project. This project has now been expanded to include Japanese investment in Brazil and Chile. In connection with this project, Székely recently visited Japan under the auspices of the Japan Society for the Promotion of Science.

Ernani T. Torres is a Brazilian economist who works at the Federal University of Rio de Janeiro and the Brazilian National Development Bank (BNDES). He is part of a team in Brazil, which is collaborating with the Institute of Developing Economies in Tokyo, on an analysis of Brazil's development strategy and the role of Japan in that country. They have published *Japanese Economic Cooperation with Brazil: A Progress Report*. Torres visited Japan in 1989 at the invitation of the Japan International Cooperation Agency (JICA).

Part I
Introduction

1 The New Trilateralism: The United States, Japan, and Latin America

Barbara Stallings and Gabriel Székely

Japan will be a dominant player on the international stage in the 1990s. Its formidable productive capacity has already made it the world's number two economic power with a $3 trillion gross national product. Its growing technological prowess helps it outsell its competitors in international markets. Its enormous capital surpluses have turned it into the world's largest asset holder as well as the leading capital exporter. In economic terms, although not politically or militarily, Japan has come to rival the United States and has surpassed any single European nation.

Within the Third World, Japan's role has expanded considerably over the past decade. It is now the largest aid donor, and it has developed a new loan facility to help middle-income countries, especially those whose growth has been slashed by the debt crisis. In Southeast Asian countries, Japanese firms have established many branch plants, and Japan serves as a model for how their economies might develop. Even in Latin America, Japan has become a significant economic actor, despite geographical distance and tenuous historical and cultural connections. By some measures, it is already the largest source of capital for the region, and it is likely that ties will continue to expand.

This book focuses on the growing relationships between Japan and Latin America. It discusses Nissan's automobile plants in Mexico, Brazil's iron ore exports to Tokyo, Japan's interest in building a second canal in Panama, and many lesser-known activities. These interactions, however, must be put into perspective. For geopolitical and historical reasons, the United States remains the dominant force in the hemisphere, so it is impossible to understand Japanese–Latin American relations without taking the United States into account. Each of the authors in the book recognizes this fact and deals with the US role, but as a secondary concern. Our main task of the introduction, then, is to provide the context for the later chapters by highlighting the ways in which the United States influences the links between Japan and Latin America. To accomplish this task, we divide the chapter into five sections. First, we provide a brief discussion of historical relations between the United States and Latin America, the United States and Japan, and a comparison of US and Japanese transactions with Latin America. Second, we look at three models that have been suggested for future relations among the three. Two are based on the notion of rivalry between the United States and Japan. In one case, Japan displaces the United States; in the other, the outcome is the reverse. The third model is one of US–Japanese cooperation with respect to Latin America. In each of the three models, Latin America plays a fairly passive role.

The third section of the chapter tries to evaluate the potential of the three models just described. To do so, it disaggregates in two ways. First, it focuses on the differences among actors, especially public-sector and private-sector actors. It suggests that the former are likely to favor cooperative interactions between the United States and Japan, while the latter will be basically competitive. Second, it distinguishes among countries and sub-regions in Latin America and hypothesizes that different types of relationships may prevail in different geographical areas. The fourth section posits the need for a different model – what we call a "trilateral model." In the trilateral model, the Latin American countries themselves become important actors rather than passive subjects. In addition to seeing this model as desirable, we also point to some hints that it may be emerging in a few countries, especially Mexico and Chile, and in the efforts of regional organizations. Finally, we conclude with a brief summary of the remainder of the book.

HISTORICAL RELATIONS: UNITED STATES, JAPAN, AND LATIN AMERICA

Historical relations among the United States, Japan, and Latin America can be conceptualized in terms of a triangle, where the US–Japan and US–Latin America legs represent very dense sets of interactions, especially in the post-World War II era. Both have been dominated by the United States. The Japan–Latin America leg of the triangle, by contrast, has represented a much lower level of interaction.

Nevertheless, as we will show, those links have been more important than observers generally realize. Although the historical patterns are beginning to change, the presence of the United States cannot help but influence current and future relationships between Japan and Latin America. Geographical, as well as historical, factors guarantee a "mediating" US role.

United States and Latin America

Relations between the United States and Latin America have typically been conflictual as befits a situation where one nation in a region enjoys overwhelming power. Latin Americans have been resentful when the United States has intruded in their affairs, and they have been frustrated when they have been ignored. Both have occurred frequently since 1823, when the United States declared Latin America to be in its zone of influence through promulgation of the Monroe Doctrine.

Although sporadic conflicts were recorded throughout the nineteenth century, the earliest period of intense interaction began in the last years of the century and lasted until the depression. Security concerns loomed large in this period, especially with respect to sea lanes in the Caribbean. Military occupation of various countries in the Caribbean and Central America (including Cuba, Haiti, the Dominican Republic, and Nicaragua), intervention in Mexico, and annexation of the Panama Canal Zone were at least partially justified on political and security grounds. The Roosevelt Corollary of the Monroe Doctrine expressed the feeling of the times when it said that "the exercise of an international police power" might be forced on the United States by "flagrant cases of wrongdoing or impotence" in the hemisphere.[1]

Early trade and investment links were also concentrated in nearby areas. In what has been called "spillover investment,"[2] US firms built railroads in Mexico and Central America, established plantations in Central America and the Caribbean to raise fruit and sugarcane, and drilled for oil in Mexico. The term "dollar diplomacy" was coined to describe the activities of US investment banks, which floated bonds in the name of Central American and Caribbean nations occupied by US marines. Gradually, US firms moved into South America too. During the 1920s, banks set up branches in and made large loans to Brazil, Argentina, Chile, Peru, and Colombia. Direct investment also became important in South America: copper mining in Chile and Peru, tin in Bolivia, petroleum in Peru and Venezuela, utilities in many countries.[3]

With the onset of the depression, both economic and political relations contracted. US investors pulled out of Latin America as many countries defaulted on their bonds. Under the presidencies of Hoover and especially Franklin D. Roosevelt, US troops were withdrawn from the Caribbean protectorates, and unilateral US intervention in the hemisphere was renounced. With the end of World War II, Latin America was eager to resuscitate relations in order to obtain US assistance for economic development, but the United States was preoccupied by the onset of the Cold War and the reconstruction of Europe and Japan. Interest in Latin America remained low.[4]

The panorama changed in the 1960s as the Cold War moved to Latin America. The Castro victory in Cuba ushered in one of the most controversial periods in hemispheric relations. In order to provide a counterbalance to Castro's Cuba, the Alliance for Progress was to provide $20 billion over the decade to stimulate economic development. In return, the Latins were expected to undertake social reforms ranging from redistribution of land to expanded access to education. Military assistance to provide a "stable environment" was also part of the package. Although begun with a great fanfare, the Alliance fell far short of expectations. The money made available was much less than initial promises, and the reforms were largely abandoned under attack from both right and left. After Johnson succeeded Kennedy, attention shifted to other parts of the world, especially the growing conflict in Vietnam.[5]

As US government aid fell off, private-sector financing took its place in the form of loans from large private banks. Bloated by deposits from OPEC governments, US and other banks lent these "petrodollars" to Latin American governments, who wanted to find a way to pay their increased oil bills without sacrificing their large-scale investment projects. Latin America flourished and a number of countries, together with South Korea and Taiwan, were hailed as "newly industrializing countries" (NICs). In the Latin American case, however, the debt subscribed was more than could be serviced because of the regions's import-substitution industrialization policies that played down exports.[6]

While the East Asian NICs continued to grow rapidly in the 1980s, Latin America was mired in the debt crisis with its disastrous impact on the economic and social fabric of the region. The United States took the lead in establishing policies to manage the crisis, but the emphasis was on dampening the negative impact on the banks and the international financial system; thus most of the cost of adjustment was passed onto the debtor countries. Ironically, while the United States substantially increased its aid budget during this period, the money did not go to help resolve the debt crisis but to finance an anticommunist war in Central America as the calendar appeared to be turned back to an earlier part of the century.[7]

Not surprisingly, these on-again, off-again relationships over the last 170 years have created significant strains between Latin America and what is often described as the "colossus of the North." Latin Americans – especially from the political left but not limited to these groups – have blamed the United States for their economic as well as their social and political problems. Sometimes these criticisms have been entirely justified; on other occasions, the United States has simply provided a convenient scapegoat. The interesting point, however, is that one of Japan's advantages in Latin America is the *lack* of history – a blank slate on which to write. This blank slate increases the eagerness with which Japanese involvement is sought.

United States and Japan

The United States and Japan have also been closely linked through relations of domination and subordination. They began when Admiral Perry forced open the Japanese market in 1854 and continued sporadically through the early part of the twentieth century. Since World War II, however, with the Occupation and its aftermath, the US–Japanese relationship has become the centerpiece of Japanese policy, both domestic and foreign. During most of the last 45 years, the relationship has been dominated by the United States, since the latter was stronger economically as well as politically and militarily. Thus Japan followed the US lead and avoided any actions that might be perceived as a challenge to US interests, generating much less open political conflict than in the US–Latin American case.

This relationship was spelled out initially through the US–Japan Mutual Security Treaty of 1951, which gave the United States the right to maintain troops "in and about Japan so as to deter armed attack on Japan."[8] The treaty was revised somewhat and renewed in 1960, amid the biggest protests of the period, and has remained the lynchpin of Japanese defense policy. The relationship was further elaborated by the so-called Yoshida Doctrine, named after former prime minister Shigeru Yoshida. It indicated that Japan's prime national goal was to be economic development; rearmament should be avoided as far as possible. The corollary to those two goals was close economic, political, and military collaboration with the United States. Several of Yoshida's successors elaborated on the doctrine with the basic idea being separation of politics and economics in order to avoid ideological conflict at home and abroad.[9]

Although Washington's original plan was to limit Japanese re-industrialization to prevent the restoration of war-making capacity, trends in the Cold War brought a change toward stimulating growth. Indeed Japanese economic growth in the postwar period was among the highest in economic history. With *per capita* income similar to many Latin American countries in the mid-1950s, it had increased to 3–4 times that of Latin America by 1980. Causes for the spectacular growth are many, and they pose a stark contrast to Latin America. On the one hand, the Occupation forced many structural changes on Japan, including a land reform, break-up of the large conglomerates, and legalization of labor unions. (These were the kinds of reforms tried without much success during the Alliance for Progress.) On the other hand, foreign capital played a minor role in Japan's resurgence as domestic savings and exports provided for investment and foreign exchange needs.[10]

With the success of the postwar development drive, the economic underpinnings of the US–Japanese relationship changed dramatically. Just as the Latin American economies became mired in depression in the 1980s, Japan began to rival the United States on many fronts. The most obvious was trade. By 1983, a symmetrical imbalance between the two countries had developed: Japan had a $30 billion surplus that rose to $100 billion by 1988, while the United States had a matching deficit of $67 billion that increased to $150 billion by 1988. The other side of the trade imbalance was capital flows. Japan became the world's largest capital exporter, while the United States became the largest debtor. Indeed, the United States came to depend on Japan for the savings its own citizens were unwilling to provide, and Japan to depend on the US market. The two economies became intertwined in a way that Robert Gilpin has called the "Nichibei economy."[11] At a deeper level, differential trends in productivity and other measures of competitiveness arose, even in high-technology fields, and US firms encountered serious problems in matching their Japanese rivals.[12]

Not surprisingly, political conflicts began to accompany these economic changes. US corporations and their congressional supporters charged that Japan was not playing fair with its restrictions, both formal and informal, which allegedly prevented foreigners from participating in the Japanese market. While the US executive branch tried to temper the resulting calls for protection, congressional ire was aroused and "Japan bashing" increased. For its part, the Japanese government claimed that it was making changes and that the real problem was not a closed Japanese economy but lack of effort on the part of US firms. The two governments engaged in various rounds of negotiations, at both sectoral and macro levels, but conflicts continued and even escalated.[13] American citizens and government officials alike insisted that Japan not only open its market but also do more on the international level, commensurate with its growing economic power. Increased military expenditure and foreign aid were the two principal demands, but the memory of past Japanese military adventures placed an emphasis on aid. Thus both US demands and Japan's own interests led to a larger Japanese role in the Third World, including Latin America.

United States and Japan in Latin America

In comparison to the long, intense history between the United States and Latin America, Japan's relations with the region are more recent and less dense. Most of Japan's interactions with Latin America date from the beginning of the century when the Japanese government was looking for a location to place some of its surplus population. Seeking new sources of labor, Latin American governments responded positively, and the migration flows began that eventually produced the largest group of ethnic Japanese outside Japan itself.[14]

Migration was renewed after World War II, when Japan also became interested in the possibilities of trade and investment relations with Latin America. Latin America's extensive supplies of natural resources made the region appear very attractive to Japan with its dearth of raw materials. Thus the Japanese government and private sector joined forces in large-scale "national projects" to produce for use in Japan such items as petroleum, iron ore, aluminum, wood, and grains. Many of the largest projects were located in Brazil, which was also the home of the largest group of immigrants. Other countries of particular interest to Japan included Peru, Venezuela, and Mexico. During the latter half of the 1970s, Japanese banks began to join their US counterparts in supplying loans to Latin American governments.[15]

By the 1980s, Japan had acquired a surprisingly large stake in Latin America. It is usually thought that Japan has confined its Third World economic interests to Asia, but a look at the data suggests otherwise. Some idea of the size of Japan's stake in the region can be obtained through Table 1.1, which compares US and Japanese direct investment and bank loans in different parts of the world. While the United States had about $72 billion of direct foreign investment (DFI) in Latin America in 1990, Japan had a surprising $40 billion. By this measure, the United States has about 80 percent more foreign investment in the region. If we exclude financial investment in the Caribbean (the main type of investment for both countries in the 1980s) and Japan's flag-of-convenience investment in Panama, however, the gap increases substantially to $35 versus $11 billion.

For bank loans, the picture is more complicated. US banks held twice as much medium and long-term debt in Latin America when the debt crisis struck in 1982, but by the end of the decade the situation had

Table 1.1   US and Japanese investment stock and bank debt by region, 1990 (billion dollars)

Type	United States ($)	United States (%)	Japan ($)	Japan (%)
Direct Foreign Investment				
Advanced industrial nations	312.2	(74.7)	213.7	(69.0)
Third World	105.7	(25.2)	95.8	(31.0)
Latin America	72.5	(17.3)	40.4	(13.1)
(On-shore[a])	(35.4)	(8.5)	(10.9)	(3.5)
Asia	24.7	(5.9)	47.5	(15.3)
Africa	3.8	(0.9)	4.6	(1.5)
Middle East	4.8	(1.1)	3.3	(1.0)
Total	417.9	(100.0)	309.5	(100.0)
Private Bank Debt[b]				
Advanced industrial nations	26.2	(43.4)	245.6	(73.9)
Third World	34.1	(56.6)	86.6	(26.1)
Latin America[a]	28.3	(46.9)	31.2	(9.4)
Asia	3.8	(6.3)	48.7	(14.7)
Africa	1.1	(1.8)	5.5	(1.7)
Middle East	0.9	(1.5)	1.2	(0.4)
Total	60.3	(100.0)	332.2	(100.0)

[a] Excludes Panama and Caribbean tax havens.
[b] Medium and long-term debt only.
Sources: Country Exposure Lending Survey for December 31, 1990 (US bank loans); Japanese Finance Ministry, *Annual Report of International Finance Bureau*, 1990 (Japanese bank loans and direct foreign investment); *Survey of Current Japanese Business*, August 1991 (US direct investment).

reversed so that Japan had $46 billion and the United States $36 billion. The reason was that, as the debt reschedulings of the 1980s progressed, Japanese banks provided the agreed share of "new money," while their US counterparts looked for various ways to withdraw from their Latin American loans. Now, in the early 1990s, the two creditor countries have converged with similar portfolios of about $30 billion as the Japanese banks have also begun to sell off their Latin American loans.[16]

To put these figures into perspective, we need to compare them to the share for other regions. Latin America's share of DFI is roughly similar for the United States and Japan, 17 and 13 percent respectively. If we look only at on-shore investment, the share falls sharply for both (to 8.5 and 3.5 percent). In terms of bank debt, Japan's Latin American share is now slightly lower than the DFI share (9.4 percent), while US banks have an astounding 47 percent of their medium and long-term debt in Latin America. The difference arises because Japanese banks have over five times the US volume of loans outstanding world-wide.

We can see a somewhat different picture if we concentrate on the last few years, rather than the cumulative effect of many years' history. Table 1.2 shows a comparison of US and Japanese economic transactions with Latin America in the last half of the 1980s. Using *net* average annual flows for the period 1985–90, it becomes clear that neither country has provided much new capital (leaving aside the financial investments in the Caribbean that have little or nothing to do with Latin America itself). Nevertheless, the surprising conclusion emerges that Japan has provided more resources to Latin America than has the United States. Excluding flows to Panama and Caribbean tax havens, Japan has provided an annual average of $1.8 billion, while US flows have *contracted* by $0.4 billion per year. The difference is entirely due to net negative bank lending, however, as Japan continues to trail the United States in both DFI and government loans.[17]

While the DFI relationship is not likely to change dramatically, the public-sector flows probably will. With respect to Official Development Assistance (ODA), most Latin American countries have been ineligible for Japanese ODA because they have been above the *per capita* income ceiling. Adjustments are taking place in this requirement, and the overall amount of Japanese ODA is expected to double in the next 5 years, so Latin America's inflow should increase in absolute terms even if the share remains low. US ODA, which is distributed on a more political basis, has been heavily concentrated in Central America; this

Table 1.2   US and Japanese economic transactions with the world, 1985–90 (annual averages, billion dollars)

Type of flow	United States		Japan	
	($)	(%)	($)	(%)
Trade[a]				
Advanced industrial nations	454.4	(63.3)	227.3	(56.4)
Third World	263.0	(36.7)	175.7	(43.6)
Latin America	94.2	(13.1)	15.9	(3.9)
Asia	126.7	(17.7)	118.9	(29.5)
Africa	17.4	(2.4)	7.7	(1.9)
Middle East	24.9	(3.5)	33.3	(8.3)
Total	717.4	(100.0)	403.0	(100.0)
Private Bank Loans (net)[b]				
Advanced industrial nations	−1.8	(n.a.)	35.0	(83.7)
Third World	−5.0	(n.a.)	6.8	(16.3)
Latin America[c]	−3.4	(n.a.)	0.4	(1.0)
Asia	−1.3	(n.a.)	6.0	(14.4)
Africa	−0.2	(n.a.)	0.3	(0.7)
Middle East	−0.2	(n.a.)	0.1	(0.2)
Total	−6.8	(n.a.)	41.8	(100.0)
Direct Foreign Investment				
Advanced industrial nations	25.8	(75.1)	29.9	(77.3)
Third World	9.3	(24.9)	8.8	(22.7)
Latin America	7.9	(22.2)	4.5	(11.6)
(On-shore[c])	(1.8)	(4.4)	(0.7)	(1.7)
Asia	1.6	(3.7)	4.0	(10.3)
Africa	−0.2	(−0.3)	0.3	(0.8)
Middle East	–	(−0.6)	0.1	(0.3)
Total	34.2	(100.0)	38.7	(100.0)
Government Loans (net)[d]				
Advanced industrial nations	0.0	(0.0)	0.3	(6.4)
Third World	7.3	(100.0)	4.4	(93.6)
Latin America[c]	1.6	(22.2)	0.7	(14.9)
Asia	1.4	(19.4)	3.2	(68.1)
Africa	1.0	(13.5)	0.4	(7.4)
Middle East	3.3	(44.9)	0.2	(3.2)
Total	17.3	(100.0)	4.7	(100.0)
Total Capital Flows (net)[e]				
Advanced industrial nations	22.6	(68.5)	65.2	(76.5)
Third World	10.4	(31.5)	20.0	(23.5)
Latin America	5.4	(16.4)	5.6	(6.6)
(On-shore[c])	−0.4	(−1.2)	1.8	(2.1)

Type of flow	United States		Japan	
	($)	(%)	($)	(%)
Asia	1.3	(3.9)	13.2	(15.5)
Africa	0.7	(2.1)	1.0	(1.2)
Middle East	2.9	(8.8)	0.4	(0.5)
Total	33.0	(100.0)	85.2	(100.0)

[a] Exports plus imports.
[b] Medium and long-term loans.
[c] Excludes Panama and Caribbean tax havens.
[d] ODA plus Export–Import Bank loans.
[e] Total of private bank loans, DFI, and government loans.
Sources: IMF, *Direction of Trade Statistics* (US and Japanese trade); OECD, *Development Cooperation* (US and Japanese aid); *Country Exposure Lending Survey* (US bank loans); Japanese Finance Ministry, *Annual Report of International Finance Bureau* (Japanese bank loans and direct investment); *Survey of Current Business* (US direct investment).

amount may decline in the near future. In addition, while the US Export–Import Bank has almost ceased providing direct loans to Latin America, the Japanese Eximbank has become increasingly important. It has changed its functions from an emphasis on promoting exports to becoming primarily a source of aid for middle-income countries. Over $4 billion of these new loans have been committed to Latin America since 1987, and the amount will grow over the coming years.[18]

The other kind of economic transaction shown in Table 1.2 is trade. Unlike capital flows, trade with Latin America is an area where Japan has little quantitative importance. As the sum of exports plus imports, Latin America accounts for only $16 billion of Japan's international trade (4 percent) compared to $94 billion of US trade (13 percent). The United States is the dominant trade partner for almost all Latin American nations. Nevertheless, the region is an important source of raw materials for Japan, and Japan is the second largest trade partner for Brazil, Mexico, Chile, Peru, and several smaller countries.[19]

Overall, Table 1.2 suggests that Latin America is of only modest significance for both the United States and Japan. Moreover, that significance has generally been declining for both during the 1980s as more of their trade and investment has turned toward other advanced industrial countries. Insofar as the Third World remains important, the focus has shifted toward the booming Asian economies. In relative terms, Latin America remains more important for the United States as a trade and investment partner, but the data for financial flows suggest that Japan is already providing more capital to the region. In addition, it has been with respect to Latin America's deepening economic problems during the 1980s that the United States has put especially heavy pressure on Japan to become more active. The Japanese have been reluctant for a number of reasons – their lack of experience in the region, their doubts about the possibility of overcoming the current problems, and their concern about real US views on other countries' involvement in the area long considered its own sphere of influence – but they have been responding.

FUTURE MODELS: UNITED STATES, JAPAN, AND LATIN AMERICA

Moving from a brief assessment of the past to what the future may hold, three models are being discussed regarding the likely evolution of relations among the United States, Japan, and Latin America. The three are special cases of overall models of US–Japan relations. In each instance, Latin America is assumed to play a largely passive role in the relationship.

The first two models are based on a notion of rivalry between the United States and Japan. In one case, the establishment of a free trade area in the western hemisphere leads to a situation where the United States effectively prevents Japan from playing any significant role in Latin American affairs. The second model envisions a successful Japanese strategy in penetrating the larger economies of the region to the detriment of the United States, eventually displacing the latter from its traditionally dominant role in Latin America. A third model is based on cooperation between the United States and Japan with respect to Latin America. Both countries provide assistance to bring about economic reform and sustained recovery; likewise, both benefit in tangible and intangible ways.

A Western Hemisphere Trade Bloc

An increasingly influential analysis of the international political economy suggests that the world will be broken up into three trade blocs: Europe, East Asia, and the Americas, led respectively by Germany, Japan, and the United States. Typical of this type of prediction, MIT economist Lester Thurow argues that the world is heading toward a situation where trade will flow more freely within emerging trading blocs, but that it will become increasingly managed between these blocs.[20] Developments in the world economy, especially the deep conflicts in the Uruguay Round of trade negotiations, have provided governments with a rationale for pursuing policies with a strong regional flavor. With multilateralism on the decline, the world's leading industrial powers will seek to strengthen their position by rallying around them their neighbors and their closest allies.

According to this view, several trends will increase tensions within the international trading system. A comprehensive liberalization of agriculture will be resisted because it would put millions of farmers out of business in Europe. Likewise, Third World nations oppose a liberalization of the service sector, which would leave them at a great disadvantage. Moreover, all industrial powers are now competing within the same industries to expand exports, and there is growing resentment in the United States and Europe about the extensive role of the public sector in Japan's economy. These unresolved issues do not augur well for the future of a liberal world trading system.

Within this overall panorama of growing regionalism, the United States and Mexico began discussions of a free trade area. When Canada – which already had such an arrangement with the United States – joined forces, the path was opened for a North American Free Trade Area (NAFTA). Such a continental free trade area would include a total population of 360 million and a combined output of $6 trillion, which exceeds the 12-nation European Community. The NAFTA idea was further expanded in June 1990, when President Bush unveiled his "Enterprise for the Americas" initiative (EAI). The Bush initiative called for reduction of bilateral debt and some new investment funds, but the centerpiece was a free trade area for the entire hemisphere. As an indication of the new rapprochement with the United States, Latin American governments enthusiastically applauded the initiative, and "framework agreements" have been signed with almost all countries in the hemisphere.[21]

The question of concern here is the nature of a future NAFTA (and perhaps, eventually, a western hemisphere arrangement). Will it be a "Fortress America," attempting to discriminate against outsiders such as the Japanese, or will it be an area open to all on an equal basis? The answer may well depend on US *perceptions* of its economic strength. If the United States perceives that it is losing its competitive edge, it could well attempt to compensate by increasing dominance in its sphere of influence. This is the fear of the Japanese themselves and the basis for the first of the three models.[22] In particular, the Japanese are concerned that in response to pressure from organized labor, industries that have been hurt by Japanese competition, and politicians who have accused them of "using Mexico as a backdoor or export platform," the final treaty will impose a stiff local or regional content law for duty-free exports in either direction. The US–Canada agreement has a 50 percent local content requirement, and early drafts of the NAFTA treaty call for rates to rise to 62.5 percent over an 8-year period. Such a local content requirement would strongly discourage Japanese firms interested in investing in Mexico for markets in the United States and Canada.[23]

As a forerunner of things to come, a ruling in early 1991 by US Customs authorities had introduced new restrictions even before the free trade talks with Mexico got under way. Before this ruling, many Japanese-made products entering the US market were exempted from tariffs under the General System of Preferences (GSP) as long as they included 35 percent of value added in Mexico. It did not matter whether a large proportion of the parts and components in these products were imported from Japan or the Far East. Now, such parts and components must undergo one substantial transformation within Mexico for products to qualify as originating in Mexico, and a double substantial transformation for these products to qualify for GSP treatment.[24]

There are also other instances of potential constraints on Japanese investment in Latin America, arising from unresolved issues between Japan and the United States. Again, Mexico provides a case in point. The Mexican government has drastically reduced bureaucratic red tape and has diminished its regulatory powers, with the objective of luring foreign investors to participate in the drive to privatize inefficient, capital-starved public firms. Yet the giant telecommunications conglomerate Nihon Telephone and Telegraph (NTT) decided not to bid for Teléfonos de México concerned that, if it succeeded in gaining control of a leading Latin American service firm, businesses in the United States would complain that Japan itself should open its own market to this type of investment.[25]

The prospect of a "Fortress America" in which Japanese business activities are severely restricted will grow stronger should international trade conflicts deepen, or should US–Japan economic tensions continue to escalate. If forced to choose sides, there is little doubt that Latin America will support the United States – even if that means giving up a potential source of capital and technology.

Japan's Headquarters Strategy

While the previous model suggests that the United States might be able to overcome Japanese competition, at least in the Western Hemisphere, a second model sees Japan continuing its successful ascent. In global terms, it portrays Japan as displacing the United States through protection of its own market combined with government support for export-related activities. A well-known advocate of this line of analysis is Ezra Vogel of Harvard University, who speaks of a possible "Pax Nipponica" and who has written a book called *Japan as Number One*. "Future historians," says Vogel, "may well mark the mid-1980s as the time when Japan surpassed the United States to become the world's dominant economic power . . . America's GNP may remain larger than Japan's well into the 1990s (depending on exchange rate measurements), but there are many reasons to believe that Japan will extend its lead as the world's dominant economic power in the years ahead."[26]

Vogel points to several trends that give Japan an edge over the United States: better use of technologies of the new industrial revolution in microelectronics and lasers, which will lead to an increasing productivity gap; new Japanese competitiveness in services, an area long dominated by the United States; and a vastly expanded Japanese research and development capacity. Japan's singleminded determination to pursue its perceived national interest – manifested in such varying ways as the strong emphasis on education, the premium on company loyalty, and public-sector support for economic information and technology – has given the country a perhaps unsurmountable lead over the United States. This lead will be translated into great economic leverage in determining the future structure of the world economy, one that will certainly redound to Japan's own advantage.

A complementary Latin American-centered version of this model has been advanced by Leon Hollerman. Although using Brazil as an example, he implies that many Third World countries, especially the NICs, are likely to follow a similar path. Hollerman speaks of a "headquarters scenario," which is said to be Japan's strategy for assuring its economic security in the new world context. "In its broadest aspect, the headquarters country scenario transcends bilateral complementarities as a rationale for Japan's relations with other countries . . . ; the strategy contemplates the coordination of sets of complementary relations among third nations. In this perspective, Japan emerges as an orchestrator of complementarities rather than as a . . . 'locomotive' in the world economy."[27]

The model sees Japan exporting its low and medium-technology industries to Brazil and other NICs – unlike the United States, which tries to protect such sectors – while maintaining high-technology, high value-added production facilities at home. Key to this international dispersion of industries are the giant *sogo shosha* (trading companies) with branches in all important countries of the world. As Japan becomes an importer of low and medium-technology goods, its merchandise balance will turn to deficit, while its service balance (including profits and interest) will move into surplus. "Japan's strategy will have contrived to smother its bilateral trade frictions with the United States while promoting multilateral frictions between the United States and the 'new Japans.' "[28] Market-sharing deals can then be struck between high-tech firms in the United States and Japan.

As one of the "new Japans," Brazil (and some other Latin American countries) would receive Japanese assistance to develop their productive facilities. Some might export to Japan itself, but mainly they would supply their own and third markets, while generally keeping prices low for raw materials and low/medium-technology goods. Japanese investments in Brazil in the 1960s and 1970s are seen as forerunners of such a strategy; investments ranged from iron ore and steel to soybeans and wood chips to shipbuilding. The Japanese government and private sector joined forces to provide Brazil with some of the best facilities in the world.[29]

Such cooperation, according to Hollerman, was facilitated by shared values between Japan and Brazil. These values included a hierarchical view of society, the need for a powerful state to guide the economy, and protection for new industries. Hollerman claims that some Brazilian policy-makers specifically indicated that they were following a "Japanese model." In addition to positive Japanese steps, a Japanese–Brazilian alliance was helped by the failure of the United States to have any clear policy toward Brazil. After the debt crisis in 1982, the apparent lack of US concern further alienated the Brazilian government and opened up opportunities for the Japanese. "The ultimate implication for the United States is that instead of being *confronted* by Japan, it will be *outflanked* by Japan in accordance with the headquarters strategy."[30]

US–Japan Cooperation

The third model is the cooperative scenario, officially endorsed by both the United States and Japan. One influential advocate of US–Japanese cooperation is C. Fred Bergsten, director of the Washington-based Institute of International Economics. Saying that "it is obvious that the United States can no longer play the role of global economic benefactor," Bergsten goes on to suggest that "the development of a new means of pluralistic security leadership, as well as of a more cooperative economic leadership, may finally be made inevitable by the massive economic shifts in the 1980s."[31] In particular, Bergsten advocates the formation of a Group of Two (G-2 or "bigemony") to deal with major world economic problems. Although recognizing that Japan and the United States could follow either a confrontational or a cooperative path, he argues that the latter is more likely because of the growing interdependence between the two countries. The G-2 should first concentrate on resolving the current imbalances between the two economies themselves, but it could then move on to tackle broader economic issues such as managing the world currency system and promoting economic development in the Third World.

Similarly, Zbigniew Brzezinski has argued for a US–Japanese "global partnership – which one can perhaps call 'Amerippon' – with farsighted acts of statesmanship that in themselves would be beneficial to the international community while advancing the special interests of the partnership itself."[32] The two pillars of this new global partnership advocated by the former US National Security Advisor are of particular significance to our discussion: "a comprehensive strategy for the development of the Latin American economy as a whole, or at least of its Central American and Mexican portions . . . in an area of great potential importance to both (the United States and Japan)." Further, "an even more ambitious goal might involve jointly setting a target date for an American–Japanese free trade zone . . . creating the world's paramount economic unit but also inevitably enhanced global political consultations and joint strategizing."[33]

In the particular Latin American context, most of the proposals for cooperation have been more modest than Brzezinski's "comprehensive strategy." In a book sponsored by the Americas Society, an organization of US corporations with investments in Latin America, Susan Kaufman Purcell and Robert Immerman suggest expanded consultations by a wide range of government officials from the United States and Japan with respect to Latin American problems.[34] These should involve political issues (such as democracy, arms sales, nuclear non-proliferation and human rights) as well as economic problems. Purcell and Immerman also advocate increased contacts among academic experts and between academics and government people. In broader terms, Purcell and Immerman imply that virtually all Japanese activities in Latin America can be interpreted as an attempt to cooperate with the United States. This is because they believe the Japanese government wants to use its policies toward the region as a means to dampen bilateral economic tensions.[35]

Specific steps toward US–Japanese cooperation have focused on aid and debt policies. Most of the collaboration on aid has taken place in Asia. Several meetings have been held, bringing together field staff and aid policy officials from Washington and Tokyo to discuss mutual concerns in the Philippines, Indonesia, and India. Activities have also focused on greater cooperation in incorporating each nation's private sector into development initiatives. Seminars were held in California and Florida to discuss ways that US firms could win a larger share of contracts funded by Japanese aid.[36]

Likewise both parallel and joint projects have been undertaken in some Asian countries. Examples include an institute of postgraduate studies in agriculture in Bangladesh, an agricultural development research center in Thailand, an education program in Western Somoa, and agricultural development projects in Zaire and Indonesia. Only recently has such cooperation begun in Latin America. A pilot project underway right now, involving a tourism infrastructure project in Jamaica, includes construction of roads, sewage facilities, and ports. Japan is providing most of the money, including loans for the purchase of capital goods, while the United States supplies project management, oversight, and "know-how." An understanding has been reached to the effect that the Japanese will not tie equipment loans to purchases in Japan.[37]

More important than aid for Latin America, since neither Japan nor the United States gives a large volume of aid money to the region, is cooperation on debt problems. Ever since the debt crisis erupted in 1982, the Japanese have explicitly or implicitly been cooperating with the United States, which took the lead in formulating international debt policy. The Ministry of Finance, together with the Bank of Tokyo, lined up Japanese banks to participate in the refinancing negotiations and to provide "new money" to those governments that followed economic policies approved by the IMF and World Bank. Ironically, in fact, the Japanese banks followed US policy more closely than did banks from the United States itself.[38]

In 1987, Japan went further and established a program to recycle some of its balance-of-payments surplus to highly indebted countries. Over the course of the last 5 years, $65 billion has been allocated to this fund. Some goes directly to Third World countries via the Japanese Export–Import Bank and the Overseas Economic Cooperation Fund (OECF), some supports co-financing with the World Bank and Interamerican Development Bank (IDB), and some is allocated to these multilateral agencies for distribution to country recipients through their normal channels. Latin America has received about 28 percent of the Eximbank loans, though a much lower share of those from OECF. Money also accrues to the region indirectly, through the multilateral agencies and especially the IDB.[39]

In 1989, the Japanese undertook another debt initiative and put forth the Miyazawa Plan to securitize some bank loans in order to lower debt service payments and increase the value of bank assets. Although the Japanese saw their plan as complementary to the Baker Plan being followed by the Reagan administration, the latter did not perceive it as a cooperative venture. Under the Bush administration, however, Treasury Secretary Brady adopted many of the ideas from the Miyazawa Plan, expanded them, and made them official US policy known as the Brady Plan. The Japanese quickly applauded the new program and pledged money to underwrite the bonds that would be a key component of the new policy; Mexico and Venezuela have been among the main beneficiaries.[40]

EVALUATION OF THE THREE MODELS

Which of the three models – rivalry with US domination, rivalry with increasing Japanese presence, or cooperation – is most likely? To begin to answer this question, we need to stop talking about "Japan" and "the United States" and look at groups within the two countries. At a minimum, we need to distinguish between the public and private sectors in both countries. To borrow a phrase from *The Economist*, there are "those who deal in power" and "those who deal in money." Likewise, we need to differentiate among geographical regions within Latin America. It is quite likely that future relationships may be different in Mexico, Central America and the Caribbean, and South America.

Public Versus Private Sector

There is a fair amount of evidence available on the activities of US and Japanese public and private actors in Latin America during the postwar period, which can cast light on the merits of the three models. In addition, we can draw on more general research pertaining to the behavior of US and Japanese business firms and governments. To be sure, this evidence is not completely clear or unequivocal, but it does provide some significant clues to future trends.

At the most general level, we argue that public-sector actors (especially the executive branch in the two countries) will try to follow a cooperative strategy, while private businesses are more likely to engage in competitive behavior. Thus, an important determinant of the overall trend will be whether businesses or governments take the lead, which in turn will depend on whether there is a return to growth and political stability in Latin America. If dynamic growth returns, private businesses are likely to renew their interest in the region and become the dominant actors on both the US and Japanese sides. In the absence of growth and stability, the governments will take the lead by default. In the event of head-on competition, evidence in other regions, including the United States itself, suggests that US firms will have a hard time beating out their Japanese competitors. But, as we will argue in the next section on "trilateralism," the Latin Americans may have an interest in controlling competition.

The US and Japanese governments have different reasons for wanting to cooperate in the Latin American context. For the Japanese, Latin America offers a relatively low-cost opportunity to show that they are "team players" and that they are trying to meet demands in the US congress and elsewhere with respect to "burden-sharing." (It will be remembered from Table 1.2 that total Japanese government money to Latin America, including both ODA and Eximbank loans, has averaged only about $700 million annually over recent years.) At the same time, this money helps to stabilize a region where Japanese businesses have a substantial stake, even if they are not investing much at the moment. (Cumulative investment levels are $11 billion in direct investment and $31 in bank loans; see Table 1.1.)

For the US government, the latter motive is also relevant since US corporations have an even larger stake in Latin America than do the Japanese ($35 billion in DFI and $28 billion in bank loans). Furthermore, Latin America is an important export market for US firms, and the debt crisis of the 1980s had a strong negative impact on the US trade balance. Finally, geographical proximity provides other motives for trying to help Latin America: migration, environment, and drugs. At the same time, despite its greater reasons for wanting to assist Latin America, the United States has fewer means. USAID flows to

Latin America are expected to decline substantially in the coming years, the Eximbank is already a minor player, and military assistance has been cut back and will continue to go down. Where can replacement funds be found? Europe is unlikely to contribute much because of demands in its own region, so Japan is the most obvious source.[41]

Even with the two executive branches inclined to cooperate, however, the way ahead is not necessarily clear. First, there are dissenting voices within each government, particularly among those who see their mission as representing business or groups who might be alternative users of government funds. In the US case, this includes most congresspeople plus the Commerce Department and perhaps the US Trade Representative. In Japan, the Diet has become more hesitant to appropriate money for foreign aid, and the Ministry of International Trade and Industry (MITI) has conflicts with other ministries because of its close relations with Japanese firms.

Second, a problem that exacerbates the first is different views in Japan and the United States about what constitutes "development assistance." For the United States, it is now mainly government grants for small-scale projects related to basic human needs. For Japan, it is loans for large-scale projects, especially infrastructure. Moreover, the Japanese concept of "economic cooperation" involves business as a crucial component. Even if the loans are "untied," the inclusion of Japanese business raises suspicion in the United States.

Third, a key aspect of a cooperative strategy, which has not really been addressed until now, is how decisions should be made. The preferred US method – Japan provides the money and the United States spends it – will clearly be unacceptable to the Japanese over the long term, although they have been doing something approaching it in recent years. In the longer run, if Japan is to continue to provide resources, it must also have a say in how they are spent. The United States has been reluctant to admit that power-sharing must accompany burden-sharing, but that cost must eventually be paid.

Turning to private businesses, much more rivalry than cooperation is likely *if they are interested in Latin America*. In both the United States and Japan, the main goal of private-sector actors is profits, although with the important difference that US firms take a much shorter-term view of the profit-making process. It is this struggle for profits that creates competition among firms. Some are strong enough to compete on their own, while others demand help from their home government. The latter, in turn, puts pressure on the governments, as indicated above.

Beyond these general statements that are true of all business enterprises, there are also significant differences across sectors of business. At a minimum, we need to distinguish among banks, natural resource producers, and manufacturing firms. Table 1.3 shows the relative importance of these and other sectors for US and Japanese firms investing in Latin America. Given lack of uniformity in definitions and data-collection methods, these figures should be taken as only rough indicators. Even so, they suggest some interesting comparisons that need to be analyzed.

Within the banking industry, a convergence of negative opinion about prospects in Latin America seems to include most US and Japanese institutions. Since Latin American loans have not been

Table 1.3   US and Japanese direct foreign investment in Latin America[a] by Sector, 1989

Sector	United States (%)	Japan (%)
Manufacturing	65.7	43.9
Food	(7.6)	(1.8)
Chemicals	(14.2)	(4.8)
Metals	(5.6)	(15.6)
Non-electrical machinery	(8.9)	(3.1)
Electrical machinery	(3.6)	(4.0)
Transportation equipment	(10.3)	(8.5)
Textiles	(b)	(3.5)
Wood/pulp	(b)	(1.6)
Other manufacturing	(15.6)	(1.1)
Petroleum	7.8	c
Mining	c	12.6
Fishing/agriculture	c	2.7
Trade	3.0	12.2
Finance/banking	11.4	6.4
Other non-manufacturing	12.1	22.3
Total	100.0	100.0
Total ($ billion)	$31.5	$12.4

[a] Excludes Panama and Caribbean tax havens.
[b] Included in "other manufacturing."
[c] Included in "other non-manufacturing."
Sources: US Department of Commerce, *Survey of Current Business*, August 1990; Japanese Ministry of Finance, *Annual Report of International Finance Bureau*, 1990.

profitable during the last decade, the bankers say it would be hard to justify new loans to their shareholders. The possible exception is short-term trade credits. The recent Brady negotiations, which gave banks the opportunity to choose between increasing their exposure or reducing their Latin American portfolios and taking a loss, saw all Japanese banks take the latter option; most US banks did the same although a few chose to put up new money. Country risk exposure, however, must be separated from local financial services in which a number of banks and related institutions are interested. For example, all four of Japan's major securities firms have decided to open offices in Mexico, and the booming stock markets in many Latin American countries are attracting brokers and investment bankers. As Table 1.3 indicates, financial services are an important sector for both the United States and Japan.[42]

Unlike banking, natural resource investment arouses differential responses among US and Japanese corporations. US firms suffered a large number of nationalizations in the 1970s, some negotiated and others on a hostile basis. Oil in Venezuela was the most important example of the former, while Chilean copper and Peruvian oil were instances of the latter. Since the Japanese had engaged in different types of arrangements – especially the use of joint ventures – they had less trouble in the natural resource sector. Obtaining natural resources is also more important for Japan, which has very few of its own. Thus Japanese firms are still active in mining, agriculture and fishing, while US DFI is limited to small amounts of petroleum investment (see Table 1.3).[43]

Manufacturing accounts for the largest single chunk of foreign investment in Latin America for both the United States and Japan, as Table 1.3 shows, but it is relatively more important for US corporations. Both countries are continuing to invest in this sector but at a much slower rate than the 1960s or 1970s. It is in the manufacturing sector where rivalry might be most likely to occur between US and Japanese firms, especially competition for limited domestic markets in the Latin American region. Until now, however, there seems to have been an implicit division of labor: US firms have concentrated in food processing, chemicals, and non-electrical machinery, while Japanese businesses have been most prominent in metal products. Only in transportation equipment is there a current basis for direct rivalry.

Before finishing this section, a word is warranted on the inter-relationship between the public and private sectors in Japan. It is sometimes difficult to know where the one leaves off and the other begins. Many examples of public – private interaction were seen in the big natural resource projects in Latin America in the 1960s and 1970s. In the early 1980s, it took a different form as the Ministry of Finance twisted the arms of the Japanese banks to get them to participate in the debt reschedulings for Latin American countries. As the 1980s ended, however, it became clear that large corporations were obtaining much more independence from the government. MITI, in particular, was losing some of its clout as firms rejected its attempts to provide "guidance," but the Ministry of Finance was also under pressure to free the banks to follow their own course with Latin debtors. When it did so, the banks quickly began to unload their debt.[44]

The irony is that one of the main reasons for the declining influence of the Japanese government is that the United States pushed it toward liberalization, especially in the financial markets but also elsewhere. Thus, the United States, which would benefit most under a cooperative approach with Japan in Latin America, has limited the possibilities of its coming about. The Japanese government can no longer bring overwhelming influence to line up private firms with foreign policy goals. The full implications of this development will not become obvious until growth resumes in Latin America because, without growth, there is little interest in the region on the part of private business, whether US or Japanese.

Geographical Divisions

Further insight about cooperation or rivalry can be obtained by disaggregating Latin America by countries and sub-regions, since the relative interests of Japan and the United States vary along this dimension. Table 1.4 presents the country distributions of US and Japanese economic activities in Latin America. It shows a wide variation in the three fields of trade, DFI, and debt, but several constants can be identified. First, Japan always has its greatest presence in South America, ranging from 64 percent of its trade relations to 71 percent of its DFI. A closely related point: Brazil is Japan's single most important partner in the region. Second, Mexico is the most important country for the United States. This pattern is not as clear as that between Japan and Brazil, since US firms have twice as much DFI in Brazil as in Mexico, but Mexico's dominance among US trade partners is striking. Third, neither country has much of an economic stake in Central America and the Caribbean area, once the tax-haven/flag-of-convenience "investments" are eliminated.

Based on these quantitative indicators and other more qualitative data, we can begin to sketch a likely pattern of alignments for the future. In Central America and the Caribbean, the most probable

Table 1.4   US and Japanese economic transactions with Latin America by sub-region, 1989

Type of transaction	United States (%)	Japan (%)
Trade[a]		
South America	35.8	63.7
(Brazil)	(12.6)	(29.0)
Mexico	48.2	24.6
Central America/Caribbean[b]	16.0	11.6
Direct Foreign Investment[c]		
South America	74.7	79.8
(Brazil)	(46.6)	(62.8)
Mexico	22.4	18.8
Central America/Caribbean[b]	2.8	1.5
Private Bank Debt[d]		
South America	64.0	65.8
(Brazil)	(25.4)	(27.3)
Mexico	34.3	31.9
Central America/Caribbean[b]	1.8	2.3
Average[e]		
South America	58.2	69.8
(Brazil)	(28.2)	(39.7)
Mexico	35.0	25.1
Central America/Caribbean[b]	6.4	5.1

[a] Annual figures for 1989.
[b] Excludes Panama and Caribbean tax havens.
[c] Cumulative through 1989.
[d] Medium and long-term, cumulative through 1988 (Japan), 1990 (US).
[e] Unweighted average of trade, DFI, and debt percentages.
Sources: IMF, *Direction of Trade Statistics* (US and Japanese trade); *Country Exposure Lending Survey* (US bank loans); Japanese Finance Ministry, *Annual Report of International Finance Bureau* (Japanese bank loans and direct investment); *Survey of Current Business* (US direct investment).

scenario is a close alliance between Japan and the United States. There are several reasons to justify such a hypothesis. First, since there is little foreign private involvement in these countries, governments are likely to take the lead and we have argued that they will tend to cooperate. Second, the high level of poverty – and destruction in some cases – means that there is not much chance for private involvement any time soon. Third, these are countries that have traditionally been closely associated with US security interests, so Japan is highly unlikely to risk independent actions, especially with so little to gain. Steps are already being taken to form an alliance in this sub-region. The United States has requested that Japan join in providing assistance to Panama, Nicaragua, and Honduras to help them eliminate their arrears to the multilateral agencies and thus become eligible for new loans. In broader terms, the Partnership for Democracy and Development will unite the United States and Japan with European countries in a large-scale reconstruction program.[45]

In South America, Japan may take a more independent role. The United States has traditionally been less involved there, and the size of the markets and availability of natural resources make those nations much more attractive than Central America. Chile and Venezuela are two countries the Japanese continually cite as attractive investment locations, and indeed they have begun investing in both. Brazil, of course, has the greatest potential for Japan, and the Japanese population has given Japan more confidence to act there than in other parts of Latin America. The poor management and performance of the Brazilian economy over the past decade, however, has led to declining capital inflows from all sources. Peru poses a particular challenge for the Japanese. They have made it clear that they want to assist the Fujimori government, but they have hesitated to take the lead for fear of being accused of helping a fellow Japanese. In addition, the state of the economy and political relations are so bad that very little private-sector participation can be expected, so the government must be prepared to put up most of the money. The Peruvian situation, at least in the short run, is likely to be similar to that in Central America.[46]

Mexico is the most interesting case. Its geographical proximity to the United States would suggest caution, but the potential for economic gain is enormous. Japan's role toward Mexico will be the most telling in terms of predicting its overall attitude toward Latin America. Although investment has increased substantially over the past decade, it started from a very low base. Even now Japan accounts for only 6 per cent of Mexico's foreign investment. Nissan Motors has announced a $1 billion expansion of its auto facilities in Mexico, which will include exports back to Japan itself, but most firms appear to be waiting to see the outcome of the free trade negotiations and especially the local content rules.[47]

In summary, some aspects of all three models may be found in Latin America over the coming years, with geographical location an important determinant of which will be most prevalent in a given country. The economic conditions of the region as a whole and of individual countries will also be relevant to whether rivalry or cooperation predominates. At the same time, it seems unlikely that any of the three will appear in a pure form. The two models of rivalry are unlikely because of their high costs in terms of more important Japanese and US goals: access to the giant US market and the booming Asian area respectively. A pure cooperation model is also unlikely because of different perspectives in the United States and Japan on many issues pertaining to development as well as the distribution of power. Finally, the three models are deficient because they leave out a crucial actor: Latin America itself. It is to this issue that we now turn.

A NEW TRILATERAL MODEL?

A striking point about all three models is their concentration on what Japan and the United States will do with respect to Latin America, giving very little emphasis to Latin American desires and initiatives. This approach is unsatisfactory for two reasons. From a descriptive point of view, it gives an incomplete account of what is happening in the world; it fails to include initiatives that are coming from Latin America. From a prescriptive viewpoint, such passive strategies are unlikely to bring about development; a more active role by both public and private actors in the region will be necessary. Thus, we conclude by proposing an alternative model, which we call "trilateralism." We will first discuss the characteristics of trilateralism and its historical record in parts of the Third World. Then we will see how it may be emerging now in Latin America through the efforts of some governments and regional organizations.

What is "Trilateralism?"?

Trilateralism, by our definition, is a particular variant of a general strategy of diversification. It has two essential components. First, it involves a decision by a Third World country/region to pursue a development strategy involving active participation in the world economy but to seek a diversified set of international "partners." Such a strategy maximizes the advantages to be obtained from international relations, while minimizing the control of any one foreign power. In our case, we are talking about Latin America in "partnership" with the United States and Japan. The industrial nations can provide resources, technology, and expertise, but development policies must be conceived and carried out by Latin Americans themselves. Only then are the policies likely to have the domestic support necessary to make them successful.

The second element focuses on the nature of the relationship between the external actors. While it might appear that a rivalry between them would be preferable from the perspective of the Third World – allowing the latter to play off the former to increase its own benefits – we are skeptical about the outcome. As an old African saying goes, when two elephants fight, the grass gets trampled. The possibility for a beneficial outcome for the weakest party is especially limited in a situation like that in the Western Hemisphere, where one of the external actors is clearly dominant. Latin Americans stand to gain more if the United States does not feel threatened by Japan. If it does, retaliation could drive the Japanese out, at least in the short-to-medium run, thus narrowing the potential for economic and political diversification.

It might be argued that Latin America is in such a weak position with respect to the United States and Japan that it could not play a leading or even an equal role. This argument ignores the fact that the governments of the region devote comparatively more time and resources to thinking about how best to manage their external economic and political relations. The reason is simple: the stakes are higher viewed from the perspective of the Latin nations. If they are to reduce the vulnerabilities that result from overdependence on exports of a few products, limited access to foreign markets, and the concentration of investment and loans in a few sources, they must learn to manage their external environment better. In the 1990s, this is likely to mean primarily the United States and Japan.

There are many historical precedents, both within the region and outside, to support the hypothesis that trilateralism is a model that can work. If we look elsewhere in the world, there are instances in which small and medium powers have succeeded at establishing such trilateral arrangements. Indeed, much of the Third World has attempted to do so. The most successful cases are found in East Asia. Rapidly-growing

South Korea and Taiwan were extremely skillful at getting support from both the United States and Japan. Between 1971 and 1986, for example, South Korea got 30 percent of its foreign capital from the United States and 44 percent from Japan, while Taiwan received 51 percent from the United States and 39 percent from Japan. These figures contrasted with Mexico, where 65 percent of foreign capital was of US origin.[48] East Asian trade has also had a strong bimodal pattern. Together this diversification of economic relations meant that the East Asian NICs were able to maintain substantial control over their own economies.

Other Third World areas have tried to follow similar paths. The Non-Aligned Movement embodied some elements of this concept, especially for the founding countries like India, Egypt, and Yugoslavia in the early postwar period. Some countries in Africa have tried to maintain relations with their former colonial powers while diversifying toward the United States. Even in Southeast Asia where Japanese economic relations have come to dominate, governments have sought to keep strong US involvement as a balancing factor.[49]

The pursuit of trilateralism also has historical precedents in Latin America, but the outcomes have been mixed. Some countries, especially in the Southern Cone, were successful early in the twentieth century. Although European powers were displaced from their prominent position in Latin America by a rising United States, Latin Americans continued to seek special alliances with Europe. They hoped that cultivation of these ties would strengthen their negotiating leverage with the United States. Brazil and Argentina's attempts to maintain relations with Britain, while establishing them with the United States, helped those countries considerably. Less successful were Chile and Argentina's attempts to court Germany in the early 1940s, which elicited a harsh US response. After World War II, the United States assumed a political role in world affairs commensurate with its economic power, and it consolidated its hegemonic position within Latin America as well, thus increasing the difficulties of diversification.

Postwar attempts have been of two types. Some countries tried to obtain resources from the Soviet Union and its allies. Cuba, of course, is the most dramatic example. Whether Castro's original intent was to form a trilateral relationship with the Soviet Union and the United States is unclear; if so, it was a failure and merely substituted one dominant power for another. Chile, Peru, Nicaragua, and several smaller countries also attempted to gain greater control over their development prospects by establishing links with the Soviet Union. All of the governments that did so were eventually displaced, however, in part because of their attempts at greater independence, showing that the costs of defecting from the US alliance are very high for small and medium-size powers within the immediate sphere of influence of the United States.[50]

In a less dramatic fashion, many Latin American governments in the 1970s made efforts to diversify their international economic and political relations within the capitalist world. Rising prices of their export commodities and the availability of loans from commercial banks supported this drive, and as a result several Latin nations considerably expanded their trade, investment, and financial ties with Europe, Japan, and the Middle East. Brazil was particularly successful in this regard.[51] The progress achieved, however, was stalled or even reversed during the 1980s. As the region plunged into economic crisis precipitated by missing payments on its foreign debt, Latin America found its profile of foreign economic relations not more diversified but rather more dependent than ever on the good will and resources of the United States.[52]

Despite its patchy record, diversification will undoubtedly continue to be a fundamental component of Latin America's strategy to redefine its position within the world political economy. Since Europe has its own concerns, which make it unlikely that it will devote much attention and resources to Latin America, and the former Soviet Union is no longer a viable partner if it ever was, Japan has become the main alternative.[53] We have argued that a general environment of cooperation and not an escalation of conflict with the United States is a necessary condition for trilateralism to work. As long as Japan is not perceived as a threat to the United States, Latin America may search for innovative and ingenious ways to enhance its leverage with its powerful neighbor through a closer association with Japan.

It must be pointed out that there are critical domestic ingredients for a trilateral strategy including Japan to work. The Japanese have made it clear that there are prerequisites for obtaining their investment funds and access to their markets. Trade requires consistently high-quality products plus a record of meeting obligations in a timely fashion. In order to attract Japanese capital, public or private, Latin American governments must bring inflation and budget deficits under control, promote exports and perhaps liberalize imports, and provide a welcoming attitude toward foreign investment. More generally, the Japanese want clear rules to be established for the operation of foreign capital and maintained over time and across changes of government. This implies the creation of a domestic consensus about a new development strategy focusing on openness to the international economy.[54]

Steps Toward Trilateralism?

Of all the countries in Latin America, the two that most closely approximate our notion of trilateralism are Chile and Mexico. Both have taken aggressive steps to increase their relations with Japan as a way of diversifying away from dependence on the United States. Yet neither has tried to substitute the former for the latter, nor even to play off the one against the other. Rather they see the two as complementary – and complementary to their own development policies.

Chile is engaged in a sustained effort to lure Japanese firms to participate in its economic success. Since the US share of foreign investment is so overwhelming, the small Japanese role is not seen as any threat. This is especially true since Japanese investment has been concentrated in natural resources, an area where the United States has not been very active in recent years. In addition, following a decade of hard work, several firms owned by Chilean citizens have been among Latin America's first to break into the relatively protected Japanese market for non-traditional exports. Thus, fruit, wood, and fish products have joined the traditional copper in Japan's imports from Chile. This trade venture ironically began during the military government, in reaction to Chile's loss of many privileges in the US market.[55]

In 1990 Chile signed letters of intent with both the United States and Mexico for opening free trade talks in the near future. Although the Chilean economy is comparatively small, it was the first nation in South America to join the movement toward region-wide trade and investment liberalization. The Japanese, who are fully aware of Chile's aspirations, see their involvement in that country as an opportunity to strengthen their own position as insiders in a potential hemispheric trade bloc. The challenge for Chilean leaders is to turn to their advantage the Japanese perception of the future importance of their country.

Mexico presents an even more interesting case. For President Salinas and his team, a crucial assumption underlying the current Mexican strategy is that a closer association with the United States through the NAFTA will enhance Mexico's chances of effectively diversifying the country's economic relations with the rest of the world. European and Asian investors will look at Mexico in a much more favorable light if it formally joins the North American economy. By the same token, expanded relations with industrial powers like Japan may enhance Mexico's negotiating leverage with its powerful northern neighbor. In this sense, the Mexican case perhaps best illustrates the possibilities of pursuing a trilateralist strategy.

Like Chile, Mexico's trade and investment are so dominated by the United States that increasing relations with Japan are not seen as posing a generalized threat. What has caused concern among organized labor and in the US Congress is the high profile of Japanese *maquiladoras* and the concentration of Japanese-owned plants in the automobile and electronics industries. Both of these issues receive constant attention in the US media because US producers in these industries are being displaced by their more successful Japanese competitors. This example implies that, in certain cases, tensions may develop in a trilateral relationship. While the US government has until now been willing to let Japanese assembly plants located in the border area ship goods to the US market under special facilities, a crucial test will be how "rules of origin" are handled in the eventual NAFTA treaty. Restrictive rules would result in lower Japanese investment in Mexico and thus more tensions with the United States, since one of Mexico's goals in negotiating a free trade agreement is to attract investors from around the globe.[56]

Beyond individual country efforts to take a more active role in shaping the future of US–Japanese–Latin American relations, several regional organizations have also been working along similar lines. Both the Interamerican Development Bank (IDB) and the UN Economic Commission for Latin America and the Caribbean (ECLAC) have had joint activities with Japan dating back to the 1970s. More recently, the Latin American Economic System (SELA) and the Andean Pact have also begun to initiate activities with Japan.

Japan's role in the IDB began in 1976 when it became one of first non-regional members of the Bank. Contributions since that time have totaled $10.7 billion, including paid-in and callable capital, contributions to the Fund for Special Operations and the Japan Special Fund, borrowings from Japan's capital markets, and project co-financing with the Export–Import Bank of Japan, the OECF, and Japanese private banks. A symbolic gesture of the interaction was the holding of the IDB's 32nd Annual Meeting in Nagoya, Japan, in April 1991. Beyond financial activities, the IDB and Japan's Export–Import Bank have jointly sponsored four symposia (in 1979, 1982, 1985, and 1989) to encourage economic and financial relations between Japan and Latin America. The increased role of Japan (as well as the other non-regional members) has moderated to some extent the influence of the United States in the IDB.[57]

ECLAC's activities with Japan have been geared toward research incorporating the development experience of Japan (and other East Asian countries) into their policy analysis and recommendations. As early as 1978, ECLAC and the International Development Center of Japan formed two teams of researchers to analyze development problems in Latin American countries and the possibilities of cooperation between Japan and Latin America to resolve them. The report of the research teams posited the twin goals of high economic growth and greater social equity for Latin America and drew on experiences in East Asia to construct an analytical framework for Latin American development policy. In addition to the researchers involved in the above projects, ECLAC has almost continually had a Japanese economist working in its Santiago headquarters, and ECLAC researchers have joined Japanese colleagues in a number of other endeavors. A recent project was a comparative study of Latin American and East Asian development experiences.[58]

SELA and the Andean Pact have become interested in working with Japanese counterparts in the last few years. After publishing a series of reports on Japan and Latin America, SELA has recently hired one of Latin America's premier Japan experts as a member of its permanent staff. In December 1991, it held an international symposium of experts on Japanese relations with Latin America; from this meeting came recommendations to SELA's Board of Governors about possible ways to increase Japanese cooperation with Latin America.[59] The Andean Pact likewise has commissioned reports on Japanese interactions with its member countries (Bolivia, Colombia, Ecuador, Peru, and Venezuela) and possible future joint activities. It, too, has a permanent staff member who specializes in relations with Japan.[60]

In summary, a trilateral model linking the United States and Japan with Latin America offers the latter the opportunity to decrease its vulnerability to external shocks and pressures by diversifying its external relations. Since the interwar period, the United States has dominated both Latin America's foreign trade and investment flows, which arguably has limited the amount of resources obtained and increased their price monetarily and in terms of strings attached. Thus, the possibility of increasing Japan's involvement, both as a market and a supplier of capital, has a real attraction for the region. In the case of Chile and Mexico, governments and private businesses are actively and successfully seeking contacts with Japan; other countries are doing so to a more limited extent. Several regional organizations have also been promoting relations with Japan. These actions do not mean that anyone sees Japan as replacing the United States but as participating in a complementary relationship. This trend is likely to accelerate during the rest of the 1990s and – if played out skillfully – should help Latin America recuperate and move ahead again after the "lost decade" of the 1980s.

JAPANESE PERSPECTIVES AND LATIN AMERICAN CASE STUDIES

One of the most interesting aspects of our experience in editing this book has been to discover how different the emerging relationships look, depending on the observer's location within the triangle. In many instances, there is a similarity in the views presented by our Japanese and Latin American colleagues, but the relative importance attached to certain trends can vary substantially. Likewise, the conceptual and analytical interpretations are sometimes difficult to reconcile. These differences are a testimony to the complexities involved when it comes to understanding social phenomena within and across diverse cultures and across political and economic structures.

In Part II of the book, three Japanese scholars offer their perspectives on their country's past and present economic and political relations with Latin America, as well as on the large migration of Japanese nationals to the region over the last century. In general, these authors downplay the importance of Latin America for Japan in comparison to the United States, Asia, and even Europe.

Chapter 2, by Kotaro Horisaka, analyzes Japan's economic interactions with Latin America. After tracing the postwar history of trade, direct investment, and financial links, Horisaka says that the 1980s have been a period of Japanese withdrawal from the region. Part of the explanation he offers is the debt crisis, but he also points to the one-sided nature of the relationship until now. Latin Americans have rarely taken any initiative, so when Japanese interest fell, the relationship atrophied. In the last few years, the Japanese government began financing the region through its recycling program; the question is whether the business sector will follow suit. Horisaka concludes by identifying three scenarios that would increase business interest: renewal of growth in Latin America, a rise in commodity prices, and greater initiatives by Latin Americans to attract Japanese investors

In a complementary analysis to that of Horisaka, Hiroshi Matsushita in Chapter 3 discusses Japan's diplomatic relations with Latin America. Somewhat paradoxically, as Japan has lost economic interest in the region, it seems to have increased its political interests there. Contrary to its traditional principle of shunning politics in favor of economics, the Japanese have recently become concerned with issues like democratization and military spending. In another more gradual shift, Matsushita sees Japan as becoming more independent of the United States, globally and even in the US "backyard." This independence, he admits, is still very partial, but it has encompassed positions different from its main ally with respect to Cuba, the Malvinas/Falklands, Panama, and Peru. Nonetheless, Matsushita cautions that the changes are likely to progress slowly since Japan does not want to endanger its relations with the United States.

Part II closes with an analysis of Japanese migration to Latin America, a topic of particular importance in Japan. Iyo Kunimoto points out in Chapter 4 that Latin America is the region of the world where we find the largest community of Japanese descendants. In the early part of the twentieth century and immediately after World War II, the Japanese government took the initiative in sending people abroad to alleviate domestic social pressures. Many Latin American countries were eager to receive them to deal with labor shortages in agriculture and other sectors. The migrants' experiences in Latin America were not always positive, especially during World War II, as Kunimoto reports, but most of them have become quite successful. In the process, they frequently served as intermediaries for Japanese businesses wanting to trade or invest in the region. Even the Japanese Latin Americans have experienced difficulties during the 1980s, however, and a substantial number have begun a reverse migration (*dekasegi*) returning to the country of their ancestors at least for a temporary period.

Better to understand their countries' relationships with Japan, we have turned to colleagues in Latin America, who in Part III also offer their perspectives on what the ties with Japan may mean for relations with the United States. Here we can see the international asymmetry as Japan is more important to Latin America than vice-versa. Even a small share of Japan's capital exports could make a significant difference for Latin America.

The five countries include Brazil, Mexico, Peru, Chile, and Panama. Together they account for four fifths of Japan's trade with Latin America and two thirds of Japanese foreign investment in the region. As will be seen, the five have had different patterns of historical relationships with Japan. Brazil and Peru were the most important countries through the 1970s, but Mexico and Chile have now replaced them as the focus of Japanese interest. Panama continues to be important because of its geographical location and its role as a shipping registry and free trade zone.

Ernani Torres in Chapter 5 undertakes the task of explaining why Japanese relations with Brazil have turned "from fever to chill." From the 1950s through the 1970s, Brazil was one of Japan's favorite Third World nations. Some of the biggest Japanese projects in the world were located in Brazil: iron ore and steel complexes, Latin America's biggest shipyard, aluminum refineries, vast agricultural projects. One of the reasons for the negative shift in Japanese opinion, Torres suggests, was poor macroeconomic management in Brazil. In addition, however, international economic trends including the debt crisis as well as lower commodity prices, the development of futures markets, and the rise of Southeast Asia also contributed. Torres believes that the way to reverse the current stagnation of Japanese investment and trade with Brazil is for the country to develop a realistic plan for restoring the economy; regional integration might be a part of such a strategy. While Brazil would like to diversify its economic relations through increased links with Japan, he does not see this as challenging the dominant role of the United States.

In his analysis of Mexico's relations with Japan in Chapter 6, Gabriel Székely argues that oil has provided the Mexican government with a tool systematically to pursue a policy to attract Japanese capital and technology to encourage domestic development. While previous efforts in the 1960s and early 1970s achieved limited progress, the expansion of petroleum exports led Japanese commercial banks, trading companies involved in large state-sponsored joint ventures, and some manufacturers to raise their stake within the Mexican economy. Paradoxically, even though Mexico experienced a prolonged domestic recession in the 1980s as a result of the debt crisis, there was a sharp increase of Japanese investment in manufacturing. A very large proportion of the output of these new plants was geared to the US market, a development that both gave a new shape to the emerging trilateral relationship and raised a series of challenges and opportunities. At the heart of Mexico's trilateral strategy is the pursuit of two paths simultaneously: accelerating the pace of economic integration with the United States and continuing to expand economic relations with Japan.

Noting that the election of Alberto Fujimori as President of Peru aroused a great deal of interest in Japan, Pablo de la Flor in Chapter 7 points out that Peru has a long prior history of relations with Japan. Beginning with large-scale immigration in the early twentieth century, these relations later shifted toward economics, especially the mining sector. Under the military government that came to power in 1968, Peru and Japan appeared to have complementary interests. Japan wanted access to minerals and devised a "resource diplomacy" strategy, which meshed well with Peruvian desires to obtain capital for development. These relations soured in the 1980s, especially after Alan García severed links with the international financial community, but de la Flor suggests they may be strengthened again in the 1990s as Japan seeks to help Fujimori restructure and rejuvenate the Peruvian economy.

Chile, the country in the Southern Cone that occupies the largest geographical area facing the Pacific Ocean, and the nation that has gone furthest in adopting a liberal economic program, is a newcomer in terms of attracting the attention of Japan. It also holds a great potential for the future. Neantro Saavedra-Rivano in Chapter 8 notes two differences in Chile's relations with Japan in comparison with other Latin American nations. One is the emphasis on trade. Chilean trade with Japan is of much greater importance than investment (although some big natural resource projects are being developed). Even in non-traditional exports, Chile has made substantial inroads into the difficult Japanese market. Second, unlike other countries except Mexico, Chileans themselves have taken important initiatives toward Japan in order to diversify and amplify their international links. Since growth has also resumed in Chile, the country thus fulfills two of Horisaka's three conditions for a revival of Japanese interest.

Finally, the book concludes with a look at the most anomalous set of relations within the Japanese–Latin American context: Panama. Looking at the statistics on Japan and Latin America, it appears that a very large share of both trade and investment are in that small country. As Charlotte Elton explains in Chapter 9, however, this is because of the Japanese ships registered in Panama. The large volume of exports consists of sales of boats to the shipping companies, while the investment is loans to finance the sales. Japan's real interest in Panama has been in the canal, the main subject of Elton's analysis.

Given its geographical location in the Pacific Northwest and its heavy dependence on foreign trade, Japan has traditionally considered international waterways, such as the Panama Canal, to be of utmost strategic importance. While the Japanese government shares with the United States concern for the canal's safety, it has tried to distance itself from the more heavy-handed US attempts to influence changes in local government. At the same time, Japanese business interests in Panama have dwindled as a result of the instability and lack of confidence that ensued after General Manuel Noriega was arrested. It should not be surprising that Japan continues to explore alternative sites for the construction of a new canal, with a view to meeting the requirements of the Japanese economy in the twenty-first century.

Notes

1. The classic statement of early US–Latin American American relations is Samuel Flagg Bemis, *The Latin American Policy of the United States: An Historical Interpretation* (New York: Harcourt Brace, 1943). For a Latin American view of that period, see Alonso Aguilar, *Pan-Americanism from Monroe to the Present: A View from the Other Side* (New York: Monthly Review Press, 1968), especially chs. 1–5.
2. This term comes from Mira Wilkins, *The Emergence of Multinational Enterprise: American Business Abroad from the Colonial Era to 1914* (Cambridge, MA: Harvard University Press, 1970), chs. 6–8
3. One of the most authoritative studies of early US investments is Cleona Lewis, *America's Stake in International Investments* (Washington, DC: Brookings Institution, 1938).
4. An account of US – Latin American economic relations during the early postwar years is Raymond Mikesell, (ed.), *US Private and Government Investment Abroad* (Eugene: University of Oregon Books, 1962).
5. On the Alliance for Progress, see Jerome Levinson and Juan de Onis, *The Alliance that Lost its Way* (Chicago: Quadrangle Books, 1970).
6. Private bank loans to Latin America in the 1970s are contrasted to those of the 1920s in Barbara Stallings, *Banker to the Third World: US Portfolio Investment in Latin America, 1900–86* (Berkeley: University of California Press, 1987).
7. For a comparison of US relations with Central America and the rest of the region during the 1980s, see Abraham Lowenthal, *Partners in Conflict* (Baltimore: Johns Hopkins University Press, 1987).
8. The treaty provisions and related documents can be found in R.K. Jain, *Japan's Postwar Peace Settlements* (New Delhi: Radiant Publishers, 1978) pp. 149–221.

9. An important analysis of the "Yoshida Doctrine" is found in Kenneth Pyle, "Japan, the World, and the Twenty-first Century," in Takashi Inoguchi and Daniel Okimoto, (eds.), *The Political Economy of Japan: The Changing International Context* (Stanford: Stanford University Press, 1988).

10. The major reference for analyzing the postwar economic growth of Japan is Hugh Patrick and Henry Rosovsky, (eds.), *Asia's New Giant: How the Japanese Economy Works* (Washington, DC: Brookings Institution, 1976).

11. Robert Gilpin, *The Political Economy of International Relations* (Princeton, NJ: Princeton University Press, 1987) p. 6.

12. On recent US–Japanese economic relations, see C. Fred Bergsten and William R. Cline, *The United States – Japan Economic Problem* (Washington, DC: Institute for International Economics, 1987), and Bela Belassa and Marcus Noland, *Japan in the World Economy* (Washington, DC: Institute for International Economics, 1988).

13. Examples of political analysis reflecting the frustration of many in the United States are James Fallows, *More Like Us: Making America Great Again* (Boston: Houghton Mifflin, 1989); Clyde Prestowitz, *Trading Places* (New York: Basic Books, 1988); and Pat Choate, *Agents of Influence* (New York: Alfred K. Knopf, 1990). A balancing frustration on the Japanese side is seen in Shintaro Ishihara, *The Japan that Can Say No* (New York: Simon & Schuster, 1991).

14. For a summary of Japanese migration to Latin America, see Iyo Kunimoto, "Japanese Migration to Latin America" (ch.4 this volume).

15. An overview of Japanese economic relations with Latin America is found in Kotaro Horisaka, "Japanese Economic Relations with Latin America" (ch.2 this volume).

16. On Japanese banks in Latin America, see Barbara Stallings, "The Reluctant Giant: Japan and the Latin American Debt Crisis," *Journal of Latin American Studies* 22, 1 (February 1990), and Kotaro Horisaka, "Japanese Banks and Latin American Debt Problems," *Latin American Studies Occasional Papers*, No. 4, Georgetown University, 1990. On the recent beginning of Japanese withdrawal, see Stephen Murphy, "The Purge Is On," *LatinFinance* (March 1991).

17. It is important to realize the complexity involved in interpreting contractions in US (or other) bank holdings of Latin American debt. There are at least four possible processes on the creditor side that would produce this statistical result, with different implications for the debtors: (1) US banks could sell their debt to non-US banks; this would have virtually no effect on the debtors since they would merely owe the money to someone else. (2) US banks could write down the debt on their books but still try to collect it; again the pressure for interest and amortization would continue much as before. (3) US banks could forgive the debt, i.e. cease trying to collect, as in the Brady Plan; only in this way would the debtors obtain relief. (4) US banks could demand (and obtain) repayment of the loans and not issue new debt; in this way, money is actually taken out of the region. Since it is virtually impossible to determine which combination of the four was taking place at any given time, knowing how to interpret the contracting exposure is extremely difficult.

18. On the new loans by Japan's Export–Import Bank, see Toshihiko Kinoshita, "Developments in the International Debt Strategy and Japan's Response," *EXIM Review*, 10, 2 (1991).
19. Barbara Stallings, "Japanese Trade Relations with Latin America: New Opportunities in the 1990s?", in Mark Rosenberg (ed.), *The Changing Hemispheric Trade Environment: Opportunities and Obstacles* (Miami: Florida International University Press, 1991).
20. Lester Thurow, *Head to Head: The Coming Economic Battle among Japan, Europe, and America* (New York: William Morrow & Co., 1992).
21. On the North American Free Trade Area, see Gary Clyde Hufbauer and Jeffrey Schott, *North American Free Trade: Issues and Recommendations* (Washington, DC: Institute for International Economics, 1992). On the Enterprise for the Americas Initiative (EAI), see Sylvia Saborio *et al.*, *The Premise and the Promise: Free Trade in the Americas* (New Brunswick, NJ: Transaction Books, 1992). A surprisingly favorable Latin American response to the EAI is Latin American Economic System, *The Enterprise for the Americas Initiative in the Context of Latin American and Caribbean Relations with the United States* (Caracas: SELA, 1991).
22. Early views are explored in Dianna Solis and Matt Moffett, "Japanese Firms Fear Change in Mexico," *Asian Wall Street Journal*, November 13, 1990. For Japanese views after the NAFTA draft treaty was completed, see Andrew Pollack, "Japan Reacts Cautiously to 3-Nation Trade Pact," *New York Times*, August 14, 1992; Al Nakajima, "North America Trade Pact Called Worrisome Trend," *Nikkei Weekly*, August 22, 1992; and "Cautious Responses Greet Conclusion of North American Trade Pact Talks," *JEI Report*, 32B, August 21, 1992.
23. On provisions of the US – Canada Free Trade Agreement, see Arlene Wilson, "US Free Trade Agreements with Canada and Israel: Comparison of the Major Provisions," *CRS Report for Congress*, March 12, 1991.
24. David L. Kimport, "Doing Business in California," mimeo, Baker & McKenzie, n.d.
25. Interviews in Mexico City, March 1991.
26. Ezra Vogel, "Pax Nipponica?," *Foreign Affairs* (Spring 1986) p. 752.
27. Leon Hollerman, *Japan's Economic Strategy in Brazil: Challenge for the United States* (Lexington, MA: Lexington Books, 1988) p. 18.
28. Ibid., p. 17.
29. Ernani T. Torres, "Brazil–Japan Relations: From Fever to Chill" (ch. 5 this volume).
30. Leon Hollerman, "The Role of Brazil in Japan's Economic Strategy: Implications for the United States," paper presented at a conference on Japan and Latin America, University of California-San Diego, April 1990, p. 4.
31. C. Fred Bergsten, "Economic Imbalances and World Politics," *Foreign Affairs* (Spring 1987) p. 772.
32. Zbigniew Brzezinski, "America's New Geostrategy," *Foreign Affairs* (Spring 1988) p. 698.
33. Ibid., pp. 698–99.
34. Susan Kaufman Purcell and Robert M. Immerman, "Japan, Latin America, and the United States: Prospects for Cooperation and Con-

flict," in Susan Kaufman Purcell and Robert M. Immerman, (eds.), *Japan and Latin America in the New Global Order* (Boulder, CO: Lynne Rienner Publishers, 1992).

35. Ibid. For a similar line of analysis, see also Peter H. Smith, *Japan, Latin America, and the New International Order* (Tokyo: Institute of Developing Economies, V.R.F. Series 179, 1990).

36. "Japan–US Aid Cooperation: The Prospects for Collaboration," *JEI Report*, 12A, March 29, 1991.

37. Interviews with officials of OECF, Tokyo, February 1991 and USAID, Washington, DC, July 1991.

38. Stallings, "The Reluctant Giant."

39. Kinoshita, "Developments in the International Debt Strategy."

40. Ibid.

41. On declining US aid flows, see James H. Michel, Statement before Subcommittee on Foreign Operations, Committee on Appropriations, US House of Representatives, Washington, DC, March 13, 1991. On new US relations with Latin America, see Abraham Lowenthal, "Rediscovering Latin America," *Foreign Affairs* (Fall 1990).

42. The data problems referred to in the text are especially serious with respect to financial services. We have tried to eliminate supposed "direct investments" that are really part of banking tax–haven operations. Regardless of the exact numbers, however, it is clear that a major new area of interest for investors in Latin America is the new local capital markets. See, for example, recent issues of the journal *Latin Finance*.

43. On differing US and Japanese strategies with respect to natural resource investments, see Charles Oman *et al.*, *New Forms of Investment in Developing Countries* (Paris: OECD, 1989) and Oliver Bomsel *et al*, *Mining and Metallurgy Investment in the Third World* (Paris: OECD, 1990).

44. A debate has been raging for a number of years now on the relative weight of the Japanese bureaucracy compared to other groups in Japanese society. For a case study of the issue in the financial sector, see Frances McCall Rosenbluth, *Financial Politics in Contemporary Japan* (Ithaca: Cornell University Press, 1989). See also comments by Kotaro Horisaka, "Japan's Economic Relations with Latin America" (ch. 2 this volume).

45. On Japan and Central America, see Charlotte Elton, "The New Japanese Presence in Central America: Challenges and Opportunities," paper presented at XVI Congress of the Latin American Studies Association, Washington, DC, April 1991. See also Elton's conclusions in "Panama and Japan: The Role of the Canal" (ch. 9, this volume).

46. See Ernani Torres, "Brazil–Japan Relations: From Fever to Chill;" Neantro Saavedra-Rivano, "Chile and Japan: Opening Doors through Trade;" and Pablo de la Flor, "Peruvian – Japanese Relations: The Frustration of Resource Diplomacy" (chs. 5, 8 and 7 this volume).

47. See Gabriel Székely, "Mexico's International Strategy: Looking East and North" (ch. 6 this volume).

48. Barbara Stallings, "The Role of Foreign Capital in Latin America and East Asia," in Gary Gereffi and Donald Wyman, (eds.), *Manufacturing Miracles* (Princeton: Princeton University Press, 1990) pp. 64–66.

49. An analysis of the Non-Aligned Movement and its relations with the superpowers is found in Archie Singham, *The Non-Aligned Movement in World Politics* (New York: Lawrence & Hill, 1977). On the Southeast Asia position, see Lee Poh-ping, "Japan and the Asia – Pacific Region," paper presented at the Woodrow Wilson Center conference on Japan and the World, Washington, DC, January 1992.

50. On problems encountered by small countries trying to follow socialist development strategies, see Richard Fagen, Carmen Diana Deere and José Luis Corragio, (eds.), *Transition to Socialism in Small Peripheral Societies* (New York: Monthly Review Press, 1988).

51. On Brazilian diversification, see Sylvia Ann Hewlett, *The Cruel Dilemmas of Development: Twentieth-Century Brazil* (New York: Basic Books, 1980), ch. 7; Werner Baer, *The Brazilian Economy: Growth and Development* (New York: Praeger, 1983), especially ch. 8; and Peter Evans and Gary Gereffi, "Foreign Investment and Dependent Development," in Sylvia Ann Hewlett and Richard Weinert, (eds.), *Brazil and Mexico* (Philadelphia: ISHI, 1982).

52. Laurence Whitehead, "Debt, Diversification, and Dependency: Latin America's International Political Relations," in Kevin Middlebrook and Carlos Rico, (eds.), *The United States and Latin America in the 1980s* (Pittsburgh: University of Pittsburgh Press, 1986).

53. European and Soviet relations with Latin America are discussed, respectively, by Alberto van Klaveran, "Europe and Latin America in the 1990s," and Sergo Mikoyan, "Russia and Latin America in the 1990s," in Abraham Lowenthal and Gregory Treverton, (eds.), *Latin America and the United States in a New World* (forthcoming).

54. See discussion in Barbara Stallings and Kotaro Horisaka, "Japan and Latin America in the 1990s," in Lowenthal and Treverton, *Latin America and the United States*.

55. See Neantro Saavedra-Rivano, "Chile and Japan: Opening Doors Through Trade" (ch. 8 this volume).

56. On the existing trilateral relations among the United States, Japan, and Mexico, see Gabriel Székely, (ed.), *Manufacturing across Borders and Oceans: Japan, the United States, and Mexico* (San Diego: Center for US – Mexican Studies, 1991).

57. See "The Interamerican Development Bank and Japan," brochure prepared for the XXXII Annual Meeting of the Board of Governors, Nagoya, Japan, April 1991. The latest symposium volume is Interamerican Development Bank and Export–Import Bank of Japan, *The Fourth Symposium on Financial and Business Cooperation between Latin America and Japan* (Washington and Tokyo: IDB and Export–Import Bank of Japan, 1989).

58. The joint volume is *Towards New Forms of Economic Cooperation between Latin America and Japan* (Santiago: ECLAC, 1987). The more recent collaboration is reported in Takao Fukuchi and Mitsuhiro Kagami, (eds.), *Perspectives on the Pacific Basin Economy: A Comparison of Asia and Latin America* (Tokyo: Institute of Developing Economies, 1989).

59. SELA's Japan expert is Carlos J. Moneta. His most recent publication on Japan and Latin America is *Japón y América Latina en los años noventa* (Buenos Aires: Planeta, 1991).
60. See Toru Yanagihara, *Relaciones Grupo Andino/Japón* (Lima: Junta del Acuerdo de Cartegena, 1991).

Part II
Perspectives from Japan

2 Japan's Economic Relations with Latin America

Kotaro Horisaka

With the recent sweeping changes in the world, scholars are reconsidering many of their ideas about international relations. New topics are emerging, such as the relationship between Japan and Latin America, which had hardly attracted any interest before. This interest has derived largely from the decade of economic crisis in Latin America, US inability to deal with Latin American financial problems, and the emergence of Japan as a major economic power. Indeed, there are even expectations among some Latin American government officials and businesspeople that Japan represents a viable alternative to the United States as a source of capital and technology.

While Latin America remained mired in crisis and the United States experienced serious fiscal and trade deficits, Japan enjoyed the longest economic boom in the postwar era, lasting until the end of 1991. After consecutive years of tremendous trade surpluses, it became the country with the world's largest financial reserves. In 1989, Japan's total outstanding foreign assets reached $1.7 trillion, equivalent to 60 percent of its Gross National Product (GNP). At the same time, Japan became the fastest growing industrial and financial market as well as the research and development center of the world. Japan's industrial investment in the private sector amounted to $498 billion in 1988 (17 percent of GNP), exceeding that of the United States with $488 billion (10 percent of GNP).[1]

Can Latin Americans expect Japan to work more closely with them in their economic recovery? Will Japan's economic presence in Latin America really be a threat to US business, as feared by some Americans? Is it realistic to foresee a scenario in which Japan becomes an economic superpower in Latin America? In order to answer these questions, it is necessary to consider the recent changes in the Japanese economy and polity, as well as alterations of the business environment in Latin America. Japan's economic and political systems have grown

49

in complexity, and the policy-making process is much more differentiated than it used to be. Not only is the political base of the Liberal Democratic Party (LDP) starting to shake after 35 years of uninterrupted rule, but the rules of the political game itself are also starting to change. Nobody expects a continuation of political stability through LDP–bureaucracy–business domination. The leaders of the Japanese business community, with the strengthening of their financial base, have sought more independence from domestic politics. With the multinationalization of business activities, the integrated package offered by "Japan Inc." is becoming less attractive for them.

This chapter will present a framework of Japan–Latin American economic relations based on a historical perspective, an analysis of reasons for Japanese interest in Latin America, and a study of government–business relations. It consists of four major parts. The first section traces different stages in the historical evolution of the relationship, ending with the present when little activity is going on. The second analyzes the current characteristics of the relationship. The third looks at new features that seem to be emerging. Finally, the conclusion identifies several conditions under which Japan–Latin American relations might be revived from their current stagnation and the implications for a trilateral relationship.

FOUR STAGES OF ECONOMIC RELATIONS

The economic relationship between Japan and Latin America is surprisingly long. A student of Japan–Mexican relations published a book in 1989 throwing light upon the Silver Road, not the Silk Road, between Mexico and Japan via the Philippine Islands in the late sixteenth century.[2] According to this analysis, one of the major reasons why the Tokugawa Shogunate closed the door to foreigners in 1603 was to avoid the inflationary price impact of silver discoveries in the highlands of Mexico. The commonly accepted explanation of *sakoku*, or closure of Japan, has been the elimination of the religious influence of Christianity.

Mexico is also important in Japan's history as the first western nation with which the modern Japanese government attained its cherished hope of signing an equitable trade treaty; this event occurred in 1888, two decades after the Meiji Restoration. The Chilean government's turning the warship *Esmeralda* over to the Japanese government during the Sino–Japanese War (1894–95), and the

Argentine government's transfer to the Japanese navy of the rights to two warships, *Rivadavia* and *Moreno*, on the eve of the Russo–Japanese War (1904–05), became foundations for friendship. Moreover, the biggest community of Japanese descent abroad is found in Brazil.

Japan–Latin America relations, however, are very different from the relations between the United States and Latin America. The importance of political dialogue and diplomatic bargaining, as well as of cultural exchanges between Japan and Latin American nations in the past decades, cannot be ignored. Nevertheless, as will be seen, Japanese relations have been predominantly economic and business oriented. Japan has had little involvement in the domestic politics of Latin American nations or in regional conflicts such as those of Central America. The Japanese establishment and foreign policy-makers have always tended to think that "Latin America is the backyard of the United States, and its problems should be primarily managed by the United States." Thus, they tried to ignore the political issues of the Western Hemisphere or to act in harmony with the United States.

Economic relations between Japan and Latin America can be roughly divided into four stages. Bilateral relations before and immediately after World War II mainly focused on immigration and trade. Later came a stage of investment, starting in the late 1950s. Although trade remained important, direct investment became the major interest of the Japanese business community. In the latter half of the 1970s, loans by private banks became the driving force of interaction. Then came a period of inactivity in the 1980s, due to the economic crisis in most Latin American countries and to changes in the business environment for Japanese companies.

Stage 1: Immigration and Trade

Latin America is the region that has accepted the most immigrants from Japan. While this topic is discussed extensively in Chapter 4, it is worthwhile noting that Japanese immigrants moved to the new world for economic rather than for religious or political reasons. They looked for job opportunities, while Latin Americans were interested in obtaining both a labor force of good quality and new technologies, especially for agriculture. Although several trading companies, such as Mitsui and Kanematsu, were engaged in the import of raw materials from Latin America, most of the investment and trade activities before World War II were related to immigration and immigrants.

Having given priority to economic recovery at home after the war, Japan's stance in foreign affairs was based on the principle of separation of economics from politics. This was especially true in a remote area like Latin America, whose political problems do not directly affect Japan's domestic affairs. As discussed in Chapter 3, for example, Japan maintained diplomatic relations with Cuba after its revolution in 1959 and signed a trade treaty in 1961, although Japan's closest ally, the United States, broke diplomatic relations and declared an embargo on Cuba.

In the postwar period, Latin America played a modest, and even declining, role in Japanese trade. As seen in Table 2.1, exports to Latin America represented 7.5 percent of Japan's total exports in the 1950s, 6.3 percent in the 1960s, 7.2 percent in the 1970s, and 4.1 percent in the 1980s.[3] Imports from Latin America accounted for 9.8 percent of the

Table 2.1 Japan's trade with Latin America, 1938–90 (million dollars)

Year	Exports (FOB)		Imports (CIF)	
	($)	(%)	($)	(%)
1938	25.4	(3.3)	27.9	(3.7)
1948	2.6	(1.0)	88.5	(13.0)
1950	47.1	(5.7)	67.1	(6.9)
1955	185.6	(9.2)	243.4	(9.8)
1960	298.3	(7.4)	309.6	(6.9)
1965	457.9	(5.4)	707.9	(8.7)
1970	1,112.2	(5.8)	1,368.7	(7.2)
1975	4,667.0	(8.4)	2,510.0	(4.3)
1980	8,572.0	(6.6)	5,702.0	(4.0)
1981	10,119.0	(6.7)	6,595.0	(4.6)
1982	8,726.0	(6.3)	6,201.0	(4.7)
1983	5,902.0	(4.0)	6,368.0	(5.0)
1984	7,899.0	(4.7)	7,097.0	(5.2)
1985	7,753.0	(4.4)	6,188.0	(4.7)
1986	8,716.0	(4.1)	6,087.0	(4.8)
1987	8,151.0	(3.5)	6,221.0	(4.1)
1988	8,673.0	(3.3)	8,070.0	(4.3)
1989	8,836.0	(3.2)	8,507.0	(4.0)
1990	9,729.0	(3.4)	9,371.0	(4.0)

Note: Numbers in parenthesis are Latin American participation in Japan's total exports and imports.
Source: IMF, *Direction of Trade Statistics Yearbook.*

Japanese total in the 1950s, 8 percent in the 1960s, 5 percent in the 1970s, and 4.5 percent in the 1980s. There is no doubt that trade was seriously affected by the economic crisis of the 1980s.

Brazil with 11.6 percent of Japan's exports to Latin America in 1981–90 and 30.8 percent of Japan's imports from Latin America, and Mexico with 16 and 24.5 percent respectively, are the two major trade partners. Chile (4.1 percent of exports and 11.2 percent of imports), Venezuela (6.2, 7.5), Argentina (4.1, 6.3), Colombia (5.5, 3) and Peru (2.2, 6.4) constitute a second group. The other countries accounted for less than 2 percent of Japan's trade with Latin America. Panama is an exception. Its imports from Japan represented 32.9 percent of Japan's exports to the region, but this was mainly because of the registration of freighters in that country by Japanese shipping companies seeking tax benefits (see Chapter 9 in this volume).

For many Latin American countries, Japan is in second or third place as a trading partner, though there are important differences among them. Japan represented 5.9 percent of the total exports of Latin America and 5.8 percent of its total imports in 1990, almost the same as the amount to and from Germany.[4] The trade balance was generally favorable to Latin America until the beginning of the 1970s. Then it turned in Japan's favor, with the surplus diminishing after the Latin American debt crisis took place. Brazil, Chile, and Peru enjoy large trade surpluses with Japan.

In general, trade between Japan and Latin America has been of the "traditional" type. That is, Japan exports industrial goods in exchange for raw materials. The main changes over the postwar period have been an increase in the sophistication of the Japanese industrial exports and occasional moves to semi-process the Latin American raw materials before shipping them to Japan. The main items that Latin America exports to Japan include petroleum, iron ore and steel, ferroalloys, copper, aluminum, coffee, salt, wood pulp and chips, and fish products.

Stage 2: Direct Foreign Investment

Japan's postwar foreign investment started in the mid-1950s, and the first wave of massive investment in Latin America came later in that decade. This investment wave occurred while Japan was still under severe balance-of-payments constraints, but it was exactly when Latin American nations made a great push to promote industrialization through import substitution.

Usiminas (Usinas Siderúrgicas de Minas Gerais) in Brazil, the largest steel complex in Latin America, was one of the four biggest Japanese foreign ventures of the 1950s.[5] Brazil's Ishibrás (Ishikawajima do Brasil), the biggest shipyard in the region, was also an undertaking by Japanese industrial capital, started in the decade when Japan's shipbuilding industry was still in the stage of reconstruction. Car manufacturers, also in their early stages, established knockdown plants in Brazil (Toyota started operations in 1958), and then Mexico (Nissan in 1966) and Peru (Toyota and Nissan, both in 1966). The textile industry, which expanded rapidly after the war, was interested in cotton-spinning (in Brazil), woollen manufacture (in Argentina), and weaving machine production (in Mexico and Brazil).[6]

From the late 1960s to the early 1970s, the second great wave of Japanese investment was seen in Latin America. Investment increased not only in value (see Table 2.2), but also in number of companies involved and number of countries receiving investment. According to a survey done by *Toyo Keizai*, a leading business magazine in Japan, there were 847 Japanese subsidiaries in Latin America at the end of 1990.[7] This was 7 percent of total Japanese subsidiaries in the world. Among the 847 companies, 130 were established before 1970 (12 percent of total Japanese subsidiaries established in the period), 366 were established during the 1970s (11 percent), and 314 were established in the 1980s (4 percent). The rest did not specify their date of establishment.

In the first half of the 1970s, Brazil was the major target of foreign direct investment for Japanese companies as well as for American and European multinationals. There were 251 Japanese subsidiaries established in Brazil in that decade, followed by Panama with 58 and Mexico with 35. At the same time, a geographical expansion of investment targets could be observed. From the late 1960s, Japanese companies started to set up production bases in Central America and in the Andean nations, taking advantage of the regional integration movements in the Central American Common Market and the Andean Community.

Large Japanese firms invested heavily, sometimes with government support and in groups, in manufacturing and also in natural resource production. The development abroad of a stable supply of natural resources for domestic use was one of the key objectives of foreign investment policy at that time. Especially after the 1973 oil crisis, the term *kaihatsu yunyu* (development for import) became a catchphrase among government officials in charge of international economic

Table 2.2   Japan's direct foreign investment by region, 1951–90 (million dollars)

Region	1965	1970	1975	1980	1985	1990	Total from 1951
North America	44	192	905	1,596	5,495	27,192	136,185
Europe	5	335	333	578	1,930	14,294	59,265
Latin America	62	46	371	588	2,616	3,628	40,483
Argentina	11	2	0	8	8	213	215
Brazil	17	20	271	170	314	615	6,560
Chile	6	1	0	9	0	30	311
Mexico	9	1	30	85	101	168	1,874
Panama	0	8	13	222	1,533	1,342	16,244
Peru	16	2	8	3	10	0	696
Venezuela	0	1	10	12	2	77	341
Other	3	11	39	79	648	1,183	14,722
Asia	35	167	1,101	1,186	1,435	7,054	47,519
Middle East	11	28	196	158	45	27	3,431
Africa	2	14	192	139	172	551	5,826
Oceania	0	123	182	448	525	4,166	18,098
Total	159	904	3,280	4,693	12,217	56,911	310,808

Note: Japan's foreign direct investment was calculated on approval basis until FY1977; reported and approval basis from April 1978 to November 1980; reported basis after December 1980.
Source: Ministry of Finance, *Annual Report of International Finance Bureau.*

relations and the business world. The complementary structure of the Japanese and Latin American economies was emphasized to justify joint activities. Japan's strength in capital and technology was conceived as being complemented by Latin America's raw materials and human resources.[8]

As a first step, Japan invested in and/or financed the development of natural resources, such as Peruvian non-ferrous metal mines, Brazilian iron ore exploitation, and Mexican salt deposits. With increased demand for industrialization in the host countries, however, Japanese investment shifted toward semi-processing of raw materials in the locale, in the form of joint ventures. Production of iron ore dust pellets (Nibrasco), pulp (Cenibra), aluminum (Albrás), and semi-finished steel billet (Tubarão Steel) in Brazil and aluminum (Venalum) in Venezuela are examples of those joint ventures. Eventually, most of the smelting sector of the aluminum industry, which became unprofitable in Japan because of high electricity costs, was transplanted abroad, including to

Brazil and Venezuela. These investments continue to produce relatively important results as foreign-currency earners despite the sluggishness of Latin American economies.

The total value of Japan's accumulated investment in the region was $40.5 billion at the end of FY1990, 17 percent of the total Japanese direct investment abroad (see Table 2.2). Panama was the top recipient with $16.2 billion, mainly due to the registration of freighters in that country by Japanese shipping companies seeking tax benefits. For this reason, Panama is usually treated as a special case and is subtracted from the total in order to reach the actual size of foreign direct investment in Latin America. The Bahamas and other "tax havens" such as the Cayman Islands and Curaçao, where financial companies established "paper companies," are also treated this way. In fact, tax havens often mislead us about the actual size of Japanese investment in Latin America. It should be noted that the transportation and financial sectors accounted for annual average of 31 percent ($1.5 billion) and 52 percent ($2.6 billion) respectively out of a total average annual investment of $5.0 billion in 1986–90; the manufacturing sector was responsible for less than 7 percent ($344 million).

If we discount Panama and other tax havens, Brazil is the top recipient, followed by Mexico (see Table 2.2). Brazil is placed seventh after the United States, the United Kingdom, Australia, the Netherlands, Indonesia, and Hong Kong as Japan's overseas investment sites (although it has been much less important in recent years). There are no data that show the ranking of countries investing in Latin America as a whole, but Japan is third in accumulated foreign direct investment in Brazil, fourth in Mexico, and fifth in Peru and Venezuela.[9]

Stage 3: Private Bank Lending

Japan has now become the country with the world's biggest trade surplus and highest financial reserves, but Japan's private banks have only relatively recently moved into foreign financial markets. Compared with foreign activities by trading firms, which quickly expanded their overseas networks after World War II, or manufacturers who became internationally active in the 1960s, the banks were latecomers in the early 1970s.[10]

For the Japanese banks, major Latin American nations such as Brazil, Mexico, Argentina, and Venezuela became important custo-

mers because of their flourishing demand for development funds
(Table 2.3). Having started with participation in syndicated loans
organized by American or European banks, Japanese banks gradually
accumulated financial know-how and, early in the 1980s, some of
them began to act as managers of syndicated loans. In this process,
Latin America can be said to have played an important "test tube"
role in efforts by Japanese banks to acquire international financial
experience.

Compared with American and European banks, the lending attitudes
of Japanese banks showed particular characteristics. A tendency to
follow the lead of American banks was the chief characteristic,
prompted by the Japanese banks' limited knowledge about Latin
American countries and general immaturity in international finance.
Emphasis was placed on sovereign lending for which state banks and
firms were borrowers, with little lending to the private sector. High
priority was given to project financing for resource development and
industrial investments in which groups of Japanese firms participated.
These characteristics are manifest in the limited lending of Japanese
banks to the Alfa Group, Mexico's biggest private conglomerate, in
which the US private banks invested heavily, and again in the Japanese
banks' willingness to provide a large loan to Tubarão Steel, the joint
venture of Japan, Brazil and Italy in northeastern Brazil. Though the
composition of creditors for Latin American debtor countries differs
from country to country, Japan is today the second-ranking creditor
nation after the United States.

Table 2.3 Japan's medium/long-term loans outstanding by region, 1982–90
(billion dollars)

	1982		1984		1986		1988		1990	
OECD Countries	24.3	(36)	35.9	(38)	64.0	(42)	155.0	(55)	245.6	(68)
Latin America	21.3	(32)	28.6	(30)	36.8	(24)	45.5	(16)	31.2	(9)
Asia	7.6	(11)	12.5	(13)	22.2	(15)	38.2	(14)	48.7	(14)
Middle East	0.3	(–)	0.5	(1)	0.9	(1)	0.9	(–)	1.2	(–)
Africa	3.7	(6)	3.8	(4)	5.4	(4)	7.0	(2)	5.5	(2)
Eastern Europe	4.9	(7)	5.2	(6)	11.4	(7)	16.3	(6)	10.9	(3)
International Organizations	4.8	(7)	7.8	(8)	11.3	(7)	19.1	(7)	16.7	(5)
Total	67.1	(100)	94.4	(100)	152.2	(100)	282.5	(100)	360.5	(100)

Note: Figures in parentheses are percentages of total loans.
Source: Ministry of Finance, *Annual Report of International Finance Bureau.*

Stage 4: Inactivity

The severe economic crisis in Latin America in the 1980s has seriously affected Japan–Latin American economic relations. The impact of Mexico's debt crisis of August 1982 in Japanese financial circles was as dramatic as in the United States and Europe. Private banks immediately halted lending to Latin America. In order to avoid a crash of the Japanese financial system, the Ministry of Finance issued tight lending and procurement guidelines to private banks. The Bank of Japan took the emergency measure of extending short-term bridge loans to debtor countries through the Bank for International Settlements (BIS), and the government agreed to delay payments on official loans through the Paris Club. Japanese private banks promptly joined debt rescheduling committees formed by the international banking community.

Here, too, in most cases, Japanese private banks followed American initiatives. Japan strongly supported the Multi-Year Rescheduling Agreements (MYRA), which were suggested in 1984 by the United States; the Baker Plan of October 1985; and the Brady Plan of February 1989. Once an agreement was concluded between a Bank Advisory Committee and a debtor country, Japanese banks as a group were the most faithful in implementing it. Because of this, although the Latin American share of loans outstanding by Japanese banks decreased from 32 percent in 1982 to 16 percent in 1988, the absolute amount increased from $21.3 billion to $45.5 billion.[11] The absolute amount fell significantly only from 1990, as seen in Table 2.3, when the Brady Plan was implemented for the first time in Mexico.

The basic stance that Japanese banks took toward Latin America's debt problem can be summarized by the following points. First, they generally followed market mechanisms, avoiding measures such as debt reduction. Second, they emphasized the importance of unity among creditor banks. When rescheduling of debt payments and providing of new money were implemented, the number of Japanese banks that dropped out was far smaller than for American and European banks. Third, Japanese banks promoted a role for governments and international financial institutions, similar to standard Japanese practice in cases of domestic debt problems. They especially valued the International Monetary Fund's (IMF) function of reviewing the policies of debtor countries. Overall, Japanese banks helped to implement agreed schemes, but at the same time, they were severe toward debtor countries and became extremely reluctant to finance Latin American economic development.[12]

Japanese banks were slower than American and European banks to increase reserves for bad debts and to reduce loans outstanding, using such mechanisms as debt–equity swaps. Nevertheless, the risks of credit to Latin America have been largely reduced. A substantial reduction in yen terms has been obtained through appreciation of the yen after 1985. Further, Japanese banks' assets have greatly increased because of the favorable expansion of the Japanese economy, sharp increases in real estate and stocks, and the growth of Tokyo as an international financial center.

It goes without saying that trade and investment stagnated with the debt crisis of Latin American nations. In addition to the lack of financing and reduction in consumer demand, the debt crisis of the region affected traders and investors psychologically. It was at this moment that the Japanese business community started to think seriously of country risks, in addition to individual business risks, for trade partners and investment markets. Through much of the 1980s, Japan's trade with Latin America stagnated; now, with the attempts by Latin American nations to increase and diversify their exports, Japan has become an important target. These efforts have begun to bear fruit only for countries like Chile and Mexico. Latin America as a whole depends on the United States for 40 percent of its trade.

Although official statistics show a continuous increase in Japan's foreign direct investment to Latin America (see Table 2.2), the major part has shifted to the transportation and finance sectors; manufacturing accounted for less than 10 percent by the late 1980s. Among the 314 Japanese subsidiary companies established in the 1980s, 139 were in Panama and the tax-haven islands. These data clearly indicate the declining importance of the region for Japanese investors. *Toyo Keizai* listed 45 Japanese subsidiaries as "sleeping" (not functioning) or withdrawn from Latin America between 1982 and 1990.[13] In addition, Toyota and Nissan stopped their automobile assembly operations in Peru in June 1991 and January 1992, respectively. Makita, the top Japanese industrial toolmaker, is also reported to have stopped their production in São Paulo at the beginning of 1992.[14] Although these trends do not suggest a wholesale withdrawal of Japanese business from Latin America, they do indicate a cautious attitude on the part of investors.

Generally speaking, investment interest in natural resources, in ferment in the 1970s, has also cooled because of the relatively easy procurement of raw materials through international commodity markets. Interest in Latin America among Japanese businesspeople is no longer as high as it was in the 1960s and 1970s, except for those who already have a big stake in the region or those who are interested in *maquiladora* production (in bond plants in Mexico on the US border), which is an important strategic point to penetrate the US market.

Debt–equity conversions are offered in many countries as a mechanism to attract foreign capital as well as to reduce the debt burden. Japanese companies participated actively in Mexico, mainly to raise funds for *maquiladora* investments. They were also active in Brazil for the purpose of getting operational funds and/or funds for expansion of existing facilities, not for new investment.[15]

MAJOR FEATURES OF JAPAN–LATIN AMERICAN RELATIONS

Structural Characteristics

Japan–Latin American relations have been predominantly economic, and they have been heavily one-sided. Japan has played the active role, while Latin American nations have been rather passive. Japan sent thousands of people to Latin America as emigrants. Those who started and expanded trade between the two partners were primarily Japanese businessmen. Japanese companies, sometimes with government support, looked to Latin America for export markets and investment opportunities, and Japanese private banks were eager to lend money.

As a consequence of the one-sidedness, when Japan lost interest in Latin America, relations stagnated. The complex feelings of envy, hostility, superiority, and inferiority commonly observed between the United States and Latin American nations cannot be found between Japan and Latin America. Trade conflicts, which sometimes imperil Japanese relations with the United States, the European Community and Asian neighbors, are seldom seen in relations with Latin America. National security and common defense, whether from the Communist bloc or the "drug mafia," were never on the agenda at a summit meeting of these two partners. The Panama Canal is an exception, perhaps, but it was taken up from the "economic security" rather than from the political perspective.

This simplicity helped to facilitate relations, but it turned out to be a weak point when the interests of the two sides failed to coincide. This was especially true when the situations of the two partners were extremely different as in the late 1980s: Japan was flourishing and

Latin America was in crisis. There was much rhetoric, but few concrete actions were taken to promote the relationship.

In addition to simple, Latin American economic relations with Japan can also be characterized as unbalanced. Figure 2.1 gives an idea of the Latin American position in Japanese foreign economic relations in comparison with Southeast Asia. Participation by Latin America and Southeast Asia are shown as percentages of Japan's total by categories: trade, aid, direct investment, and debt. While Southeast Asia has a roughly even distribution across categories, Latin America has a strongly biased pattern.[16] There is a disproportion between the small amount of trade and Official Development Assistance (ODA) for Latin America, matched by an overemphasis on foreign direct investment and loans by private banks.

In the case of Japan's economic relations with Southeast Asia, the interrelationship between trade, investment, loans, and ODA is clear. For example, trade expansion led to direct investment in Southeast Asia, which in turn led to more trade. The recent industrial development of Asian NIEs and ASEAN (Association of Southeast Asian Nations) countries is accelerating. Japanese firms are rapidly changing their management strategy of producing everything from raw

Figure 2.1 Japan's economic relations with Latin America and Southeast Asia

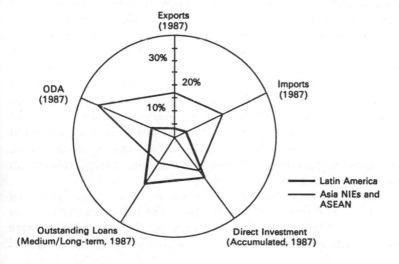

materials to finished products at home. Instead, they are pursuing a division of labor with neighboring Asian countries. The relationships with Latin America are less integrated and reinforcing.

In Southeast Asia, lending by Japanese banks is still a driving force of bilateral relations. In Latin America, by contrast, loans are an overwhelming fetter to relations. Although the Asian countries are very cautious about not repeating the errors committed by Latin American countries in the 1970s, they are in need of borrowed money for industrialization (see Table 2.3). There is no doubt that the expansion of trade and investment encourages lending, and vice-versa.

Business Motivations in Latin America

What motivated the Japanese to promote economic relations with a remote area like Latin America? Obviously, each company and each project has its own specific motivation. An examination of the activities, however, suggests three general motivations: (1) to acquire a secured position (or market share) in the host country's market; (2) to develop stable supply sources abroad of natural resources for domestic use; and (3) to establish production bases for export to the countries of North America, Europe, neighboring South America, Africa, and the Middle East.

Major motivations have changed over time, as can be seen in Figure 2.2. In the 1950s and 1960s, most manufacturing firms as well as trading companies were interested in Latin America as a new market for rapidly-growing Japanese industries. Their main concern was how to penetrate the Latin American market. They exported products as a first step. Then, with the introduction by the host countries of import-substitution policies and common market mechanisms, such as the Latin American Free Trade Association, the Central American Common Market, and the Andean Pact, Japanese companies were obliged to increase production inside the market in order to overcome tariff and non-tariff barriers. The timing of the different investments was based not only upon the import-substitution policies of host countries but also upon the product cycle. Thus there was a stress on basic industries in the 1950s and 1960s, while investments in home appliances, such as television and stereo, motorcycles, communication and informatic equipment, started mainly in the 1970s.

Japanese direct investment in Latin America during that period served quite different goals than in neighboring Asian countries. In

Figure 2.2   Changes in Japanese business motivation in Latin America

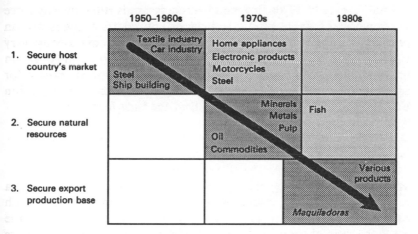

general, Japanese companies looked at Asia as a source of cheap labor. Investments by the electronic parts makers in export-processing zones in Taiwan in the late 1960s were typical examples. Materials produced in the mother company were exported to subsidiary companies in Taiwan for assembly and then sent back again to Japan for final processing. The objective of their direct investment was cheap labor, not the market itself. Latin America, by contrast, offered prosperous markets for Japanese goods, although the market size did not expand as was expected due to the big income disparities among the people in the region. At the same time, Latin America was geographically too distant to function as a processing zone for Japanese industries. This explains why Japanese capital in Latin America was generally interested in free trade zones, such as in Manaus (Brazil), Ushuaia (Argentina), and Colón (Panama), but did not show any interest in the idea of export-processing zones until the late 1970s. Contrary to the expectations of the Panamanian government, for example, Japanese companies did not start processing in the Colón Free Zone; they merely used this facility as a distribution center for Japanese-made products to Latin American and Caribbean markets. The advantage for Japanese companies of the Manaus Free Trade Zone in the Amazon area has been the growing Brazilian market in the south, along with favorable tax incentives for investment.

From the early 1970s, a second business motivation emerged: the development of stable supply sources of natural resources and food products for domestic use. A precursor of this trend was the long-term trade agreement for iron ore export signed between Japan and Brazil in the mid-1960s. This was the first international long-term sales agreement for iron ore for the Brazilian state company, Companhia Vale do Rio Doce (CVRD); it constituted the basis for the the big joint ventures in the 1970s.

Nibrasco (iron ore dust pelletizing), Cenibra (pulp), and Albrás (aluminum) are Japanese–Brazilian joint ventures planned with the participation of CVRD. The Tubarão steel complex was also established through the legacy of the iron ore trade, although CVRD did not participate as a share holder. Kawasaki Steel's original purpose for participating in Tubarão Steel was to secure raw materials for domestic use in the form of semi-manufactured steel billet. Zinc, lead and copper smelting in Peru; aluminum production in Venezuela; pulp ventures in Chile; financing of an oil pipeline in Peru; and construction of oil–shipping installations in Mexico also reflect the second motivation. The same is true of the development of Brazil's semi-arid plateau, Cerrado, into coffee and soybean farms, and the cooperation in the fishing industries of Argentina, Chile, and Peru; all were intended to increase sources of food products. Although these projects were not necessarily intended to supply the Japanese market directly, they were expected to benefit Japan indirectly by increasing the total world supply.

The third motivation of Japanese business was to use Latin America as a production base for export to third countries. This motivation can be divided into two sub-categories: (a) self-interest of Japanese business in promoting exports and (b) changes in Latin American political and economic conditions. The Mexican *maquiladoras* are the best-known example of the first category. The flower growing business in Colombia and Costa Rica for export to the United States are other examples. There are several Japanese manufacturing sectors – such as cotton yarn, electronic parts, and chemicals – which utilize Latin American factories as suppliers of products to developed countries. The prerequisite for this type of business is the combination of a big US or European market, local resources (labor power, raw materials, natural environment such as climate) and/or industrial capacity, and Japanese technology and capital.

The second circumstance that motivated exports is found among Japanese trading companies. A study done by the Japanese Chamber of Commerce and Industry of Brazil shows that exports from Brazil to third parties by Japanese trading companies in 1983 accounted for 43 percent of their total exports from the country.[17] Indeed, most Japanese and other multinational companies are trying to promote exports because of the deterioration of local markets, the difficulties in acquiring foreign exchange for imports of raw materials, and the pressures and incentives from local governments. For these type of exports, nations in Latin America, Africa, the Middle East, and Japan (usually the mother company) are the principal markets.

Japanese Actors in the Arena

Private companies, quite naturally, are the actors that have played the principal role on the Japanese side in economic relations with Latin America. A first type of private company is the big trading firm (*sogo shosha*).[18] The *sogo shosha* served as an "advance detachment" for Japanese business in the first stage of investment. They set up offices in Latin America, collected information on the market, transmitted it back to Japanese producers, and took charge of export operations. They were important in the second stage as well. Trading companies sometimes acted as intermediaries in the formation of joint ventures, and they themselves invested in many projects.

The most noteworthy function of the trading companies in the second stage, however, was as organizers of big projects. It is usually said in Japan that *sogo shosha* have four basic functions: trading, financing, business-related intelligence, and organization. They never appeared as the "prima donna," but their presence was visible behind the scenes in all the big projects as an organizer (or a director), utilizing fully the functions of intelligence and financing, and competing among themselves to be a main trader in the new business. Many projects like Cenibra and Albrás were developed by *sogo shosha*, especially when manufacturing companies and banks were weak in international activities. At times, they also acted as intermediaries between governments in the formation of ODA projects.

The second actor that should be noted is the business community itself. In the case of big projects, apart from individual investment projects, Japanese companies have participated in groups with various different combinations: groups composed of a manufacturing company, trading company, and/or bank; groups composed of *keiretsu* (companies with close working relationships); or groups composed of competing companies from the same industry. The third combination is the most confusing case for non-Japanese businesspeople.

Again, Albrás constitutes an interesting example, especially when compared with the single-company investment project in the same aluminum sector in the same Amazon area by the American firm, ALCOA.[19] In the case of Albrás, major Japanese smelting companies formed an investment company (NAAC), together with trading companies and private banks. This newly-formed investment company established a joint venture, Albrás, with the Brazilian state company, CVRD. Usually, in this type of investment, Keidanren (the federation of leading industrial organizations) or the Japanese Chamber of Commerce played an important coordinating role in order to reach a consensus among business participants.[20] In the cases of two steel projects (large diameter steel pipe and forged steel) planned in Mexico at the beginning of the 1980s, two Japanese investment companies were formed to organize joint ventures with Mexico. Some 52 companies from various sectors, including the top five steel makers, and a government agency (the Overseas Economic Cooperation Fund, OECF), participated in each of the investment companies.

A third notable actor is the Japanese government. Besides the role the Japanese government played as a donor of economic assistance to poor nations, it also financed infrastructure, such as port facilities, which could serve the big projects. There are also a few cases in which the government participated as an investor using OECF funds, such as the two Mexican steel projects. The Export–Import Bank of Japan was, of course, eager to provide suppliers' credits for those big projects, and it also offered financing for natural resources using a payment-in-advance mechanism.

A CHANGE OF FRAMEWORK?

Let us now return to the questions raised in the Introduction to this volume about the Japanese presence in Latin America under new international and domestic circumstances. There are at least two major changes underway in Japan, which began in the late 1980s and are likely to affect the future of Japan–Latin American relations. In many senses, the changes are two sides of the same coin. On the one hand, the government is taking a more active role, independent of the old activities revolving around large projects in collaboration with the private sector. On the other hand, the private sector itself wants more independence from the government.

Fund Recycling by Japanese Government

The Japanese government has said on many occasions that Japan will cooperate with Latin America in its economic recovery by recycling accumulated trade surpluses and increasing technological assistance. The government has recognized the Latin American economic crisis as one of the most urgent international economic issues, as well as a problem from the viewpoint of the Japanese national interest. For government officials, Latin American issues are important to Japan because they "share the view that the economic stability and development of Latin American countries are crucial to the United States economy and security, and hence to the interest of Japan."[21]

Japanese government finance has been of two main types: the traditional ODA for poorer countries and the new recycling funds for middle-income countries. In May 1988, the government unveiled the Fourth Medium-Term ODA Target, which promised ODA of more than $50 billion over the 5 years ending in 1992, more than doubling the aggregate volume of ODA disbursed over the previous 5 years.

Most of Japan's bilateral aid has been concentrated in the Asian nations. As seen in Table 2.4, 60–70 percent of its total bilateral ODA is extended to that region. Japan favors Asia partly because of geographic and economic proximity. Of equal importance is the fact that Japanese-style ODA, composed mainly of yen loans, is more heavily in demand in that area than in other developing regions because of close ties with Japan in exports and investment.

Aid to non-Asian countries is divided almost evenly among Africa, the Middle East, and Latin America, but the share provided to Latin America has been declining in recent years from a peak of 10 percent in 1983. According to the explanation of the Ministry of Foreign Affairs, this is due to the relatively high *per capita* income level in Latin America, which results in a small number of countries eligible for financial assistance. In addition, many of the highly-indebted Latin American nations had fallen behind in their payments and were thus ineligible for Japanese government assistance.[22]

In addition to the ODA-doubling plan, the government has taken a series of measures to facilitate capital recycling to debtor countries, through the so-called Nakasone Fund. In May 1987, then Prime Minister Nakasone announced the recycling of $30 billion over 3 years,

Table 2.4   Japan's bilateral ODA by region, 1975–90 (net disbursement, million dollars)

	1975		1980		1985		1990	
Asia	638	(75.0)	1,383	(70.5)	1,732	(67.8)	4,177	(59.3)
Middle East	90	(10.6)	204	(10.4)	201	(7.9)	705	(10.2)
Africa	59	(6.9)	233	(11.4)	252	(9.9)	792	(11.4)
Latin America	47	(5.6)	118	(6.0)	225	(8.8)	561	(8.1)
Oceania	5	(0.6)	12	(0.6)	24	(0.9)	114	(1.6)
Europe	0	(0.0)	−1.5	(–)	1	(0.0)	158	(2.3)
Unallocable	11	(1.3)	1	(1.2)	122	(4.8)	494	(7.1)
Total	850	(100.0)	1,961	(100.0)	2,557	(100.0)	6,940	(100.0)

Note: The figures in the parentheses are the share of bilateral ODA distributed to each region.
Source: Ministry of Foreign Affairs, *Japan's Official Development Assistance, Annual Report 1991* (Tokyo, Association for Promotion of International Cooperation, 1991).

including $10 billion committed to international financial institutions in 1986, as a part of Japan's effort to reduce its huge trade surplus. By June 1989, when nearly 90 percent of the $30 billion recycling program had been committed, the government decided to expand the program from $30 billion to $65 billion over a 5-year period (see Table 2.5). There are three main channels for recycling. The first is funds made available to international financial institutions, such as the World Bank, the IMF, and the Interamerican Development Bank (IDB). The second channel is through the OECF, the Export–Import Bank of Japan (JEXIM), and the Japanese commercial banks in co-financing arrangements with the international financial institutions. The third is direct, untied loans by OECF and JEXIM.

The capital recycling plan indicates implicitly Japan's new way of thinking about economic cooperation. Although bilateral cooperation will be strengthened with the increase of the ODA budget, substantial emphasis is being attached to cooperation with the international financial institutions. This is due to the following factors: (1) a lack of operational capacity and information about recipient countries, because of the small size of the economic assistance organizations in Japan compared with the rapidly increasing ODA budget; (2) a desire to avoid the direct risk of lending by using the multilateral mechanism and its authority over recipient countries; (3) an awareness of the utility

Table 2.5   Japan's expanded capital recycling program, 1987–92 (billion dollars)

Period	Original program 1987–90	After expansion 1987–92
EXIM-Japan	10.0	23.5
OECF	5.5	12.5
Others*	14.5	29.0
Total	30.0	65.0

* Contributions and/or subscriptions to multilateral development banks by Japanese government.
Source: Export–Import Bank of Japan.

of multilateral organizations to Japan, a country with weak political power and no military forces, in expanding its sphere of influence; and (4) a need to maintain the present international economic system, which is the foundation of Japanese prosperity.

Beyond co-financing, the Japanese government has been an ardent supporter of the IMF as the pivot for the debt-rescheduling agreements still being negotiated, although it has not expressed its support in as blunt terms as the US government has. In this context, it is likely that the Japanese government will prefer an increase in fund recycling rather than a commitment to large-scale bilateral development projects for Latin America, assuming there are no basic changes in international economic circumstances, such as new oil crises or the emergence of economic blocs.

The End of Japan Inc.?

With regard to private companies, it is necessary to consider their qualitative changes during the decade of the 1980s and their main concerns today. From the late 1980s, the international presence of Japanese companies has increased dramatically. This increasing presence has been especially noticed in the United States, and has sometimes been an irritant to the American people. The acquisition of Columbia Pictures by Sony and the Rockefeller Center by Mitsubishi Real Estate are prominent examples. Honda's Accord took the title of top-selling car in the United States in 1989, and the total number of "Japanese cars" assembled in the United States is approaching one third of the US market. The Dai-Ichi Kangyo Bank, the largest bank in Japan, acquired 4.9 percent of the capital of Manufacturers Hanover, a major money center bank of the United States, in 1989. The latter sold a part of its shares in an affiliated investment company to the former in order to increase loan-loss reserves, preparing for a possible default by Latin American countries.

The big companies enjoyed very high economic growth during the 1980s. For example, the top five Japanese car makers (Toyota, Nissan, Honda, Matsuda, and Isuzu) doubled their total assets in the 1980s in yen terms, and increased them more than three-fold in dollar terms. Their total assets in FY1990 were $93.4 billion (¥13.2 trillion). The same can be said for the top five electric/electronic products firms (Matsushita, Hitachi, Toshiba, NEC, and Mitsubishi). Their total assets in FY1990 were $117.1 billion (¥16.5 trillion).[23]

These big companies, which accumulated tremendous financial power from recent economic growth, want to be much more independent of domestic politics. That is, they want to be free from political parties, which are fettered by particular domestic social and economic problems, and from control by Japan's powerful bureaucracy. They are now in transition from the old stage of "internationalization," in which the decisions of enterprises were outgrowths of the national interest, to a new stage of "multinationalization."

The big businesses have started to establish regional headquarters, in North America and Europe, to administer local subsidiaries. Some of them are setting up research and development centers in the United States and Europe in order to utilize the expertise, know-how, and information that each country possesses. Research done by Yamaichi Securities shows that the number of successful foreign mergers and acquisitions by Japanese companies in 1989 was 404, 89 more than the previous year.[24]

The Ministry of International Trade and Industry (MITI) explains this phenomenon as "globalization" of Japanese companies as well as economies, demonstrating implicitly its fear of losing control of them. And, indeed, it seems that the big companies are escaping the control of the government. Liberalization and deregulation in developed economies in recent years have accelerated the phenomenon of multinationalization even more.[25]

In general, the orientation of Japanese companies is toward greater participation in all markets. Japanese companies traditionally compete with each other in sales rather than profits or assets. They are intent on expanding their share of existing markets and in finding and developing new markets domestically and abroad. For this purpose, they are keen to strengthen the competitiveness of their products by cost cutting and technological development. It is quite clear in this context that, for them, the major fields of investment are in growing consumer markets, whether at home or in foreign countries, and in new technologies.

Japan's overseas direct investment began to rise rapidly in 1983, with the migration of the automobile and electronic companies to the United States to start local production. Since that time, foreign direct investment has increased at a skyrocketing pace every year. For FY1989, total investment hit $68 billion, eight times more than in 1983, and it was $57 billion in FY1990. The main targets for new investment have been the big consumer markets of the United States and the European Community and, to a lesser extent, Asian NIEs and ASEAN countries with relatively cheap labor and expanding local markets. In FY1990, about 50 percent of Japan's investment went to the United States.[26]

It seems naive to imagine that major Japanese companies will relocate much of their surplus to Latin America in anticipation of potential economic power beyond the year 2000, except for those who already have substantial investments in the region.[27] The *maquiladora* sector may represent an exception to this rule, because it offers Japanese business a strategic point of entry into the US market. This process, however, is on hold right now, awaiting the outcome of the North American Free Trade Area (NAFTA) negotiations. The "integrated package approach," a lion of the 1970s, is also an unlikely alternative. Individual manufacturing companies are becoming stronger today in comparison with government bureaucrats, Keidanren, or the trading companies that previously played coordinating roles from the standpoint of "national interest." Business investors are more sensitive to their own strategies and more cautious about country risks. It seems that the "Japan Inc." approach is not as attractive for them as it once was. In summary, the Japanese establishment sees Latin America today primarily in connection with the United States and with the world economy. As a result, Japan's direct interest in the region continues to contract in comparison with the 1970s.

CONCLUSIONS: THREE SOURCES OF REACTIVATION

It is quite difficult to draw a scenario today, no matter what the subject. Nonetheless, Japan's business motivations toward Latin

America, as discussed earlier, reveal some sources for a reactivation of Japan–Latin American economic relations. They include strong local and regional market development, utilization of rich natural resources, and stronger Latin American initiatives. To produce this reactivation, policy dialogues between the two partners are indispensable.

The first source is the reactivation and expansion of the Latin American market. There are many discussions that point to foreign direct investment as a necessary condition for economic recovery, but it seems doubtful that Japanese companies will invest where there is no market growth. It must be recognized that relaxation of investment restrictions and economic liberalization are not sufficient conditions for Japanese companies to invest. Latin American governments and leaders must seriously consider social and economic reforms to end income disparity and realize the potential consuming power of their people, and they must implement measures to integrate and expand regional markets. Once the Latin American market becomes active again, Japanese companies will become interested, regardless of the intentions of local governments to invite them; the converse is not true.

The second source is the effective development and marketing of Latin America's rich mineral and agricultural resources. Low petroleum prices, low commodity prices, low inflation, and liberalization of economic systems provided the economic circumstances by which developed countries, especially Japan, prospered in the past decade. If these circumstances were to change, it is quite certain that the conflicts centering on natural resources will again emerge. Recent rapid growth of East and Southeast Asian countries, economic liberalization of East Europe and the former Soviet Union, and serious famine in Africa raise questions about the continuation of present circumstances in the world economy. Japan is fundamentally vulnerable to a shortage of natural resources.[28] Latin America, with effective development and utilization of natural resources, can initiate policy dialogues with developed countries, above all with Japan.

The third source concerns Latin American initiatives. As this chapter has tried to make clear, Japan–Latin American relations have been almost entirely one-sided. This type of interrelationship must be corrected in order to have a stable partnership. Fortunately, Latin American business people are taking more initiative today than in the past to market their products in Japan, one of the world's largest consumer markets, and Latin American government officials are much more keen to sell business opportunities in Latin America to Japanese businesspeople. As pointed out in the Introduction to this volume, Mexico and Chile have become especially aggressive in trying to attract Japanese investment and break into the Japanese market. Another example concerns Brazil. Four Brazilian orange juice companies, which together account for 60 percent of the world orange juice trade, will be investing $40 million in Japan to construct a huge juice deposit installation of 18,000 tons. Their aim is to market directly in Japan's big consumer society, especially after 1992, when the government will open the Japanese orange juice market completely to foreign products.[29] The *dekasegi* phenomenon, the temporary movement of Japanese and their descendants living in Latin American countries to Japan looking for job opportunities, is also important from this perspective. Their numbers are estimated at more than 150,000 in 1991, and they are certainly contributing to an increased Latin American presence in Japanese society.

Beyond these issues concerning Latin America itself, analysis of the future of Japanese–Latin American relations needs to be placed within a broader context that includes the United States. This is especially true with the US–Mexico–Canada negotiations for a NAFTA and President Bush's announcement of support for a hemisphere-wide trade area. These events indicate recovery of US special interest toward the region, which had receded since the early 1970s. Although the results of the plan are not yet clear, there can be no doubt that these plans, if unilaterally pursued, pose a serious challenge not only to Japan, which is very worried about the formation of regional economic blocs, but also to Latin American nations, which want to pursue economic independence by diversifying their business partners.[30] To deal with this new challenge in a positive way, Japan and the Latin American nations need to reactivate mutual and diversified contacts.

Notes

1. On investment, see Yoshiyasu Ono and Hiroshi Yoshikawa, "Setsubi tōshi" (Industrial Investment), in Kenichi Imai and Ryutaro Komiya, (eds.), *Nihon no kigyo* (Japanese Companies) (Tokyo: Tokyo University Press, 1989). According to the US National Science Foundation, the research and development expenditure of the United States was $100.8 billion and Japan was $39.1 billion in 1987. However, Japan's R&D

represents 2.9 percent of GNP, whereas that of the United States is only 2.6 percent (*Nihon Keizai Shimbun*, New York, August 6, 1989).

2. M. Kimura, *Sakoku to Silverroad, sekai no nakano Jipang* (Why Japan Closed its Doors: The Price Revolution in the Pan-Pacific, 1600–1650) (Tokyo: Simul Press, 1989).

3. IMF, *Direction of Trade Statistics Yearbook*, various issues. The IMF has varied the division and and designation of areas over the past four decades. For Table 2.1, the trade value of Latin America was calculated as follows:

    1950–55 Mexico + Central America + South America
    1956–57 (North America − US − Canada) + South America
    1958–59 Latin America + Other Western Hemisphere
    1960–70 Latin America + Other Western Hemisphere + Cuba
    1971–72 Other Western Hemisphere + Ecuador + Venezuela + Cuba
    1973–80 Other Western Hemisphere + Venezuela + Cuba
    1981–90 (Western Hemisphere − Greenland) + Cuba

4. IMF, *Direction of Trade Statistics Yearbook*, 1991. Cuba is excluded in these numbers. According to the data, in 1990 Latin America exported to Japan $7,663,000 and imported $6,844,000.

5. The other three were pulp development in Alaska; oil development on Sumatra Island, Indonesia; and oil in Kuwait.

6. The company withdrew from Argentina in the late 1970s.

7. Toyo Keizai, *Kaigai shinshutsu kigyō sōran, 1991* (Japanese Overseas Investment: A Complete Listing by Firms and Countries, 1991) (Tokyo: Toyo Keizai, 1991).

8. Usage of the term "complementary structure" became a controversial diplomatic issue on the occasion of the visit to Japan of the Brazilian president, Ernesto Geisel, in 1976.

9. JETRO, *Hakusho tōshihen 1991: sekai to Nihon no kaigai chokusetsu tōshi* (White Paper on Japan's Foreign Direct Investment, 1991). Due to differences in criteria, the accumulated value of Japanese investment announced by Latin American governments is different from that of the Japanese government. The Central Bank of Brazil, for example, listed Japanese investment as $3.146 billion in 1989. SECOFI statistics (Ministry of Commerce and Industrial Promotion of Mexico) showed Japanese investment in Mexico to be $1.334 billion in 1989.

10. For more detailed analyses of Japanese lending to Latin America, see Kotaro Horisaka, "Japanese Banks and Latin American Debt Problems," *Latin American Studies Occasional Papers*, No. 4, Georgetown University, 1990, and Barbara Stallings, "The Reluctant Giant: Japan and the Latin American Debt Crisis," *Journal of Latin American Studies* 22, No. 1 (February 1990).

11. The medium and long-term loans outstanding of American banks increased less than those of Japanese banks, from $36.8 billion in 1982 to $47.0 billion at the end of 1987. Short-term loans (1 year and under) outstanding for 1987 were $29.0 billion, compared to $51.6 billion at the end of 1982 (*Country Exposure Lending Survey*, various issues). This cut had a tremendous negative impact on the financial situation of Latin American countries. Although no data are available on Japanese short-

term loans, these were probably less significant than those of American banks.

12. This attitude was clearly expressed in the Mexican rescue plan that was finalized in February 1990. Japanese banks chose the debt reduction or interest reduction options, even though these implied a loss, rather than agreeing to lend additional funds to Mexico.

13. Toyo Keizai, *Kaigai shinshutsu kigyō sōran*.

14. *Nihon Keizai Shimbun*, New York, July 2, 1991; January 16, 1992; and March 1, 1992.

15. According to data compiled by a Dutch bank from Brazilian official announcements, Japanese companies were second with 15.2 percent ($224 million), after American companies with 29.6 percent ($436 million), in Brazil's international auctions of debt – equity conversions that came into operation in 1988. See NMB Bank, *Brazilian Debt–Equity Conversion Program: 1988 Results* (São Paulo: NMB, 1988).

16. Trade and ODA are calculated as annual averages, but direct investent and loans are shown as accumulated totals. Although methodologically inconsistent, this is the usual way to compare relations. Note that Asian NIEs and ASEAN countries, excluding Taiwan, are combined in the category Southeast Asia.

17. Japanese Chamber of Commerce and Industry of Brazil, "Brazil keizai jōhō" (Economic Information on Brazil), October 1, 1983.

18. There are nine big trading companies, which deal in almost every commercial item.

19. Although ALCOA later invited the Shell group and Brazilian local capital to be partners, the decision to establish the project was taken by ALCOA itself.

20. Big projects like Albrás were unofficially called "national projects" at that time in Japan. This was mainly because (1) projects were directly related to the national interest, (2) companies participated as a group, and (3) government organizations supported them directly or indirectly.

21. This statement came from a speech given by Hiroshi Kitamura, Japan's Deputy Minister of Foreign Affairs, before the Japan Society of Boston, February 24, 1988 (quoted in ch. 9 this volume). This explanation is quite common among government officials in Japan.

22. Ministry of Foreign Affairs, *Japan's Official Development Assistance, Annual Report*, 1988 (Tokyo: Association for Promotion of International Cooperation, 1989).

23. Calculated from companies' balance sheets.

24. *Nihon Keizai Shimbun*, New York, January 13, 1990.

25. Although more precise study is necessary, it seems to the author that the "multinationalization" of big Japanese companies signals the emergence of a new type of multinational company, different from the original American and European multinationals. One important difference is that those affiliated with Japanese companies, whether employers or employees, consider that they will be with the company permanently.

26. *Japan Economic Almanac*, 1991.

27. According to a survey conducted by Toyo Keizai in 1987, less than one percent of the listed companies on the stock exchange, which had definite

plans to invest abroad (280), were interested in investing in Latin America. While the survey may not be very accurate, it shows the reluctance of Japanese companies to invest in the region (see Toyo Keizai, *Kaigai shinshutsu kigyō sōran*).

28. Most of the new projects and ventures of Japanese business in Latin America, which have been reported in the news media in 1991–92, are in natural resources. They include the development of copper mines in Mexico and Chile, aluminum smelting projects in Venezuela and Chile, liquid natural gas and petrochemical projects in Venezuela, and forestation for pulp production in Chile.

29. *Nihon Keizai Shimbun*, New York, October 4, 1989.

30. On May 22, 1991, the Ministry of Finance announced the Japanese pledge to disburse $100 million annually for 5 years to the IDB as a part of the investment fund included in the Enterprise for the Americas Initiative (EAI). See *Nihon Keizai Shimbun*, May 23, 1991.

3 Japanese Diplomacy toward Latin America after World War II

Hiroshi Matsushita

apan's diplomatic relations with Latin America can be understood nly within the context of the country's overall postwar foreign policy. s devised by the long-ruling Liberal Democratic Party (LDP), this olicy gave top priority to the maintenance of good relations between e United States and Japan, in military as well as economic terms, us accepting the US "nuclear umbrella." This pro-American iplomacy was a response by the Japanese government to increasing nsions between West and East in an early period of the Cold War. he conservative LDP chose this alternative rather than a more neutral osition, as advocated by the Socialist Party and other groups, who pposed the pro-American policy on the grounds that it would increase nsion in Asia and the possibility of Japan entering another war. acifism had become very strong in postwar Japan as a consequence of apan's defeat and the disaster caused by the two atomic bombs. Since e government could not ignore such sentiments among the people, it ied to act very cautiously so as not to provoke international conflict at would have reverberations at home. This led Japan to take a low-rofile diplomacy in the international sphere, which is characterized by not being conspicuous," "not saying anything," and "not interfering other countries' affairs."[1]

At the same time, Japanese businessmen have been very active in reign countries, and the Japanese government has made every effort facilitate their activities. In other words, the Japanese government cted positively in the economic field but reluctantly in the field of ternational politics. As Robert S. Ozaki pointed out, postwar Japan as concentrated much of its energy on the accomplishment of conomic ends.[2] The slogan of "separation of politics from econom-s," adopted by Japan to justify trade with Communist China without xtending diplomatic recognition, is a major element of the Japanese pproach.

These features of Japan's overall diplomacy in the postwar perio
are also seen in her diplomacy toward Latin America. Perhaps it is saf
to say that these aspects appeared especially clearly in the Lati
American region for the following reasons. First of all, from th
Japanese point of view, the region is a zone of influence for the Unite
States. Thus, Japan has to refrain from interfering because an
interference would irritate the United States and hurt the US–Japa
relationship. Second, in the Latin American continent, there are mor
than a million Japanese and their descendants. Any political actio
taken by the Japanese government would provoke negative effects fo
them. Such considerations have led Japan to act more cautiously in th
region than any other. Third, partly because of the great distanc
between Japan and Latin America, Japan has not had conflicts wit
any country in the region, which permits it to concentrate on economi
goals. Consequently, Japan's presence in Latin America has bee
conspicuous in such fields as trade, investment, immigration, an
economic aid but not in political and diplomatic endeavors.[3]

In the 1980s, however, Japanese diplomacy toward Latin Americ
underwent some changes, although they were subtle ones. One exampl
is that Japan began to show more interest in political problems tha
before, declaring officially around the middle of the decade its suppor
for the democratization process underway in many countries of th
continent. If Japan had adhered to the principle of separating politic
from economics, it would not have mattered whether the continent wa
under military or civilian control. In this sense, the new policy meant
partial departure from strict application of the principle of separatio
of politics from economics. At the same time, Japan began to show
desire to contribute to Central America during the crisis there
expressing support for the activities of the Contadora Group an
taking some measures to encourage economic recovery in the area. I
short, Japanese diplomacy shifted toward a more active phase, even i
Latin America. Why did this change occur, and what does it mean fo
the triangular relations among the United States, Japan, and Lati
America? This chapter will try to answer these questions by tracing th
evolution of Japanese diplomacy toward the region since the end o
World War II.

To analyze the changes in Japanese diplomacy toward Lati
America, however, it is necessary to keep in mind those of overal
Japanese diplomacy because the former is often a reflection of th
latter. Since it is impossible to trace the evolution of the latter in deta

here, I will use a set of categories elaborated by Stephen Krasner,[4] and modified by T. J. Pempel who applied them to Japan.[5]

Krasner divided countries into three types, according to their influence in international decision-making. First, there are countries called "makers," which can exercise great influence in decision-making. Consequently, decisions about international economic policy are based more on internal politics than on the international environment. At the opposite extreme are countries called "takers," which are obliged to accept international decisions without being able to participate in the decision-making process. For these countries, internal politics does not have much relevance; international economic decisions are imposed on them from the outside. Between the two, there are countries that cannot exercise as much influence as "makers" but can produce some changes in the international economic system; Krasner calls them "breakers." Pempel accepts the overall thrust of Krasner's typology, but he labels the in-between countries "shakers" instead of "breakers." He then tries to apply these categories to explain the changes in Japanese diplomacy, pointing out that immediately after the war Japan was evidently a "taker," but around the end of the 1970s it became one of the few "makers," at least with respect to the world economic system.[6]

I agree with Pempel's periodization although I think the shift to the period of "maker" began in the mid-1970s with Japan's entry into the so-called Group of Seven (G-7) industrial countries at the summit held in 1975. Furthermore, I agree that it is more appropriate to use the term "shaker" than "breaker" to characterize the intermediate phase for Japan, because Japan in that period was characterized not by its aggressiveness in breaking the existing system but by its vulnerability to changes in the international situation. Therefore, the three categories of "taker," "shaker," and "maker" as modified by Pempel will be used here, and an attempt will be made to show the basic characteristics of Japan's overall diplomacy in each period and how its diplomacy toward Latin America was related to these features.

JAPAN AS A "TAKER": IMMIGRATION AND TRADE

After Japan's capitulation before the United Nations in August 1945, the country was occupied militarily by the United Nations armies, thus losing autonomy not only in its internal politics but also in its foreign

policy. The military occupation ended in 1952 when the peace treaties
signed in San Francisco the previous year became effective. Recovery
of Japanese sovereignty was not complete, however, because the
security treaty signed between the United States and Japan in 1951
gave the former power over the use of Japanese military bases and the
disposition of its armed forces, making Japan a subordinate partner. In
particular, Article I of the treaty gave the United States the right to use
its armed forces in Japan to put down internal disturbances if the
Japanese government requested it. Therefore, while the security treaty
continued in effect, Japan remained as a "taker," implying that this
period lasted until 1960, when the security treaty was revised to
eliminate Japan's unequal position.

During these years as a "taker," the principal objective of the
Japanese government was to encourage recovery to the economic
status of the prewar period. (As a result of the defeat, the national
product had declined almost 10 percent with respect to the years before
the war.) To achieve this objective, diplomacy was used. For example,
the payment of large-scale reparations to East Asian countries was
carried out with a view toward creating a market for Japanese
industrial products and importing raw materials from these countries. In 1953, Japan began to trade with Communist China, only a
year after Japan had recognized the government in Taiwan, demonstrating the principle of the separation of politics from economics.

This diplomacy, oriented almost exclusively to economic ends, was
also applied to Latin America in this period. The Japanese government
was especially interested in Latin America because the region was
expected to be an important recipient of Japanese migrants. After the
war, the problem of overpopulation was serious as a result of the
repatriation of 5 million people from abroad, particularly from former
colonies. Besides, due to the loss of Manchuria, which had received
slightly over one fourth of the Japanese emigrants by 1940 (Latin
America had received a little under one fourth),[7] the importance of
Latin America had increased. Therefore, the Foreign Ministry tried to
promote emigration to Latin America as one of the measures to
alleviate the problem of unemployment. As the director of the
emigration section of the Foreign Ministry, Fujio Uchida, said in
1958:

The government is making special efforts to increase emigration
[toward Latin America], not only because the internal situation
demands it, but also because the majority of the Latin American

countries receive them with favorable eyes at a moment when it is urgent to use various means to solve the demographic problems. The government should not lose this opportunity.[8]

Another role the Japanese government expected the Latin American countries to play was as trade partners: Latin America could be a market for Japanese industrial products as well as a supplier of raw materials. These trade relations represented a change with respect to the prewar period. In the 1930s, for example, Latin America's share in Japanese imports fluctuated between 0.4 percent (in 1933) and 4.8 percent (in 1936 and 1937); its share in Japanese exports varied between .2 percent (in 1931) and 6.1 percent (in 1937).[9] As was true for migration, the loss of Manchuria and the China market led the Japanese business world to pay more attention to Latin America as a substitute market. Soon after the war, then, the number of branches of Japanese trading companies exceeded the prewar level; Japan's trade volume with Latin America had recovered its prewar level by the mid-1950s.[10]

To increase trade with Latin America, the Japanese government took several initiatives in the second half of the 1950s. For example, the Ministry of Foreign Affairs helped organize the Latin American Society, whose principal objective was "to promote economic, technological and cultural exchange and to stimulate emigration."[11] In the same year, the Ministry of International Trade and Industry (MITI) founded the Research Institute for Asian Economies, which had a section for Latin American studies. Also in the same year, MITI established the Japan External Trade Organization (JETRO) as a semi-official organization to promote Japanese trade, including that with Latin America.

These policies for the promotion of trade represented the common understanding shared by many bureaucrats that Japanese economic development depended chiefly on trade. In the first volume of the *White Paper on Trade*, published in 1958 by MITI, then Minister Shigesaburo Maeo stated, "It is an indispensable condition to expand trade so that our country, which lacks natural resources, may grow."[12] The importance attributed to Latin America in this context was pointed out clearly by Keizo Shibusawa, one of the leading business-men at that time, who visited 13 countries as a special ambassador in 1957. He recognized the difficulties Japan would face in increasing trade with the region. First, the influence of the United States and some European countries was overwhelming. Second, there is a long distance between Latin America and Japan, which constitutes a big disadvantage for Japan. Nevertheless, he was optimistic concerning the future of economic relations between the two regions because of the large number of Japanese emigrants living in Latin America, who could play the role of intermediaries, and because the Latin American countries had been showing friendly attitudes toward Japan in international conferences.[13]

It is interesting to note that the new policies were begun in 1958; at that time, the Japanese economy had recovered its prewar level. The *White Paper on the Economy*, published by the Economic Planning Agency in 1956, had declared that "the postwar period is over."[14] Also Japan had acquired more export capacities by that time, which required the government to search for new markets. But there was yet another reason why the Japanese government showed more interest in Latin America in the late 1950s; the formation of the EEC as a new economic bloc was perceived as a threat to the Japanese economy. Facing this new reality in the international environment, the Japanese government tried to strengthen its trade relations. Perhaps this explains why Prime Minister Nobusuke Kishi paid his first visit to several Asian countries in 1958 and to Latin America in the following year.

In short, during the period as a "taker," Japanese diplomacy toward Latin America was motivated by economic concerns, with a view to using it as an outlet for emigrants and to turning it into a trade partner both of which were expected to help solve serious Japanese economic problems. This diplomacy, also applied to other regions of the world complemented the domestic policies pursued to achieve economic recovery and development. Thus, around the end of the 1950s, Japan was in a position to improve its international position, putting an end to its status as a subordinate partner of the United States. As was said before, this change was symbolized by the revision of the security treaty in 1960. So, it is safe to say that the period as a "shaker" began around 1960.

JAPAN AS A "SHAKER": NEED FOR NATURAL RESOURCE

During the "shaker" period, Japan's overall diplomacy did no undergo substantial change, still maintaining its economic-oriented thrust. Indeed, this characteristic was even intensified in this phase One reason was that the revision of the security treaty, which marked the transition from "taker" to "shaker," was highly controversial provoking unprecedented mass mobilization and leaving profound divisions within the population. The administration of Hayato Ikeda, which began just after the political turmoil, tried to divert public attention from politics by promising to double income within 10 years. Diplomacy was used to help achieve this national objective, and it seems to me that Robert Ozaki's previously-cited remark about the concentration of Japan's diplomatic efforts on economic ends is most relevant to this period. The Japanese economy developed so remarkably that *per capita* income doubled earlier than planned, and Japan's gross national product (GNP) in 1968 became second only to the United States in the non-socialist world. But in spite of this economic "miracle," Japan remained vulnerable to external shocks during almost all this period.

One event that put Japan in a difficult situation was the Cuban missile crisis in October 1962. When Fulgencio Batista was overthrown by Fidel Castro in January 1959, the Japanese government recognized the new revolutionary regime, as the United States had done.[15] In the early period of the Cuban revolution, then, there was no discrepancy between the US and Japanese positions. As the tension between the United States and Cuba grew after the rupture of diplomatic relations in January 1961, however, Japan faced a serious dilemma: how to maintain trade relations with Cuba without undermining its relations with the United States? This dilemma deepened when Cuba intensified the socialist and Marxist character of the revolution after the Bay of Pigs invasion in April 1961. Even under these circumstances, Japan wanted to continue her trade with Cuba because it depended heavily on the island for the import of sugar. Cuba's share in Japan's sugar imports was 32 percent in 1959, 16 percent in 1960 and 23.4 percent in 1961.[16] Besides, according to Japan's traditional policy of separation of politics from economics, there was no problem in maintaining trade relations with a communist country. The Cuban missile crisis again posed the question of whether Japan could continue such a policy, especially after West Germany broke off her diplomatic relations with Cuba.[17]

As there are limited materials available concerning Japan's attitude toward the Cuban crisis, the details on discussions within the government are not yet known. It is certain, however, that the Japanese government adopted a policy that did not differ from its traditional principle of separation of politics from economics, while trying to show understanding of the US position. In other words, Japan maintained its trade with Cuba as before, but at the same time as a non-permanent member of the Security Council of the United Nations, it supported the United States' position there on the ground that the installation of a missile base in Cuba would pose a threat to the Western Hemisphere.[18]

The reason for the Japanese policy can be understood if the internal politics of Japan are taken into account. On the one hand, the LDP leaders had adhered since the war to the policy of separation of politics from economics, and despite their staunch anti-communism, they did not see any reason to abandon that policy over Cuba. On the other hand, the Socialist Party, which was the main opposition party, had ideological sympathy with Socialist Cuba and so opposed an embargo. In short, both the conservative Liberal Democrats and the Socialists were opposed to sanctions against Cuba, which prevented the government from taking a strong anti-Cuban position. The reaction of the US government toward Japan's diplomacy is not known, but since there was no mention about it in any important Japanese newspaper, it can be supposed that the United States was satisfied with Japan's support in the United Nations Security Council, or at least did not protest explicitly.

After the Cuban crisis in the 1960s, it is difficult to find a clear difference in diplomatic stance between the two countries concerning Latin America. One incident that attracted world-wide attention was the Dominican invasion by the United States in April 1965. On that occasion the Japanese government avoided any kind of criticism against the United States. In the Foreign Affairs Committee of the House of Deputies, Socialist Kei Hoashi criticized the government's policy for its lack of understanding of the increasing demands of Third World peoples for self-determination. He also cited De Gaulle's criticism against the military intervention by the United States, demanding that the Japanese government take a similar stand. In his response, Minister of Foreign Affairs Etsusaburo Shiina did not show any sympathy to De Gaulle's policy and explicitly supported the American intervention.[19]

A problem much bigger than Cuba, which erupted during this period, was the oil crisis of October 1973. Although this crisis itself was not a Latin American phenomenon, its repercussions extended to Japanese diplomacy toward the region. The effect on Japan's Latin American policy can be seen by first analyzing the Japanese reaction in general.

One of the measures taken by the Japanese government in the wake of the oil crisis was to modify its traditional pro-Israeli stance toward a neutral or even pro-Arab one. For example, when the Organization of Arab Petroleum Exporting Countries (OAPEC) decided on November 18, 1973, to make further cuts in the oil supply to Japan, while excluding the European Community countries, Japan did not delay in declaring for the first time its support for the rights of self-determination of the Palestinian people. This naturally provoked resentment from the Israeli government but did not satisfy the Arab countries. Therefore, Prime Minister Kakuei Tanaka sent Vice-Prime Minister Takeo Miki to explain Japan's stance and ask for the same treatment toward Japan as toward the European Community. During his trip to the Middle East in December 1973, Miki promised some economic aid and succeeded in getting better treatment for Japan; a meeting in late December of the OAPEC oil ministers declared a reduction in oil cutbacks to Japan and appreciation for the Miki visit.[20] This active diplomacy was evidently motivated by Japanese concerns to assure the import of oil at any cost; to achieve this aim, the Japanese government began to take a more independent stance in the Middle East with respect to the United States. The above-mentioned declaration about the Palestinian people's rights was one example. Pempel says that in the second half of 1973 and in the first half of 1974, Japan began to take a more pro-Arab stance, "ignoring the pressure of the United States."[21]

Similar active policies were also carried out in Asia and Latin America for the purpose of assuring the supply of raw materials. Prime Minister Tanaka's visit to Southeast Asia in January of 1974 and to Mexico and Brazil in September of the same year shows clearly that Japan made much of Latin America as a supplier of raw materials. Although Latin America had been seen in these terms previously, the role became much more important after the oil crisis. Tanaka visited Mexico and Brazil with a very concrete plan to exploit raw materials. He agreed with Mexico's President Luis Echeverría on the inauguration of a new program for joint investment in the sectors most desirable for the development of the economies of the two countries.[22] These sectors were evidently resource industries. In Brazil, Tanaka agreed on joint ventures between Japanese and Brazilian private enterprises dedicated to the production of aluminum and pulp and the exploitation of agricultural resources.

Although these plans were evidently designed to confront the oil crisis and Japan's national interest was very clear, there was no strong opposition in Latin America. This was an advantage that Latin America had over the Southeast Asian countries as a supplier of raw materials from the Japanese point of view. Unlike Southeast Asia, anti-Japanese sentiment did not exist in Latin America. Tanaka's visit to the Asian countries had provoked a strong anti-Japanese movement in some places; in Jakarta it ended in a riot. In Latin America, by contrast, nationalism was principally directed toward the United States rather than Japan. Needless to say, Latin America had offsetting disadvantages in its geographical location, which prompted some businessmen to think of a new Panama Canal as a means to assure the supply of raw materials in a more secure and rapid way (see Chapter 9 in this volume).

All this did not mean that Japan could promote economic-oriented diplomacy in Latin America without any problems. For example, criticism of Japanese economic expansion began to be heard in some Latin American countries (especially Chile, Venezuela, and Colombia) around the mid-1970s, where the Japanese "import rush" was noted.[23] The United States also began to view Japan's economic expansion into this region with some concern. An analyst at the State Department made the following comment after the oil crisis:

> There is a good reason to believe that an increasing share of Japan's raw material imports will come from Latin America. Japan is thus moving into an area long regarded as our backyard, while the United States becomes more dependent on its traditional Latin American sources of raw materials and its relations with the area are bedeviled by nationalism and economic conflicts of interest. In this context, there would seem to exist a serious possibility of conflict with Japan over access to raw materials, which significantly affects the overall United States security–political–economic relationship.[24]

Although there is no evidence about how this type of concern was transmitted to the Japanese government and how it reacted, the statement shows that Japan's more aggressive economic diplomacy in Latin America was causing new frictions with the United States.

In summary, Japan's Latin American diplomacy during the "shaker" period was characterized by an even stronger economic orientation than in the "taker" years. It is notable that this tendency provoked some discrepancies between the United States and Japan with respect to Latin America, although Japan continued to be a loyal partner as shown in the case of the Dominican invasion. This emerging independent orientation became stronger in the following phase.

JAPAN AS A "MAKER": A NEW IDEOLOGICAL APPROACH

It is very difficult to define when Japan became a "maker," but as pointed out before, it seems reasonable to think that becoming a member of the G-7 summit in 1975 gave it such a status, at least in the economic field. Obviously, there are differences among "makers," and even if Japan became one, it remained a subordinate partner of the United States in the military realm. The maintenance of friendly relations with the United States also continued to be the first and foremost objective for the LDP. Therefore, the transition from "shaker" to "maker" did not imply any substantial change in Japanese diplomacy. Japan's policy toward Latin America has been especially constrained because of the latter's location in the US sphere of influence. Moreover, in this period economic conflicts between the United States and Japan became more serious, so Japan had to try to avoid further conflicts over Latin America. In short, despite Japan's becoming a "maker," there was little room for it to take a free and independent diplomatic stance with respect to Latin America. With all these limitations, however, Japanese diplomacy began to show some change in this period, reflecting a new orientation in overall diplomacy.

One of the changes in this new stage that deserves mention is Japan's recognition of its own position as a world economic power. Such recognition had been expressed in diverse forms during the 1970s, but in the 1980s, the *Blue Book* (the official report published every year by the Ministry of Foreign Affairs) began to voice the necessity to recognize Japan's position in the world and to take corresponding measures. For example, the *Blue Book* of 1984 said, "Japan has become important politically and economically in the international society, accounting for 10 percent of world production," and "Japan cannot be allowed to remain only as a beneficiary which acts passively." It further stated that it was more and more recognized internationally that "Japan ought to play a more positive role for the maintenance of world peace and contribute to the prosperity of the world by means of economic cooperation."[25] The 1983 *Blue Book* had also said that "Japan should take a more positive international role, including in the political sphere, to respond to the world's expectations of our country."[26]

These two volumes of the *Blue Book* coincided in pointing out the necessity of a more active role for Japan, even in political areas. This shift is very important because it signaled a departure from the traditional principle of the separation of politics from economics. If the Japanese government intended to adhere to that principle, it could not have recommended political action in the international arena. In this sense, it is safe to say that some important changes occurred in the general approach of Japanese diplomacy in the first half of the 1980s.

Why did this change occur? One reason was probably Japan's recognition that pursuing economic ends without any kind of political participation was no longer possible, given the country's enormous economic power. Put another way, the separation of politics from economics was possible only when the Japanese economy was small; once Japan came to represent 10 percent of world output, any action, even if purely economic, could not help having political implications. Another reason was that Japan felt responsibility as an economic power, especially after its entry into the Group of Seven. It is to be noted that Prime Minister Yasuhiro Nakasone (1982–87) was a strong advocate of Japan taking a more active role in the world.

But what did the Japanese government mean by a more active international role? According to the 1984 *Blue Book*, it meant several principles and policies, among which the most important was to reaffirm Japan's position as a member of the Western Bloc. This meant that Japan should support the values of liberty, democracy, and free market economies.[27] First, then, it is safe to say that Japanese diplomacy in this period was and is much more ideologically oriented. Second, another important policy stressed in the same document was the contribution to the stability and development of the Third World. An aid policy for the developing countries had begun during the previous period, but Japan's aid policy became much more important in the 1980s because of the growing size of its economy and the enormous trade surplus. Third, Japan began to act as a mediator in international conflicts. In particular, Japan's mediation role in the Iran–Iraq war and the Cambodian dispute would never have taken place 10 years earlier.

These changes in Japan's overall diplomacy were reflected in her policy toward Latin America. For example, a more ideologically-oriented diplomacy was shown in her critical attitude toward revolutionary Nicaragua. As we have seen, in the case of the Cuban revolution, Japan applied the principle of the separation of politics from economics, avoiding any kind of criticism of the revolution. Japan's attitude was very different with respect to the revolution in Nicaragua in 1979, 20 years after the Cuban revolution. Especially after the United States began open hostilities in 1981, Japan took a critical stance toward Nicaragua. The 1981 *Blue Book* commented on

Nicaragua, saying, "The tendency toward a single-party dictatorship became more evident through the prohibition of mass meetings to protest the Sandinista dictatorship and through restrictions on freedom of the press."[28] The 1984 *Blue Book* escalated the attack against the Sandinista regime, pointing out that "the government turned to the left, leaving almost without effect the multi-party system, mixed economy, and non-aligned diplomacy, which the revolution of 1979 had promised."[29]

The new approach was not limited to words; Japan's aid policy showed similar tendencies. The ODA given by Japan to Nicaragua in 1985 reached only $60,000 while Holland gave $15.7 million, France $7 million, Canada $5.8 million, West Germany $4.7 million, Italy $4.3 million, and Great Britain $150,000.[30] In short, among the principal developed countries, Japan was the most critical with the exception of the United States. It is interesting to note that Japan's new attitude toward the revolutionary regime coincided with that of the United States. Therefore, at least with respect to Nicaragua, Japan's more ideologically-oriented diplomacy did not produce any friction with the United States, although Japan showed some different attitudes toward the overall conflict in Central America, as we will see later.

Another case that showed Japan's new approach was the explicit support for the democratization that was occurring throughout the continent in the 1980s. This new stance was first officially stressed in the recommendations formulated by the meeting of Japanese ambassadors held in Tokyo in November 1984. On that occasion, they agreed that Japan welcomed the democratization of the Latin American countries in recent years.[31] Following this stance, the 1985 *Blue Book* expressed explicitly for the first time Japan's support for democratization, saying: "As for the recent democratization of the Latin American area, our country welcomes it, because it will be an incentive to strengthen the dialogue and cooperative relations with Latin America."[32]

More importantly, in April 1991, Prime Minister Toshiki Kaifu announced new guidelines to be taken into account in the allocation of Official Development Assistance (ODA). Negative factors, which could limit ODA, included (1) a high level of military expenditure, (2) development of nuclear and biological weapons, and (3) weapons exports. A positive factor that could increase aid was movement toward, and support for, democracy. In other words, Japan decided to tie its aid to democracy. This new policy was applied to Haiti after the military coup in September 1991.

These actions clearly show the intention of the Japanese government to retreat from the traditional principle of the separation of politics from economics; if it had been strictly maintained, support for a particular type of regime would not have been expressed. The new approach meant a very important step in Japan's Latin American policy, for in the past Japan had often maintained good relations with military or civilian dictators, such as Paraguay's Alfredo Stroessner. In the 1970s, Japan was the only industrial country that invited the Argentine military president, Jorge Rafael Videla. In this sense, Japan's Latin American policy reflected the new orientation of its overall diplomacy. Again, the effects of the new ideologically-oriented stance did not mean an increase in tensions with the United States because, when Japan began to move in favor of democratization, the Reagan administration had shifted in the same direction. Thus, in spite of Japan's increasing importance as an economic power and the growing desire to participate in international society, there were some aspects in Latin America that could promote cooperation between the United States and Japan. Nevertheless, in this stage as a "maker," Japan showed more independent and sometimes conflicting attitudes in this region.

One example was Japan's policy in the Malvinas (Falklands) conflict. Immediately after the Argentine army's occupation of the disputed islands on April 2, 1982, Japan took a critical position against the military aggression. As a non-permanent member of the Security Council of the United Nations, Japan supported a resolution that asked for the immediate cessation of the military action and the withdrawal of Argentine troops. But the criticism did not go far, and Japan soon showed a more neutral position. On April 6, the Japanese government decided not to participate in the economic sanctions which the British government asked the Western European countries to impose.

This neutral position was severely criticized by the Thatcher government but, while US Secretary of State Alexander Haig continued his mediation, Japan's neutral position did not stand out within the western bloc because the United States maintained the same neutral position. Japan was obliged to face its most difficult moment when the US government abandoned its mediation and declared its support for Great Britain on April 30. At that time British pressure on Japan mounted, but the Japanese government could not easily follow the United States for various reasons. One was that almost all the Latin American countries had supported the Argentine cause, and Japan wanted to maintain good relationships with them. In addition, there were more than 32,000 Japanese immigrants and their descendants in Argentina, who had been criticized because of a Japanese policy that seemed pro-British to the Argentines.[33] As was pointed out before, Japanese diplomacy has tended to give great importance to the Japanese immigrants in Latin America, so it is safe to suppose that this was one factor preventing Japan from taking a clear pro-British stance.

Under such difficult circumstances, the Japanese government decided to adopt an ambiguous policy, announcing the following measures on May 1: (1) the Japanese government would urge Japanese trading companies not to undermine the effects of the economic sanctions against Argentina imposed by other countries and not to use this situation to the advantage of Japanese economic interests; (2) no new requests for export credits to Argentina (requests from Japanese enterprises to the Export–Import Bank of Japan) would be welcomed.[34]

At first glance, the measures seemed like economic sanctions, and some newspapers reported that the declaration was an economic sanction.[35] From the point of the Ministry of Foreign Affairs, however, the measures did not constitute economic sanctions. After the announcement of the measures, the Ministry sent a dispatch to the mass media, saying that "these two measures are not economic sanctions."[36] This additional dispatch shows that the measures taken by the government were confusing and ambiguous. Probably such ambiguity came from the fact that the measures were a product of compromise between the pro-British group and the pro-Argentine or pro-Latin American group within the Ministry of Foreign Affairs.[37]

The measures were designed to appease the British government, because they looked like sanctions, and they were intended to avoid criticism from the Argentine side, because they had practically no effect on Argentina. In this sense, the measures can be thought of as very subtle ones. The British government, of course, was not satisfied.[38] Moreover, the government continued to take a rather pro-Argentine position, showing a clear discrepancy with the United States' pro-British stance. Thus, a difference emerged between the policies of the United States and Japan with respect to the Malvinas War. We have not yet been able to obtain any documents about the attitude of the United States toward Japan during this conflict, but judging from the fact that the Japanese mass media did not mention any complaints by the United States concerning Japan's position on the war, it seems safe to say that US criticism was not strong. In any case, the Japanese reaction toward the conflict showed that Japan had begun to act more independently, even in Latin America, without seriously harming the US–Japan friendship.

Another example that showed Japan's more independent attitude was its policy toward Central America. As we have seen, there was no important difference between the United States and Japan concerning the nature of the Sandinista revolution. Japan preferred a peaceful solution, however, and expressed its explicit support for the activity of the Contadora process, although avoiding direct criticism of the US aid policy to the Contras. Such support was expressed on the occasion of the visit paid by the Foreign Minister Shintaro Abe to Colombia in January 1985.[39] Meanwhile, the Reagan administration continued to give only lip service to the activities of the Contadora group.

This kind of difference was also shown when the Esquipulas II agreement was signed among the Central American republics in Guatemala in August 1987. While the United States continued to take a cool attitude toward the agreement, Japan welcomed it as an important step toward bringing peace to the region. Tadashi Kuranari, who visited Guatemala in September of the same year as the first Japanese Foreign Minister to visit that country, praised the agreement highly and proposed an aid plan to contribute to the peace and development of the region once the cease-fire went into effect. The plan included financial aid through the Interamerican Development Bank (IDB), a seminar for the development of human capital, and aid to the refugees.[40] In March of 1988, a seminar on human capital in Central America was held in Tokyo, and 10 representatives from Central America (two from each country, including Nicaragua) were invited.[41]

Perhaps the United States welcomed Japanese aid to these countries, given its own inability to provide much money for them. But all these activities that Japan carried out concerning Central America meant that Japan had begun to try to increase its influence, even in the US backyard, sharing some American points of view but at the same time showing some different attitudes.

In the case of Panama, also, we can see the combination of difference and coincidence, or opposition and cooperation, between the policies of the United States and Japan. From the Japanese point of view, Panama is one of the Latin American countries that had been attracting Japanese businessmen and traders since the beginning of this century, at first because of the Panama Canal and after World War II as a base for re-export of Japanese products.[42] In addition, because

of the recent discussion about the construction of a new canal, Panama
has attracted much attention from the Japanese business world.

Interest in a new canal in Panama was related to the problem of the
stable acquisition of raw materials after the oil crisis (see also Chapter 9
in this volume). As a route for the international transport of raw
materials, it seemed that the existing canal had become obsolete and
that its capacity could not meet increasing demand. The signature of a
new canal treaty between the United States and Panama in 1978 also
provoked interest in the canal problem because, in Article 12, both
countries agreed on a joint study on the feasibility of a new sea-level
canal within the Republic of Panama.[43]

Although the article did not prohibit the participation of third
countries in the construction of a new canal, the plan was evidently
considered as a US–Panama joint project. But, since the two countries
could not afford to spend much money, even for a feasibility study,
Japanese participation was accepted. Meanwhile in Japan, because of
the tenacious efforts of Shigeo Nagano, president of the Japanese
Chamber of Commerce, who had been interested in the Canal since his
trip to Panama in 1977,[44] the idea of Japan's participation in the
feasibility study was supported by the main leaders of the business
world. Since the Keidanren (the most important employers' association
in Japan) decided to endorse Japan's participation, the movement in
favor of the participation was encouraged.[45]

Finally, in October 1982, the government decided to participate in the
feasibility study, accepting the invitation extended by the United States
and Panama.[46] Since then, Japan has participated in all activities related
to the feasibility study, signing a new agreement to set up a commission
for the study of alternatives to the existing canal in September 1985.
Thus, Japan participated in a giant project in Latin America for the first
time. What is worth stressing is the fact that all the costs relative to the
feasibility study are shared equally among the three countries. In other
words, Japan's ability to participate as an equal partner with the United
States derived from the country's increased economic strength.

This new kind of cooperation reached a stalemate soon after the
Board of the Commission in January 1988 designated the international
consortium, composed of three companies (one from each country), to
carry out a feasibility study. At the end of the following month,
President Eric Arturo Delvalle was overthrown because of his intention
to cooperate with the United States in arresting General Manuel
Noriega, who had been indicted by a court in Miami for his
involvement in drug trafficking. Manuel Solís Palma, a member of

Noriega's group, was sworn in as provisional president, causing new friction between the United States and Japan. While the former did not recognize the new government, the latter tried to maintain normal diplomatic relations with Panama, accepting that the change of government was carried out according to constitutional procedure and the new government was ruling the country effectively.[47]

This attitude can be explained by several factors. First of all, the Japanese government has traditionally avoided using recognition policy as a diplomatic tool, thinking that it signified intervention in the domestic affairs of foreign countries. Second, Japanese economic interests in Panama were so huge that Japan wanted to try to avoid any kind of diplomatic conflict with that country. Third, some leading members of the ruling LDP, including Prime Minister Noboru Takeshita, had friendly relations with Noriega, who had visited Japan six times.[48]

The position of the Japanese Foreign Ministry at first provoked some strong criticism in the United States, not only in the State Department but also in the Congress. Elliot Abrams, Assistant Secretary of State for Latin American Affairs, called in Ryozo Kato, the counselor for political affairs at the Japanese Embassy, explaining the US position and asking for mutual close cooperation between the two countries concerning Panama.[49]

Under pressure from the United States, the Takeshita administration retreated to a more conciliatory policy, postponing the reopening of diplomatic relations. On this occasion, Japan once again gave higher priority to US–Japan relations than to its particular interests in Latin America. At that moment, Japan had a very severe problem with the United States over liberalization of import controls on oranges and beef. The government had been making every effort to appease the United States about Japan's delay in the liberalization schedule. It seems that the government gave in to the United States for the moment concerning the Panamanian problem, so as not to provoke additional friction. Solution of the oranges and beef problem was reached by Japan's concession on June 19, 1988, paving the way for Japan to act more independently with respect to Panama. Less than a week after the settlement of the oranges and beef issue, the Japanese ambassador in Panama informed the Panamanian Foreign Ministry of the desire of the Japanese government to maintain normal diplomatic relations.[50] When the United States invaded Panama in December 1989, however, the Japanese government took a more pro-American stance, recognizing Guillermo Endara's government on January 5, 1990.[51]

Japan again showed its independence during the Peruvian political crisis caused by President Fujimori's auto-coup in April 1992. While the United States suspended economic aid, Japan did not follow suit but showed some sympathy toward Fujimori's measures. Japan's main arguments were that a military coup was not involved because there were plans to restore democracy, and that the policies were necessary because of the problems with terrorism and drugs.[52] Japan's attitude was problematic, however, since it undermined the government's own principles to support democracy as established in the 1980s and confirmed in the ODA guidelines set out in April 1991. This dilemma prompted the Japanese government to take measures to persuade Fujimori to lessen his government's anti-democratic features. Thus, Prime Minister Miyazawa sent the director of the Foreign Ministry's Latin America Bureau to persuade Fujimori to attend the May 19 meeting of the Organization of American States (OAS). According to the declaration of the top officials of the ministry, Fujimori's attendance and speech softened the atmosphere of the meeting and avoided harsh criticism of the Peruvian government.[53]

CONCLUSIONS

In this chapter, I have tried to make clear the evolution of Japanese diplomacy toward Latin America, from the immediate postwar period until the present, by using the three ideal types of countries as "takers," "shakers," and "makers." This framework may be too simple to analyze the complicated diplomatic realities, but it enables us to define the characteristics of each stage, and to recognize some changes in Japanese diplomacy. For example, Japan shifted from strict adherence to the principle of the separation of politics from economics to a more ideologically-oriented diplomacy, stressing its role as a member of the western world. Also, Japan has begun to take a more independent diplomatic stance with respect to the United States, even in Latin America, reflecting its increasing economic power.

How far this independent policy will go in the near future remains to be seen, but it appears that while Japan stresses the importance of the global US–Japan relationship as its first priority, its action at the governmental level will continue to be restrained. It is true that some members of the LDP have begun to question the maintenance of the US–Japan security treaty with the end of the Cold War. This opinion is supported by only a small minority within the party, however, and while Japan maintains that treaty with the United States, its diplomacy will not change very much. Nonetheless, it is possible that Japan's independent attitude in Latin America may increase in the future as long as it does not endanger relations between the United States and Japan.

Notes

1. Kuniko Inoguchi, *Posuto haken sisutemu to Nihon no sentaku* (The Emerging Post-Hegemonic System: Choices for Japan) (Tokyo: Chikuma Shobō, 1987) p. 65.
2. Robert S. Ozaki, "Introduction: The Political Economy of Japan's Foreign Relations," in Robert Ozaki and Walter Arnold, (eds.), *Japan's Foreign Relations* (Boulder, CO: Westview Press, 1985) p. 3.
3. Herbert Goldhamer, *The Foreign Powers in Latin America* (Princeton, NJ: Princeton University Press, 1972) p. 225.
4. Stephen D. Krasner, "United States Commercial and Monetary Policy: Unravelling the Paradox of External Strength and Internal Weakness," in Peter Katzenstein, (ed.), *Between Power and Plenty* (Madison: University of Wisconsin Press, 1978).
5. T. J. Pempel, "Nihon no gaikō seisaku no naiseiteki kiso" (The Internal Basis of Japanese Foreign Policy), in Nobuo Tomita and Yasunori Sone, (eds.), *Sekai seiji no nakano Nihon seiji* (Japanese Politics within World Politics) (Tokyo: Yuhikaku, 1983).
6. Ibid., pp. 31–32.
7. Naomasa Oshimoto, "Kokusai ijū" (International Migration), in Minoru Izawa *et al.*, (eds.), *Raten Amerika* (Latin America) (Tokyo: Daiyamondosha, 1971) pp. 210–11.
8. Fujio Uchida, "The Policies for Foreign Migration and Latin America," *Latin America* 1, 1 (1958).
9. Iyo Kunimoto, "Historical Relations between Japan and Latin America," in Hiroshi Matsushita, Akio Hosono and Iyo Kunimoto, *Japan's Relations with Latin America* (unpublished ms.) p. 13.
10. Hiroshi Matsushita, "Japanese Diplomacy toward Latin America in the Postwar Period," in Matsushita, Hosono and Kunimoto, p. 7.
11. Latin American Society, *Raten Amerika Kyōkai no gaiyō* (A History of the Latin American Society) (Tokyo: Raten Amerika Kyōkai, 1985) p. 2.
12. MITI, *Tsūshō hakusho* (White Paper on Trade) (Tokyo: Ministry of International Trade and Industry, 1958) p. 3.
13. Ministry of Foreign Affairs, "Idō yontaishi hōkoku yōshi no gaiyō" (A Summary of the Reports Presented by the Four Non-Permanent Ambassadors), 1958, pp. 6–7.
14. Economic Planning Agency, *Keizai hakusho* (White Paper on the Economy), (Tokyo: Shiseidō, 1956), p. 42.

5. Ministry of Foreign Affairs, *Waga gaikō no kinkyō* (The Present Situation of Our Diplomacy) (Tokyo: Ministry of Foreign Affairs, 1959) p. 89; cited hereafter as *Blue Book*.
6. MITI, *Tsūshō hakusho*, 1962, p. 149.
7. Gerhard Drekonja Kornat, "Europe's Rediscovery of Latin America," in Wolf Grabendorff and Riordan Roett, (eds.), *Latin America, Western Europe, and the United States* (New York: Praeger, 1985) p. 66.
8. The declaration was made by Yasushi Kurogane, Secretary of Government, on October 24, 1962 (reported in *Asahi Shimbun*, October 25, 1962, morning edition, p. 1).
9. *Shūgiin gijiroku* (Diary of the House of Deputies), 48th Congressional Session, May 7, 1965, pp. 6–7.
10. Sukehiro Hasegawa, *Japanese Foreign Aid: Policy and Practice* (New York: Praeger, 1975) p. 94.
11. Pempel, "Nihon no gaikō seisaku," p. 55.
12. *Blue Book*, 1975, p. 79.
13. Matsushita, "Japanese Diplomacy," p. 25.
14. Cited in Heraldo Muñoz, "The Strategic Dependency of the Centers and the Economic Importance of the Latin American Periphery," in Heraldo Muñoz, (ed.), *From Dependency to Development: Strategies to Overcome Underdevelopment and Inequality* (Boulder, CO: Westview Press, 1981) pp. 84–85.
15. *Blue Book*, 1984, p. 1.
16. *Blue Book*, 1983, p. 1.
17. *Blue Book*, 1984, p. 2.
18. *Blue Book*, 1981, p. 136.
19. *Blue Book*, 1984, p. 155.
20. *Blue Book*, 1987, pp. 470, 547.
21. "Proposal of the Meeting of (Japanese) Ambassadors in Latin America for 1984," November 6, 1984, *Latin America Journal*, No. 34 (December 1, 1984) pp. 13–15.
22. *Blue Book*, 1985, p. 185.
23. *Asahi Shimbun*, April 8, 1982, evening edition, p. 2.
24. Asahi Shimbun Gaihōbu, *Kurutta sinario: Fōkurando funsō no uchimaku* (The Failed Scenarios: The Inside Story of the Falklands War) (Tokyo: Asahi Shimbunsha, 1982) p. 202.
25. *Japan Times*, May 2, 1982, p. 1.
26. Asahi Shimbun Gaihōbu, *Kurutta sinario*, p. 204.
27. *Asahi Shimbun*, May 8, 1982, morning edition, p. 2.
28. *Japan Times*, June 2, 1982, p. 1.
29. *Blue Book*, 1985, p. 185.
30. Matsushita, "Japanese Diplomacy," p. 40.
31. For information about this seminar, see JICA, "Seminario sobre el desarrollo de los recursos humanos en América Central" (Tokyo, n.d.).
32. In 1903, when Panama became independent with the United States' help, the Ministry of Foreign Affairs and the Ministry of Agriculture and Industry of Japan began research on the possibility of constructing a canal there. See Masato Kimura, "Panama unga no kaitū to Nichibei kankei" (The Opening of the Panama Canal in 1914 and US–Japanese

Relations), in *Kindai Nihon kenkyūkai nenpō, kindai Nihon kenkyū II kyōchō gaikō no genkai* (Annals of Studies of Modern Japan: The Limits of Cooperationist Policy) (Tokyo: Yamakawa Shuppansha, 1989) p. 45.

43. David N. Farnsworth and James W. McKenny, *US–Panama Relations 1903–1978* (Boulder: Westview Press, 1983), p. 291.

44. Shigeo Nagano, *Waga zaikai jinsei* (My Life at the Top of the Business World) (Tokyo: Daiyamondosha, 1982) p. 135.

45. Matsushita, "Japanese Diplomacy," p. 45.

46. *Nihon Keizai Shimbun*, October 1, 1982, morning edition, p. 3 and October 11, 1982, morning edition, p. 3.

47. *Asahi Shimbun*, March 3, 1988, morning edition, p. 3. See also Charlotte Elton, "Panama and Japan: The Role of the Canal" (ch. 9 this volume).

48. Benjamin Venegas, "El Japonés Noriega," *Periodista* (Buenos Aires), 4, 189 (22 al 28 de abril, 1988) p. 18.

49. *Asahi Shimbun*, March 5, 1988, evening edition, p. 2; *Japan Times*, March 6, 1988, p. 1.

50. *Asahi Shimbun*, June 24, 1988, morning edition, p. 1.

51. Ibid., January 6, 1990, evening edition, p. 2.

52. *Mainichi Shimbun*, April 9, 1992, evening edition, p. 1; *Asahi Shimbun*, April 12, 1992, morning edition, p. 3.

53. *Asahi Shimbun*, May 21, 1992, morning edition, p. 3.

4 Japanese Migration to Latin America

Iyo Kunimoto

Latin America has the largest Japanese community outside Japan, both first-generation migrants and their descendants. The exact numbers are impossible to determine, but best estimates suggest that well over 1 million are living in Brazil, Peru, Mexico, Paraguay, Bolivia, and a few other countries. These ethnic Japanese have not only been successfully integrated into the socio-economic mainstream of the local societies, but they have also racially mingled in many countries. The latest and most dramatic example of this successful integration was the election of Alberto Fujimori as president of Peru. Fujimori has now focused international attention on the Japanese immigrant population, but it has long been important both for Japan and for the recipient Latin American nations.

Japanese migration constituted the most important aspect of Japanese–Latin American relations until trade and investment burgeoned in the 1960s. The migration and economic trends, however, are not unrelated. It is thus not coincidence that the two Latin American countries receiving the largest amounts of Japanese direct investment in the period up till the debt crisis were Brazil and Peru, though in the latter case Japanese investment fluctuated sharply depending on the period; they were also the homes of the biggest Japanese populations. Especially in Brazil, the Japanese immigrants as well as the *nisei* (second-generation Japanese) population played an important intermediary role when Japanese firms wanted to invest. Likewise, Japanese government aid, which has become increasingly important in recent years, has been skewed toward those countries – and even areas within countries – where large Japanese populations are found. Overall, the presence of Japanese ethnic groups in Latin America continues to have a surprisingly strong impact on Japanese policy.[1]

This chapter analyzes the reasons for the large-scale Japanese migration to Latin America, both the Japanese government's perceived need to find homes for "surplus population" and the Latin American governments' complementary requirements for labor. It also discusses some of the experiences of the migrants in their new homelands and presents a sketch of Japanese communities that exist in the region. Finally, it concludes with the latest trend in the migration history – the *dekasegi* or reverse migration back to Japan. The latter can be seen as a symbol of the economic devastation that has enveloped Latin America over the last decade. Although American and Latin American scholars speak of the *dekasegi* phenomenon as the Japanese–Latin Americans returning home, both the Japanese government and the majority of the Japanese–Latin Americans view the reverse migration as temporary.

AN OVERVIEW OF JAPANESE MIGRATION TO LATIN AMERICA

The history of Japanese migration to Latin America can be divided into two distinct periods: before World War II and after it. While the Japanese government strongly encouraged migration throughout, its paternalistic attitude reached a climax in the preparation for and the organization of a massive migratory flow to Brazil in the 1920s and 1930s. The two periods differ, however, in the motivations of Japanese migrants and in the patterns of their migration. Before World War II, most migrants went abroad as contract laborers, with the clear intention of returning home after saving enough money to start a business or at least survive back in their communities. Intentions aside, however, many of them stayed in Latin American indefinitely. Some married local women and acquired land or opened businesses; others lost the chance to return home simply because they could not save enough money. In contrast, most migrants who left Japan after the war had plans to settle permanently in the new countries, deciding to leave war-torn and poverty-stricken Japan to seek their future in foreign lands.

The important role played by Latin America in the history of Japanese emigration can be seen in Table 4.1. At present Latin America has the largest Japanese community outside Japan, with 56 percent of the total. North America is second with 35 percent, and Europe is far behind with only 4 percent. The Japanese–Latin Americans are not temporary residents but permanent residents in their respective countries; some have lived there for over half a century, thus establishing a large group of second and third generations. While Latin America was an important recipient area for Japanese migrants

Table 4.1 Number of Japanese emigrants residing abroad by region, 1988

Region	No. of emigrants	% of total
Latin America	137,117	55.8
North America	86,007	35.0
Europe	10,391	4.2
Asia	7,412	3.0
Other	4,967	2.0
Total	245,894	100.0

Source: Kokusai Kyōryoku Jigyōdan, *Kaigai ijū tōkei: Shōwa 27 nendo-Shōwa 63 nendo* (Statistics on Overseas Emigration, 1952–88) (Tokyo: Kokusai Kyōryoku Jigyōdan, 1989) pp. 108–9.

before World War II, it was even more dominant in the postwar years. According to Table 4.2, over 90 percent of postwar emigrants who received government assistance went to Latin America. Table 4.2 also highlights the sharp decline in emigration as affluence replaced poverty in postwar Japan. This affluence, in turn, especially in contrast to the crisis that gripped Latin America in the 1980s, was responsible for the reverse migration flows.

JAPANESE MIGRATION TO LATIN AMERICA BEFORE WORLD WAR II

Japanese migration in the modern period of the country's history began with groups of Japanese leaving for Hawaii and Guam. From the beginning of the Meiji Era (1868–1914), there was a strong demand in other countries for Japanese laborers. The Japanese government first opposed migration because of the generally harsh conditions the earliest migrants had encountered abroad. It was not until 1885 that the government permitted 36 Japanese to migrate to Australia. The government also agreed to send over 900 laborers to the sugarcane plantations of Hawaii. A number of migration companies were organized under official supervision, and migration policy was carried out by the Ministry of Foreign Affairs. In encouraging migration, the Japanese government was increasingly focusing its attention on

Table 4.2   Japanese emigrants receiving subsidies, 1952–88

Year	Total no. of emigrants	Emigrants to Latin America
1952	54	54
1953	1,489	1,489
1954	3,741	3,741
1955	3,512	3,512
1956	6,168	6,050
1957	7,439	7,439
1958	7,606	7,594
1959	7,610	7,433
1960	8,386	8,316
1961	6,263	6,261
1962	2,201	2,193
1963	1,526	1,526
1964	1,105	1,104
1965	818	818
1966	1,531	1,059
1967	1,543	884
1968	1,129	645
1969	1,146	656
1970	1,236	632
1971	1,098	674
1972	1,012	763
1973	631	425
1974	534	389
1975	506	424
1976	502	474
1977	467	417
1978	483	428
1979	549	331
1980	597	246
1981	600	203
1982	357	123
1983	217	142
1984	137	98
1985	109	84
1986	146	91
1987	171	78
1988	157	55
Total	72,785	66,860

Source: Kokusai Kyōryoku Jigyōdan, *Kaigai ijū tōkei: Shōwa 27 nendo-Shōwa 63 nendo* (Statistics on Overseas Emigration, 1952–88) (Tokyo: Kokusai Kyōryoku Jigyōdan, 1989) p. 17.

alleviating domestic social problems such as poverty, overpopulation, and unemployment.[2]

Japanese migration to Latin America began in the last quarter of the nineteenth century. The first Japanese went to Argentina in 1886, and in 1893 another 132 Japanese workers moved from Hawaii to Guatemala. The following year a group of 499 Japanese migrated to Guadalupe in the Caribbean, as laborers on sugarcane plantations. In 1897, in what constituted the first Japanese attempt to establish a coffee plantation following the acquisition of about 65,000 hectares from the Mexican government, a group of 34 Japanese was sent to Chiapas in southern Mexico as *colonos*, or permanent settlers. These attempts, however, were individual or sporadic experiments. It was not until 1899 that Japanese laborers began to migrate in groups under contract labor arrangements with Latin American countries.[3]

According to the number of passports issued between 1899 and 1941, 244,536 Japanese officially migrated to Latin America (see Table 4.3). Brazil received the largest number of migrants, followed by Peru and Mexico. Almost 97 percent of Japanese migrants to Latin America

Table 4.3   Japanese emigration to Latin America by country, 1899–1941

Country	1899–1900	1901–10	1911–20	1921–30	1931–40	1941	Total
Brazil	0	1,714	26,947	70,914	88,134	1,277	188,986
Peru	790	7,146	12,232	9,172	3,606	24	33,070
Mexico	2	10,963	465	2,131	887	28	14,476
Argentina	0	4	807	2,100	2,363	124	5,398
Cuba	0	4	104	463	114	1	686
Paraguay	0	0	0	1	437	83	521
Chile	0	126	143	169	78	3	519
Panama	0	0	59	211	145	0	415
Colombia	0	0	0	106	121	2	229
Bolivia	0	0	17	64	112	9	202
Uruguay	0	0	0	2	16	0	18
Venezuela	0	0	0	0	12	0	12
Others	0	0	0	0	4	0	4
Total	792	19957	40,774	85,333	96,029	1,551	244,536

Source: Japanese Ministry of Foreign Affairs, *Waga kokumin no kaigai hatten: ijū hyakunen no ayumi* (The Overseas Development of the Japanese People: One Hundred Years of Japanese Emigration) (Tokyo: Gaimushō, 1975) vol. 2, pp. 140–41.

before World War II went to these three countries, but Argentina also received a substantial number. The significant flow of Japanese laborers to Brazil, Peru, and Mexico can be attributed mainly to the demand for labor as these countries pursued economic development. From the time of their independence, Latin American countries had always encouraged immigration from Europe, but in most countries, with the exception of Argentina and Uruguay, the result had proven disappointing.

As economic development accelerated, the demand for labor became very intense, leading to special efforts to attract Asian workers. First, Chinese "coolies" were brought to Peru, Cuba, and Mexico between 1850 and 1874, but this process ended because of international disputes surrounding their slave-like treatment. Some Latin American governments began to seek contact with Japanese agents in order to import a Japanese labor force. Peru was the first to succeed in bringing in a group of Japanese contract laborers. Mexico and Brazil soon followed.

Peru, which established diplomatic relations with Japan in 1873, attracted a significant flow of immigrants beginning in 1899. Approximately 800 Japanese migrated to Peru as contract laborers under an arrangement with a migration company and with the full support of the Peruvian government. But because of problems encountered by both the Japanese laborers and the Peruvian plantation owners, it took several more years for Peru to begin to receive a steady flow of Japanese laborers (Table 4.3). The need for labor was particularly high in the coastal area due to the rapid growth of sugarcane and cotton plantations, although some groups were sent to the rubber zone in the Amazonian region of eastern Peru.

In general, the Japanese laborers encountered harsh conditions and an unfriendly environment in both the coastal area and the eastern tropics. Their dreams of saving money and returning to Japan proved, in most cases, to be unrealistic. According to the earliest group's contract, prospective immigrants had to be between 20 and 45 years of age and willing to work 10 hours daily in the field or 12 hours in the mills or workshops on the sugarcane plantations. The landowners were to pay them 10 pounds for travel expenses and 2 pounds 10 shillings salary per month, in addition to providing lodging and medical care. The migration company was to retain 8 shillings every month for the return journey and was to provide an interpreter for every 50 Japanese laborers as well as a representative stationed in Peru to serve as intermediary between the landowners and the Japanese laborers.[4]

The contract, which had a 4-year term, stipulated that the Japanese were temporary workers who would eventually return to Japan. Other contracts following this first experiment were much the same. In reality, many Japanese laborers deserted their assigned plantations before they completed the term of their contract. Some of them even left Peru for neighboring countries, especially to participate in the rubber boom in Bolivia's northwestern territory. Many contract deserters – as well as many who fulfilled their contracts – came to settle in the metropolitan area of Lima–Callao. In addition, many remained in Peru against their will, although some succeeded in saving some money to bring back to Japan with them in addition to paying the cost of their return tickets.

In 1923, the Japanese and Peruvian governments agreed to abolish Japanese contract labor. Japan was concerned with the low wages being paid to its citizens, whereas Peru was concerned about the social problems caused by Japanese immigrants. Many Peruvians viewed the Japanese as troublesome because they concentrated in the metropolitan area without assimilating into Peruvian society and because they aggressively took over small businesses, damaging the economic situation of the Peruvian lower classes. Despite the end of contract immigration, Japanese nationals continued to migrate to Peru in ever-increasing numbers from the mid-1920s through 1930. These people were not agricultural laborers but small traders, artisans, cultivators, or skilled laborers such as plumbers, watchmakers, or opticians. For the most part, they were relatives or friends of established Japanese residents in Peru.

With the world depression, there was a rise in the anti-Japanese sentiment that had begun in the 1920s. In August 1930 Japanese shops in the Lima–Callao area were vandalized; the environment deteriorated further as time went by. A new immigration law promulgated on June 26, 1936, restricted the number of foreign residents to 16,000 persons of any one nationality and instituted a 20 percent limit on the employment of foreigners in any business. Although the new law did not specifically mention Japanese (or even Asians), these regulations were obviously aimed at the Japanese because only the latter exceeded the 16,000 limit among the foreign residents in Peru at that time. The 20 percent limit on the employment of foreign nationals had severe repercussions on Japanese economic activities because many Japanese enterprises were run on a very small scale, often by only husband and wife. In 1937 another legal measure was instituted that precluded dual nationality. In 1940, this measure developed into a law stipulating that the sons of foreigners, even if born in Peru, were considered to be of the same nationality as their fathers until they reached adulthood.

The last outburst of anti-Japanese feeling occurred on May 13, 1940. During anti-Japanese demonstrations by students in Lima, Peruvian mobs attacked and sacked a number of Japanese shops and bazaars in the metropolitan area and other urban centers. As a result of the rioting, over 600 claims of damage were registered in the Japanese consulate. It was reported that over 50 houses were sacked totally and over 50 families (315 Japanese people) lost all their property. As a result, many abandoned Peru for Japan in July. Total damages were estimated at 6 million soles. The Peruvian government indemnified them in the amount of 350,000 soles paid in cash and a reimbursement of 1,050,000 soles made in wool, salt, and sugar.[5]

Mexico, in contrast to Peru, received large groups of Japanese immigrants during only a very brief period. Japanese group migration to Mexico occurred during a few years at the beginning of the twentieth century. As early as 1874, the Mexican scientist Francisco Díaz Covarrubias had advocated bringing Japanese workers to Mexico, emphasizing their desirability.[6] The Compañía Japonesa–Mexicana de Comercio y Colonización, formed in 1903, filled orders for labor for Mexican mine and plantation owners. Its Japanese partner, the Tōyō Imin Kaisha (Oriental Emigration Company), recruited and transported Japanese laborers from Japan. From 1901 to 1907, groups of Japanese workers were sent to mines in the northern states, to railway construction sites in Durango and Colima, and to sugarcane plantations in the south. The sudden rise of Japanese immigration after 1901 virtually ceased in 1908 because of a political arrangement between Japan and the United States. It appears that this arrangement became the primary factor accounting for the rather low-key relationship between Japan and Mexico in the following years.

The flow of Asian immigrants had been of great concern to the United States since the late nineteenth century. Chinese entry into the United States was banned as early as 1882, and Japanese entry was being restricted with increasing frequency up until 1924, when the US Congress passed a decisive immigration law. The increasing flow of Japanese to the west coast of the United States in the early part of the twentieth century played a vital role in the US response to Japanese immigration. In 1903 anti-Japanese and anti-Korean leagues were organized in California. In December of the same year, the California state legislature approved the McKinley proposal by which the Chinese

Expulsion Law of 1882 was to be applied to the Japanese. In 1906 school segregation problems occurred in San Francisco.

The Japanese controversy became more serious and more tense every year, not only on the west coast but also in many other states. In 1907 the US Congress passed a new immigration law, under which Japanese immigrants in Hawaii were barred from moving to the mainland. In the same year, after careful consideration, Japan and the United States negotiated an agreement aimed at controlling Japanese immigration to the United States. The resulting Gentlemen's Agreement of 1907 included a clause that declared the Japanese government responsible for taking measures to stop the migration of Japanese laborers to foreign territories adjacent to the United States. Lawmakers in the United States hoped that this would effectively remove all causes of complaints over the illegal entrance of Japanese via Mexico and Canada. Japanese–US conflicts regarding migration to the United States thus led to the termination of Japanese migration to Mexico.[7] By 1908 Japanese immigration had been either prohibited or restricted in most Anglo–Saxon countries, stimulating Japanese migration to Brazil and Peru instead.

Brazil lagged behind Peru and Mexico in introducing Japanese labor, although it eventually became the country receiving the largest number of Japanese immigrants during the prewar period. Like many other Latin American countries, Brazil made efforts to attract Europeans by offering full-fare subsidies for prospective immigrants in the early 1850s. Thus, the number of foreign immigrants increased considerably in the second half of the nineteenth century. Many of those early immigrants, particularly the Germans, became independent farmers in Rio Grande do Sul and Santa Catarina, instead of working on coffee plantations. In the late nineteenth century, however, the nature of European migration changed from colonization to the importation of agricultural laborers. Faced with a serious scarcity of plantation workers, Brazil brought in over 1 million Italian immigrants during the last quarter of the century. The rapid expansion of the coffee industry in São Paulo generated a great demand for laborers, while the emancipation of black slaves in 1888 created a shortage in the labor market. Italy became the sole supplier of coffee plantation labor because most European nations did not allow their citizens to migrate to Portuguese America, given the exploitative nature of the mono-cultural economy.

With frequent coffee crises beginning in the early 1890s, Italian *colonos* were subjected to such severe hardships that in 1902 the Italian government joined other European countries in prohibiting subsidized emigration to Brazil. This resulted in an alarming scarcity of laborers, forcing the Paulista plantation owners to consider the possibility of introducing Asian labor. Before that time Brazil was not interested in bringing in Asians, who were stereotyped as semi-servile coolies because of Brazil's experience with Chinese labor. The anti-Chinese movement in the United States also discouraged the coffee planters from making serious efforts to acquire contract immigrants of Asian origin.

The earliest contacts and negotiations concerning Japanese migration to Brazil were made in the 1890s. The coffee plantations in the state of São Paulo needed labor so desperately that the coffee barons arranged the importation of Japanese contract laborers. Nevertheless, it was not until 1908 that large-scale contract labor migration started from Japan to Brazil. An agreement was signed by the state government of São Paulo and the Kōkoku Shokumin Kaisha (Kokoku Colonization Company); several other emigration companies followed their lead.

Migration from 1908–14 consisted of the experimental, and rather disappointing, introduction of Japanese labor force into Brazil. In 1915, after having received about 15,000 Japanese, the state government of São Paulo cut the subsidies for transportation of the laborers. In 1915 and 1916, only 74 Japanese laborers arrived in Brazil. Because World War I kept European immigrants from coming to Brazil, plantation owners encountered further labor shortages. As a consequence, the transportation subsidy was reinstated and continued until 1922, when the state government of São Paulo again abolished it. Meanwhile the Japanese government started subsidizing migration to Brazil in 1924.

In that year the US Congress passed the Exclusion Act, by which Japanese migrants were excluded from the United States. Analogous policies had been introduced by various other countries. Brazil remained the sole country to accept the Japanese in groups. Recognizing these conditions, the Japanese government reconsidered its migration policy and directed its attention to Brazil. The Japanese Diet passed legislation to continue subsidizing the cost of passage for migrants in September 1924. The subsidies were expanded to include transportation cost from home to the port of departure, meals and accommodation, clothing allowance, and other expenses. These subsidies were extended not only to contract laborers but also to independent farmers.

The full support of the Japanese government was characteristic of he period from 1924 to 1941, during which time 157,572 Japanese nigrated to Brazil. This migration was handled by the Kaigai Kōgyō Kabushiki Kaisha (Overseas Development Company), which was stablished in 1917 under the direction of the Japanese government. Absorbing all independent migration companies, the Kaigai Kōgyō ecame the sole business to handle these operations and was given overnmental financial assistance to promote migration.

Another characteristic of this period was the Japanese acquisition of oncessions in the unexplored Amazonian region. The Amazon Kōgyō Kabushiki Kaisha (Amazonian Development Company) and the Nambei Takushoku Kaisha (South American Colonization Comany) were formed in 1928, and the Amazonia Sangyō Kenkyūjo Institute for Amazonian Industries) was established in 1930. They btained large-scale concessions for land and began to develop them vith the Japanese immigrants.

A third characteristic was the systematization of the process of ecruiting migrants for Brazil. Stimulated by the Overseas Emigration Act of 1927, the Kaigai Ijū Kumiai (Overseas Emigration Cooperative ociety) and the Kaigai Ijū Kumiai Rengō (Federation of Overseas migration Cooperative Societies) were organized. The latter estabshed the Burajiru Takushoku Kumiai (Brazilian Colonization Cooperative Society), which acquired lands in Brazil for Japanese olonists. In addition, cooperative societies were organized in various refectures of Japan and functioned as the basic recruiting organizaons.

Candidates for migration were selected from society at large. After n applicant was selected and received authorization, he had to ndergo a medical examination and receive training in a special uigrant school, where Portuguese, tropical hygiene, tropical agricul-ure, civic behavior, and Brazilian geography, history, and economy ere taught. After this preliminary training, applicants were trans-erred to Kobe or Yokohama, where they waited for the steamer in pecially-established migrant shelters; similar homes were set up in the razilian ports of Santos and Belém. Supervision and protection were ontinually provided for immigrants in Brazil. Prospective migrants gned a contract for 4 years and were assigned to a plantation. After ey had accumulated some savings, the Cooperative bought land for em and they became independent farmers. The colonist immigrants, y contrast, went directly to a settlement already acquired by the ooperative.

Although anti-Japanese agitation had existed in Brazil since the early 1920s, Brazil did not adopt immigration policies that formally discriminated against the Japanese until 1934. This legislation, in particular Article 121 of the Constitution, restricted the annual entry of immigrants to 2 percent of the total number of entries of any one nationality for the preceding 50 years. Article 121 affected Japan more than any other country, as it limited Japanese entry to 2,849 persons for 1935. While the number of Japanese immigrants to Brazil for the 50 years from 1884 to 1933 was smaller than that of Italian, Portuguese, Spanish, or German origin, it rose sharply from 1924 to 1934. The number of European immigrants had already decreased by the early 1930s, suggesting that the newly-introduced measure mostly affected Japanese nationals. The measure was very effective. The number of Japanese immigrants dropped from 22,960 in 1934 to 5,754 in 1935, but Japanese entries for the next 3 years surpassed the allocated numbers. Instead of applying the law strictly, the Brazilian government admitted larger numbers of Japanese immigrants and exempted them from the newly-introduced restrictions.

Under the nationalist policies of the Estado Novo period, objections to the Japanese immigrants and outbursts of anti-Japanese sentiment began to appear in political debates and the media. In spite of the fact that the Brazilians and their government largely acknowledged the positive contributions of Japanese immigrants, there was resentment resulting from the Japanese attitude of non-assimilation and their insistence on retaining their own language and customs. In 1938 and 1939 several anti-foreigner laws were promulgated, in particular a new immigration law (1939) that prohibited education in a foreign language for children below the age of 14. This law virtually eliminated Japanese-language schools, which existed in almost all Japanese colonies and settlements. Another law restricted the publication of printed materials in any language other than Portuguese. Both measures had a strong psychological impact on the Japanese, who had worked hard to keep to their language, customs, and culture intact.

When the war broke out between Japan and the United States in 1941, there were about 202,000 Japanese in Brazil. Various measures restricted their activities, but in general, Brazilian attitudes toward them were relatively moderate compared with Peru, where they were seen as enemy aliens. In the immediate postwar period, the nationalistic Japanese struggled with the question of whether or not they should accept the defeat of Japan. Bloody confrontations occurred among the Japanese people in various places, and several thousand were arrested ind imprisoned by the Brazilian authorities. Although they started the postwar period with bloody incidents, the Japanese in Brazil managed to enter a new era in which they came better to integrate themselves nto Brazilian society.[8]

While Japanese migration to Latin America was a response to the urgent need for an expanded labor force, many Latin American countries banned the entry of the Japanese on racial grounds from he very beginning. Uruguay introduced restrictions as early as 1890, and Costa Rica did so in 1896. In the twentieth century, more countries followed this tendency: Cuba in 1902, Paraguay in 1903, Guatemala in 1909, and Venezuela in 1912.[9] The Japanese laborers in Brazil, Peru, and Mexico were often accused of disorderly and disruptive conduct, non-assimilation, and introducing and spreading new diseases. With he number of Japanese migrants growing and with their success in economic endeavors in the recipient countries expanding, they came to be considered by some resentful groups as detrimental to society. The Chinese had encountered the same treatment in the nineteenth century. Welcomed originally as a much needed labor supply for the large-scale production of commercial crops, the Japanese devoted themselves to hard work and often faced harsh treatment in unfamiliar countries.

After war broke out between Japan and the United States in December 1941, many Latin American countries immediately declared war against Japan. First were the Caribbean and Central American nations; then Mexico and Colombia severed diplomatic relations with Japan. Following a meeting of the foreign ministers of the American States in Rio de Janeiro in January 1942 – where the United States hoped to win unanimous support for a binding resolution calling for all Latin American governments to sever relations with the Axis – most did so, but many did not declare war against Japan right away. Indeed, many waited until as late as 1945.[10]

Wartime measures against the Japanese who resided in Latin America varied from country to country. Most common were the suspension of constitutional guarantees, freezing of funds, and black-listing; 12 countries – Bolivia, Colombia, Costa Rica, the Dominican Republic, Ecuador, El Salvador, Guatemala, Haiti, Honduras, Nicaragua, Panama, and Peru – cooperated with the US policy of deporting and interning the Japanese within the United States. About 2,200 Japanese were deported and interned in several US concentration camps. Peru's policy toward the Japanese was the harshest. It sent some 1,800 Japanese and Japanese–Peruvians to the United States, accounting for about 80 percent of all the Japanese–Latin Americans interned in the United States. Mexico and Cuba, instead of deporting the Japanese to the United States, established their own concentration camps. Other countries, such as Brazil, interned the leaders of the Japanese communities, who were considered undesirable enemy aliens, but their general treatment of and attitude toward the Japanese was relatively mild and generous.[11]

Throughout the turbulent war period and its immediate aftermath, the Japanese in Latin America faced their most difficult times economically and psychologically. Many of them lost all they had worked to build up: their property, positions, and social linkages. After the war they had to start over completely. Most decided to settle permanently where they were residing, abandoning their long-cherished desire to return to Japan with their accumulated capital. Soon they were joined by a new wave of migrants.

POSTWAR MIGRATION AND THE JAPANESE COMMUNITIES IN LATIN AMERICA

Individual migration resumed immediately after the end of World War II, but it was only in 1953 that large groups of migrants began to go to Latin America again. Migration was one of the most urgent tasks for the Japanese government to deal with in the immediate postwar period, because in a few years Japan's population had increased from 72 million to 82 million as the country absorbed the returnees from former overseas territories. Unemployment was high and poverty was severe throughout the 1950s, particularly in the rural areas.

As early as the second half of the 1940s, possible destinations for Japanese migrants were studied, and in October 1947 the Kaigai Ijū Kyōkai (Overseas Emigration Society) was established with the objective of seeking and promoting migration. When the peace treaty was signed in September 1951, Japan again became a sovereign state, in April 1952. Under a 5-year plan to promote migration (1953) and a 10-year plan of overseas migration (1954), the number of migrants, modes of transportation, costs, funds, and so on were studied in detail. Migration was considered vital if the poverty-stricken and over-populated country was to survive.

There were, however, difficulties in finding destinations. A handful of Latin American countries – Brazil, Bolivia, Paraguay, the Dominican Republic, and Argentina – were the only countries that responded to Japan's desperate pleas. Peru has not permitted Japanese immigrants in the postwar period, although it received the second largest number of Japanese before the war. About 92 percent of all Japanese migrants who received transportation subsidies or loans from the government from 1952 to 1988 went to Latin America (Table 4.2), and 80 percent of those went to Brazil. Paraguay, Bolivia, and the Dominican Republic, which had received very few Japanese immigrants during the prewar period, became important recipient countries (Table 4.4).

Brazil was the first country to which groups of Japanese began to move. In 1953 Shōtarō Tsuji, former director of the Institute for Amazonian Industries, and Yasutarō Matsubara, a successful Japanese immigrant who had close relations with Getúlio Vargas, arranged the migration of 1,498 Japanese to Brazil. They received concessions to introduce 5,000 Japanese families into the Amazonian area and 4,000 families into Matto Grosso. The Tsuji concession sent 1,036 families and 315 unmarried males between 1953 and 1963, when the concessions terminated. The Matsubara concession handled 1,279 families and 883 unmarried males during the same period.[12]

Table 4.4   Japanese emigration to Latin America by country, 1952–88

Country	Total	No. of families	Singles
Brazil	53,562	8,273	11,759
Paraguay	7,136	1,195	302
Argentina	2,735	395	1,191
Bolivia	1,905	341	110
Dominican Rep.	1,330	252	7
Colombia	55	3	46
Venezuela	49	6	21
Uruguay	46	4	31
Mexico	20	3	11
Chile	13	1	9
Peru	5	1	2
Costa Rica	2	0	2
Honduras	2	1	0
Total	66,860	10,475	13,491

Source: Kokusai Kyōryoku Jigyōdan, *Kaigai ijū tōkei: Shōwa 27 nendo–Shōwa 63 nendo* (Statistics on Overseas Emigration, 1952–88) (Tokyo: Kokusai Kyōryoku Jigyōdan, 1989) p. 23.

In 1986–88, the Japanese communities in Brazil carried out a census of Japanese descendants as a project to commemorate the eightieth anniversary of Japanese immigration to Brazil. According to this most recent census, the population of Brazilians of Japanese origin had reached 1,228,000. About 72 percent (828,000) live in the state of São Paulo and 12 percent live in the south, mostly in the state of Paraná.[13] It is known that these Japanese–Brazilians have been well integrated into the socio-economic mainstream of Brazilian society, distinguishing themselves economically, educationally, and professionally. On a nation-wide basis, Japanese farmers produced 9 percent of coffee, 14 percent of cotton, 44 percent of eggs, 50 percent of vegetables, 66 percent of soybeans, 71 percent of potatoes, 80 percent of silkworms 82 percent of peppers, 90 percent of strawberries, and 94 percent of tea in 1970.[14] Since the Japanese immigrants valued education highly many of their descendants became medical doctors, dentists, lawyers engineers, bureaucrats, and university professors.

Paraguay, which has received the second largest number of postwar Japanese immigrants, had also accepted some immigrants earlier Japanese migration to that country started in 1936 when the La Colmena colony, about 132 kilometers from Asunción, was established with 81 Japanese (11 families). This arrangement was made to accommodate those Japanese migrants who were headed for Brazi when the restrictive immigration law of 1934 was put into effect. In 1952, Paraguay permitted Japan to send 120 families to La Colmena and throughout the 1950s Ijū Shinkō Kaisha (Migration Promotion Company), a semi-official organization, purchased about 187,000 hectares of land in Paraguay, to establish agricultural colonies for the Japanese. In 1959, an agreement of immigration and colonization was exchanged between the two countries, and Japan received a concession to send 85,000 families during the next 30 years. As of 1988, however, only 1,195 families had migrated to Paraguay.

At present there are 9 centers of Japanese communities in Paraguay 6 of which are agricultural colonies. In these colonies, Japanese customs and traditions, as well as the Japanese language, are wel preserved, even among second-generation descendants. In urban centers such as Asunción, Encarnación, and the Ciudad del Este (where the Japanese came to settle after having deserted the agricultural colonies), the immigrants have mainly gone into commerce. About 80 percent of the Japanese and their descendants who reside in Paraguay at present are found in agricultural colonies, and their contributions to Paraguayan agricultural production are well known and acknowledged by the local population.[15]

Bolivia was another destination for Japanese immigrants in the postwar period. Unlike Paraguay, Japanese immigrants had moved to Bolivia in substantial numbers in the prewar period, although they did not appear in official statistics. The first group consisted of 79 Japanese, who in 1899 went to the rubber region of the upper Amazonian valley of northwestern Bolivia. By 1920, approximately 2,000 Japanese had migrated there via Peru. Most of them were single males and many of them married local women, thus establishing Japanese communities in local centers such as Riberalta, Cobija, and Trinidad. Their descendants have been so well integrated into the local society that it is difficult to find anything Japanese about them except their surnames.

In the postwar period, responding to the serious Japanese search for a destination for its surplus population, Bolivia signed an immigration agreement with Japan in 1956. It gave Japanese agricultural colonists free land concessions as a part of its colonization and development policies for the eastern tropical lowlands. Two Japanese agricultural colonies, Colonia San Juan de Yapacaní and Colonia Okinawa, were established there in the 1950s and almost all of the postwar immigrants went to these two settlements. As in the case of Paraguay, these agricultural colonies have preserved Japanese customs, traditions, and language so that the two colonies exist and function much like Japanese villages. Their achievements and contributions to Bolivian agriculture are well known.[16]

The Dominican Republic, which had virtually no Japanese in the prewar years, also became a recipient of Japanese immigrants in the postwar period. According to the agreement on Japanese immigration signed by the two countries in 1954, the Dominican Republic was to receive about 20,000 Japanese families in the Haitian border area as part of agricultural development policies. In reality, only 249 families (consisting of 1,219 people) settled in this Caribbean nation between 1956 and 1959. Immigration to this country was a failure; about 70 percent of the Japanese immigrants returned home within 4 years. At present a small number of Japanese are still found in the rural areas. Those who have deserted the agricultural colonies have remained in the urban centers and are mainly in small businesses.[17]

Argentina is one of a few Latin American countries that succeeded in introducing European immigrants on a large scale, but it imposed a restrictive immigration policy for non-Europeans. Although the policy did not specifically discriminate against the Japanese, Argentina was one of those countries that closed the door to Japanese group immigration. There was individual Japanese migration throughout the prewar period, however, and thus the bases of Japanese communities had been founded. Most of those individual immigrants settled in urban centers and engaged in small businesses. The Japanese were known as launderers and floriculturists in Argentina. The postwar period saw the entrance of Japanese immigrants attracted to Argentina by relatives or friends who had settled there earlier. The number of new Japanese immigrants gradually increased and, in 1957, Argentina admitted for the first time a Japanese colonization project of 400 families and gave them land in several frontier states. Argentina and Japan signed a migration agreement in 1961, and since then agricultural colonies have been established in the frontier states as well as on the outskirts of Buenos Aires, although the scale of each colony is very limited. Most of the Japanese in these colonies are dedicated to cultivating flowers that are marketed mainly in Buenos Aires.[18]

Japanese migration to Latin America basically ended in the 1960s, when the number of migrants fell sharply. With the explosive growth of the Japanese economy through the 1960s, the incentives for migration diminished greatly. Nevertheless, some Japanese migration to Latin America has continued with the full support of the Japanese government; the Japan International Cooperation Agency (JICA) has a monopoly on recruitment, training, and subsidies for passages and loans for the migrants.

Since the 1970s, migrants have tended to be young, single professionals who are mainly interested in the United States, Canada, and Australia. Migration to Latin America, namely to Brazil, Paraguay, Bolivia, and Argentina, is still closely monitored by Japanese authorities. Because the Japanese communities found in those countries are considered important resources for Japan, the government and its affiliate organizations extend many kinds of programs that aim to strengthen the ties between Japan and the Latin American-based communities.

THE LATEST CHAPTER: RETURN MIGRATION

In the 1980s a new phenomenon occurred in which former emigrants, or *nisei* (second generation) and *sansei* (third generation), returned to

Japan in groups looking for jobs. These so-called *dekasegi* were driven back to the land of their ancestors due to the economic difficulties that Latin American countries encountered in the 1980s. Japan's booming economy offered them jobs in which they could earn almost ten times as much as they could in their respective countries. The number of these returnees from Latin American countries reached some 150,000 as of July 1991 according to the statistics compiled by the Japanese Ministry of Foreign Affairs: 118,015 from Brazil, 18,000 from Peru, 8,500 from Argentina, 1,584 from Bolivia, and 719 from Paraguay.[19] Although not included in the figures above, there are several hundred more returnees of Japanese origin in Japan from Mexico, the Dominican Republic, and other countries.

Until around 1990, these returnees were mostly single men and women. Their sole purpose was to save up as much money as possible to repatriate to their home countries by working long hours in those jobs ordinary Japanese did not want. These were the type of jobs popularly called "the three Ks" in Japanese: *k*itsui = hard, *k*itanai = dirty, *k*iken = dangerous. Accordingly, the problems encountered by the return migrants were low wages and poor living and working conditions, partly due to exploitation by intermediaries. The situation, however, changed in 1991. The revision of the Emigration and Immigration Law in June 1990 made it possible for the second and third generations of the descendants of Japanese emigrants to stay and work in Japan. As a consequence, not only did the number of returnees increase rapidly, but their families joined them, including husbands and wives of non-Japanese origin.

Those who are returning to Japan are motivated mainly by the money they can earn, despite the fact that most were not poverty-stricken at home. In fact, many of them belong to the middle class, and their motivations vary from purchasing a better house to accumulating capital to start a new business. One Brazilian observer suggested that migrants went back to Japan because the amount of money they could earn was attractive and it was a good chance for the young to see the land of their ancestors.[20] The outflow of young people has been so phenomenal that only old people and children remain in many Japanese communities. In the case of the Bolivian Colonia San Juan de Yapacaní, a postwar agricultural establishment, around 100 Japanese immigrants and their children were working in Japan in early 1990 out of a total population of 898.[21]

In 1991, the Kaigai Nikkeijin Kyōkai (The Overseas Japanese Association) conducted a nation-wide survey with a sample of more than 3,000; its final report was published in March 1992.[22] The survey deals with characteristics and opinions of returnees from Brazil, Peru, Argentina, Bolivia, and Paraguay. Between 81 and 83 percent of returnees from Brazil, Peru, and Argentina came to Japan because of the severe economic problems in their home countries, and they plan to go back home with earnings obtained in Japan. In the case of Bolivian and Paraguayan Japanese, this type of returnee made up 52 percent and 49 percent of the migrants, respectively. The rest came to Japan with different motives: 20 percent initially came as foreign students on scholarship and another 20 percent to learn the Japanese language and culture. Only 2–5 percent of the returnees from Brazil, Peru, and Argentina came to Japan to stay permanently, while 18 percent of Bolivians and Paraguayans came to Japan with such an intention.

The level of their education is fairly high with 41 percent having at least some university training. The most highly educated group were the Peruvians, with 53 percent reporting some university education; they were followed by the Brazilians with 41 percent, the Argentines 35 percent, the Bolivians 17 percent, and the Paraguayans 18 percent. It must be added, however, that there are some doubts about whether the level of education of the returnees as a whole is as high as is indicated in the above research because of the sampling method and procedures.

This research indicates that the overall level of satisfaction of the returnees working in Japan is high, with 70 percent of both male and female respondents expressing satisfaction. Given the information available, the main problems on the receiving side involve exploitation by intermediaries and misunderstanding of Latin customs and way of thinking. On the whole, however, adequate measures are being taken by the Japanese side, aided by the acute labor shortage in Japan and the pressures on Japan to internationalize. Japanese government organizations and local municipalities are now taking active measures, and the attitude of the Japanese people towards the returnees is generally favorable. At the same time, since the returnees have some knowledge of Japanese and hold identity as Japanese–Latin Americans, however remote it may be, they are not totally isolated from the Japanese society. In many places, the workers of Japanese origin and their families are forming organizations with the help of voluntary societies among the Japanese people.

Nonetheless, it is difficult to imagine that these returnees of Japanese origin, or the former Japanese emigrants themselves, will remain permanently in Japan. Certainly the young people of the second and third generations will not stay on. They identify with their native Latin

American countries and find it uncomfortable to live in Japan, mainly because of the differences in social environment and cultural values. This observation is endorsed by the survey mentioned above. Moreover, the Japanese government believes the returnees should go back home after earning economic resources and obtaining some knowledge of Japan and some technical skills. Although the often menial character of their jobs casts doubt on the learning of technical skills by the returnees,[23] their experiences in general may help make the two areas closer, even though they have traditionally been seen as distant neighbors.

Notes

1. In ch. 3, in this volume, for example, Hiroshi Matsushita suggests that one of the reasons for Japan's pro-Argentine stance during the Malvinas/ Falklands War was worry about the Japanese population living in Argentina. The strong inclination on the part of both the Japanese government and population to help the Fujimori government in Peru is another example of the lasting impact of Japanese emigration to Latin America.
2. Japan's modern migration policy is detailed in Yasuo Wakatsuki and Jōji Suzuki, *Kaigai ijū seisaku shiron* (Historical Survey of Emigration Policies) (Tokyo: Fukumura Shuppan, 1975).
3. The history of early migration is best documented in Toraji Irie, *Hōjin kaigai hatten shi* (History of Japanese Migration Abroad), 2 vols., 1938 (Reprint, Tokyo: Hara Shobō, 1981).
4. Ibid., vol. 1, pp. 346–9.
5. Prewar Japanese experiences in Peru are well documented not only in many Japanese works, but also in these English and Spanish publications: J. F. Normano and A. Gerbi, *The Japanese in South America: An Introductory Survey with Special Reference to Peru* (New York: Institute of Pacific Relations, 1943); Toraji Irie, "History of the Japanese Migration to Peru," *Hispanic American Historical Review* 31, 3 and 4 (1951) and 32, 1 (1952); C. Harvey Gardiner, *The Japanese and Peru, 1873–1973* (Albuquerque: University of New Mexico Press, 1975); and Amelia Morimoto, *Los inmigrantes japoneses en el Perú* (Lima: Universidad Nacional Agraria, 1979).
6. Francisco Díaz Covarrubias, *Viaje de la comisión astronómica mexicana al Japón para observar el tránsito del planeta Venus por el disco del sol el 8 de diciembre de 1874* (Mexico City: Imprenta de C. Ramino y Ponce de León, 1876).
7. These works cover most of the important aspects of Japanese migration to Mexico: Nihonjin Mekishiko Ijūshi Hensan Iinkai, (ed.), *Nihonjin*

120   *Japanese Migration to Latin America*

Mekishiko ijūshi (History of Japanese Migration to Mexico) (Tokyo: Raten Amerika Kyōkai, 1971); María Elena Ota Mishima, *Siete migraciones japoneses en México, 1890–1978* (Mexico City: El Colegio de México, 1982); Nichiboku Kōryūshi Hensan Iinkai, (ed.), *Nichiboku kōryūshi* (History of Japanese-Mexican Relations) (Tokyo: P.C. Shuppan, 1990).

8. For the best accounts of Japanese migration to Brazil, see Hiroshi Saitō, *Burajiru no Nihonjin* (The Japanese in Brazil) (Tokyo: Maruzen, 1960); Tomoo Handa, *Imin no seikatsu to rekishi* (History of Japanese Immigrants' Life in Brazil) (São Paulo: Centro de Estudos Nipo-Brasileiros, 1970); Tomoo Handa, (ed.), *Burajiru Nihon imin shi nempyō* (A Chronological Table of the History of Japanese Migration to Brazil) (São Paulo: Centro de Estudos Nipo-Brasileiros, 1976); and Burajiru Nihonimin Nanajūnenshi Hensan Iinkai, (ed.), *Burajiru nihonimin nanajūnenshi* (A History of Seventy Years of Japanese Migration to Brazil) (São Paulo: Brajiru Nihon Bunka Kyōkai, 1980).

9. Japanese Ministry of Foreign Affairs, *Chūnambei shokoku ishokumin hōki* (Immigration and Colonization Laws of Latin American Countries) (Tokyo: Gaimushō, 1935). Kunimoto addresses the subject in detail; see Iyo Kunimoto, "Emigración japonesa y sentimiento anti-japonés en América Latina de la época de preguerra," *Latin American Studies* (University of Tsukuba), No. 6 (1983).

10. John J. Finan, "Latin America and World War II," in H. E. Davis, J. J. Finan and F. T. Peck, (eds.), *Latin American Diplomatic History: An Introduction* (Barton Rouge: Louisiana State University, 1977); U.S. Office of Inter-American Affairs, *The Americas Cooperate for Victory and Peace* (Washington, DC: Office of Inter-American Affairs, n.d.).

11. Specific studies have been done only on the Peruvian – Japanese. Accounts of the Japanese experience in other Latin American countries are practically non-existent, although brief accounts are found in various documents and memoirs. The best are Edward N. Barnhart, "The Japanese Scare at Magdalena Bay," *Pacific Historical Review* 24, 2 (1962) and C. Harvey Gardiner, *Pawns in a Triangle of Hate: The Peruvian Japanese and the United States* (Seattle: University of Washington Press, 1981). As memoirs, see Seiichi Higashide, *Namida no adiosu: Nikkei Peru Beikoku kyōsei shūyō no ki* (The Memoirs of Seiichi Higashide; a Japanese-Peruvian Internee in a U.S. Concentration Camp) (Tokyo: Sairyū Sha, 1981) and Yoshitaro Amano, *Waga toraware no ki: dainiji taisen to Chūnambei imin* (The Memoirs of an Internee: The Second World War and Japanese Immigrants in Latin America) (Tokyo: Chuō Kōronha, 1983).

12. Kaigai Ijū Jigyōdan, (ed.), *Kaigai ijū Jigyōdan jūnen shi* (Ten Years History of the Japanese Agency for Overseas Migration) (Tokyo: Kaigai Ijū Jigyōdan, 1973). See also Yasuo Wakatsuki and Jōji Suzuki, *Kaigai ijū seisaku shiron* (Historical Survey of Emigration Policies) (Tokyo: Fukumura Shuppan, 1975).

13. Sanpauro Jinbunkagaku Kenkyūjo, *Nikkeijin jinkō chōsa kekka* (Preliminary Report of the Population Survey of Brazilians of Japanese Origin) (São Paulo: Centro de Estudos Nipo-Brasileiros, 1989).

14. Hiroshi Saitō, (ed.), *Burajiru ni okeru Nihonjin no kōken* (Japanese Contributions to Brazil) (Tokyo: Kokusai Kyōryoku Jigyōdan, 1978).
15. Paraguai to Nihon Kankōkai, *Paraguai to Nihon* (Paraguay and Japan) (Tokyo: Paraguai to Nihon Kankōkai, 1988).
16. Nihonjin Boribia Ijūshi Hensan Iinkai, (ed.), *Nihonjin Boribia ijūshi* (History of Japanese Migration to Bolivia) (Tokyo: Raten Amerika Kyōkai, 1970); Alcides Parejas Moreno, *Colonia japonesa en Bolivia* (La Paz: Colegio de Don Bosco, 1981); and Iyo Kunimoto, *Un pueblo japonés en la Bolivia tropical* (Santa Cruz: Casa de la Cultura, 1990).
17. C. Harvey Gardiner, *La política de inmigración del dictador Trujillo: estudio sobre la creación de una imagen humanitaria* (Santo Domingo: Universidad Nacional Pedro Henríquez Urena, 1979).
18. Nihonjin Aruzenchin Ijūshi Hensan Iinkai, (ed.), *Nihonjin Aruzenchin ijūshi* (History of Japanese Migration to Argentina) (Tokyo: Raten Amerika Kyōkai, 1971).
19. Information supplied by the Ministry of Foreign Affairs.
20. *Kaigai Ijū* (Emigration Abroad), No. 506 (Tokyo: Kokusai Kyōryoku Jigyōdan, 1990) p. 13.
21. Figures were obtained in April 1990, when the author was part of an official mission to Bolivia.
22. Kaigai Nikkeijin Kyōkai, *Nikkeijin honpo shūrō jittai chōsa hōkokusho* (Report of the Survey on Working Conditions of the Japanese–Latin Americans in Japan) (Tokyo: Kaigai Kyōryoku Jigyōdan, 1992).
23. Most of the returnees are working as manual laborers, even though many are university graduates. According to the questionnaire, about 60 percent of the returnees do not believe their experiences will be useful when they go back to their home countries.

Part III

Latin American
Case Studies

5 Brazil–Japan Relations: From Fever to Chill

Ernani T. Torres

Brazil has traditionally dominated Japan's relationships with Latin America. Brazil is home to the largest group of ethnic Japanese outside Japan itself. Half of Japan's foreign investment in the region is located in Brazil.[1] Brazil is Japan's largest Latin American trading partner, providing crucial products like iron ore, steel, aluminum, and agricultural commodities. And Japanese banks have a large loan portfolio outstanding to the Brazilian central government and state corporations.

During the last decade, however, Japanese activities in Brazil have stagnated in comparison with the earlier postwar era, and Japanese business people and government officials alike express serious doubts about Brazil's future. The same is true of investors from the United States and other countries. Nevertheless, Brazil continues to attract new funds, if only because of the large stake that both US and Japanese firms have in the country. In addition, of course, Brazil's huge market and rich natural resources remain enticing to entrepreneurs the world over.

What will happen in the coming years? Will Brazil continue to be the anchor of Japan's Latin American activities, or will it be replaced by a newly-resurgent Mexico and even the much smaller, but highly successful Chilean economy? This chapter argues that Brazil can reverse the chill in its relations with Japan by stabilizing its macroeconomy and establishing a credible long-term development plan. At the same time, the argument is made that improved relations with Japan will not pose a threat to US interests. Brazil recognizes the United States as its most important economic partner, even though it will continue to seek diversification of economic relations. A version of the trilateral model discussed in the Introduction to this volume could therefore be found in Brazil in the 1990s.

This chapter reviews Japan's entry into Brazil in the early twentieth century via immigration; traces the evolution of trade, investment and financial relations during the postwar years; and then looks ahead to the 1990s to try to envision the future. It concludes with a consideration of the debate that has surfaced about the future of Brazilian–Japanese–American relations.

A HISTORICAL OVERVIEW

The fates of Brazil and Japan have been intertwined for many centuries. Brazil was "discovered" by Portugal in 1500; 40 years later, Portuguese merchants and Jesuits arrived in Japan and established Santa Maria de Nagasaki. At that time, Spain was threatening the Portuguese monopoly of trade between Europe and Asia. The trade was based on silver, and Spain controlled the main silver mines in Europe and America. Because the Portuguese had failed to find precious metals in Brazil, they looked to Japan as a source of silver they could control. Only after Portugal had to give up Japan and its main Asian colonies to Holland in the mid-1600s did it start to invest in Brazil as its most important colonial possession.

In Brazilian history, Japan stands out as the source of Brazil's fourth largest colony of immigrants. In 1990, there were estimated to be more than 1.2 million Japanese immigrants and their descendants living in Brazil, the largest Japanese colony overseas.[2] The Japanese began coming to Brazil in the early twentieth century to work on coffee plantations because, after the Russo–Japanese War, rural areas in Japan faced a severe depression. In Brazil, by contrast, coffee was booming and the government was encouraging immigration to fill labor shortages in São Paulo.

Although the earliest contacts regarding Japanese migration to Brazil occurred in the 1890s, large-scale contract immigration did not begin until 1908. Rather unsuccessful attempts to bring Japanese labor went on until World War I. When the war prevented European immigration, however, labor shortages on the coffee plantations were exacerbated, leading to subsidies to Japanese workers by the state of São Paulo.

After the war, the Japanese government increased its interest in finding homes abroad for its "surplus population," but the United States and most other countries were reluctant to receive Japanese immigrants. After the US Exclusion Act was passed in 1924, Brazil became virtually the only country willing to accept groups of Japanese. Consequently, the Japanese Diet increased subsidies to contract laborers and independent farmers going to Brazil. Between 1924 and

1941, nearly 160,000 Japanese settled in Brazil; this represented 88 percent of all Japanese going to Latin America in this period.[3]

After their contracts with coffee plantations terminated, Japanese immigrants moved to other areas in the countryside of the states of São Paulo, Paraná, and even to the Amazon region. With the agricultural know-how they had acquired in Japan, they introduced modern techniques in the production of vegetables, fruits, pepper, and jute. They also brought from Japan their experience with agricultural cooperatives. The first one was introduced in Brazil in 1927 and later grew into COTIA (Cooperativa Agrícola de Cotia), which is now the largest and most successful cooperative in Latin America.[4]

Before World War II, Japanese foreign investment was mainly centered in Asia; Brazil had no economic or strategic importance for Japan. Nonetheless, there were some small investments related to the Japanese community. The first long-term Japanese investment in Brazil was the Bratac Society for the Colonization of Brazil (Bratac Sociedade Colonizadora do Brasil), which was established in 1929 by 12 Japanese provinces and private capital; 8 years later, it was transformed into a financial institution in order to provide funds for the expansion of the activities of the Japanese–Brazilian community. The 1930s also saw the first Brazilian investments by Japanese banks and trading companies as well as the first manufacturing venture, the Tozan sake plant.[5]

Although Japanese immigrants in Brazil were generally better treated than in other Latin American countries, they also faced some discrimination. Under the nationalistic Estado Novo government, anti-foreign laws prohibited foreign-language schools and publications in any language except Portuguese. Both restrictions hit the Japanese hard, since they had tried to maintain their separate language and culture. During World War II, the activities of the Japanese–Brazilians were restricted, and Japanese investments were confiscated. After the war, then, the Japanese–Brazilians tended to move toward a more assimilationist approach, but at the same time, the number of Japanese migrants increased. The Japanese government again looked abroad for places to settle the population, and Brazil again became one of the most eager recipients. Between 1952 to 1988, nearly 60,000 new Japanese immigrants arrived.[6]

Japanese trade and investment in Brazil became much more important in the years after World War II, in part because of the presence of the large immigrant population. After the oil crisis of the early 1970s, these economic relations were expanded substantially, often through joint ventures between the two governments. Brazil became one of Japan's major investment sites in the world, and both Japan and Brazil began to see each other as a way to moderate their mutual dependence on the United States.

In the 1980s, however, Japanese–Brazilian relations soured as the two countries went in opposite directions. While the Brazilian economy was facing its first long recession in postwar history, the Japanese economy was surging. After the appreciation of the yen in 1985, Japan accelerated the globalization of its industry, but Brazil – for the first time in 30 years – was not considered a main strategic partner. As a result, bilateral relations began to chill.

Although recently Brazil has begun to take steps to resuscitate its links with Japan, this process will take a long time. Meanwhile, the most vivid symbol of Brazil's problems, and the changed relationship between the two countries, is the new migration (*dekasegi*) process. A century after the first contacts to stimulate the movement of Japanese to Brazil, the third generation of Japanese (called *sansei*) began a reverse journey to Japan because of the long period of stagnation of the Brazilian economy–the same reason their grandparents left Japan at the beginning of the century. It is estimated that 14 percent of the Brazilian–Japanese community (180,000 people), mostly young and well educated, have already left Brazil for Japan.[7]

TRADE RELATIONS

The basis for expanded trade relations between Japan and Brazil was established in the early postwar period, when Japanese trading companies arrived in Brazil. Between 1955 and 1957, all the major trading firms opened offices; they first went to São Paulo and then expanded to other Brazilian cities. This was part of the process to re-establish the world-wide trading networks they had developed in the prewar period. They were aided in the effort by the Japanese government, which was eager to promote the sale of Japanese exports.[8]

During the 1960s and 1970s, trade between Brazil and Japan soared. According to the Brazilian Central Bank, total imports and exports with Japan grew from $57.4 million in 1964 to $1.7 billion in 1974, a nearly 3000 percent increase in 10 years. In the same period, Brazilian trade with the United States grew from $910 million to $5.2 billion, a 568 percent rise. As a consequence, Japan became Brazil's second-ranked trade partner, after the United States.

Both Brazil and Japan were interested in taking advantage of the complementarity between their economies: Brazil had abundant natural resources needed by Japan, while Japan could provide capital and intermediate goods as well as technology for Brazilian industries. These relationships became even more important after the first oil crisis as Japan increased its imports of raw materials and agricultural products from Brazil, and Brazil sought Japanese machinery and equipment. In 1975, Japan's share of Brazilian external trade reached its peak at 7.8 percent for exports and 9.1 percent for imports.[9]

Conflict with the United States was also a reason for the cooperative relationship between Brazil and Japan in the 1970s. Japan was heavily dependent on US exports of some primary goods, while Brazil was a potential competitor to the United States in various markets. Once the United States decided to use its international standing in agricultural markets as a weapon against Japan, Brazil began to be seen as an alternative to the United States that should be assisted for economic–strategic purposes.[10]

One interesting example involved soybeans. In the summer of 1973, President Nixon imposed an embargo on soybeans that even included contracts already signed. This was a political as well as an economic decision. Since the United States occupied an oligopolistic position in the international soybean market, it decided to use its power as a weapon to make Japan "more cooperative."[11] At that time, Brazil was a marginal producer of soybeans, although its potential was enormous. When Japanese Prime Minister Kakuei Tanaka visited Brazil in 1974, one of the bilateral projects the Japanese government decided to fund was the development of new soybean-growing areas in Cerrado, a region in central Brazil. By the early 1980s, Brazil had become the world's second largest exporter of soybeans, after the United States.

At its outset, the Cerrado Project was funded by the Japan International Cooperation Agency (JICA), a government agency in charge of technical assistance. JICA was chosen to fund the initial stage of the project because of its long repayment period (20 years) and the low interest rates on its loans (0.75–2.25 percent). In 1985 another Japanese government agency, the Overseas Economic Cooperation Fund (OECF), began to fund the Cerrado project and a $91 million dollar concessional loan was signed at that time.[12]

Soybeans were only one of the markets in which Brazil was starting to challenge the American position. Poultry was another example. In 1976, Brazil did not export any poultry at all, but by 1983 it had become one of the five largest exporters.[13] Yet another primary processed good that Brazil began to export in the late 1970s was orange juice concentrate. When the Japanese decided to open up their orange juice market, Brazil was again used as a competitor to the United States in order to frustrate attempts by American companies to control the Japanese market.[14] Up until the early 1980s, Japan did not import substantial quantities of Brazilian orange juice concentrate, but by 1989, Brazilian exports of orange juice to Japan had reached $30 million, more than 50 percent of Japanese imports. Moreover, four Brazilian juice companies have initiated a $40 million investment to construct a huge storage facility to take advantage of the full opening of the Japanese juice market in 1992.[15]

In a symmetrical fashion, Brazilian policy-makers have regarded the Japanese as an important competitor to the United States. Brazilian leaders wanted to be more independent of the United States in international affairs. Rather than automatically supporting US foreign policy, as other military presidents had since 1964, President Geisel decided that Brazil should follow a more "ecumenical, responsible and pragmatic" approach.[16] In this context, Japan was regarded as a major partner of strategic importance, which could supply the machinery, equipment, and technology Brazil needed to implement its Second National Development Plan (1974–79). For this reason, the trade balance became extremely favorable to Japan in the 1970s. From 1974 to 1979, the Brazilian deficit *vis-à-vis* Japan reached an average of $359 million a year. The peak was $538 million in 1974 (Table 5.1).

In the 1980s, by contrast, the trade balance began to favor Brazil as a consequence of severe restrictions on all Brazilian imports in response to the external debt crisis. In order to adjust the economy to the new international environment, the Brazilian government decided to decrease total imports through direct controls, while cutting public investments and promoting an economic recession.[17] Another reason for the Brazilian trade surplus was the coming on-stream of many import-substitution investments made during the late 1970s, some with Japanese capital. Brazilian import dependency decreased for goods such as steel, non-ferrous metals, petrochemicals, fertilizers, paper, and pulp. As a result of the decline in imports, Brazil's overall trade deficit of $2.8 billion in 1981 became a $13 billion surplus in 1984. In the same period, bilateral trade with Japan went from a very small deficit to a billion-dollar surplus.

From 1982 to 1987, Brazilian–Japanese trade stagnated due to the debt crisis. Imports from Japan were cut severely and exports barely grew. This situation changed after 1987; total trade (exports plus

Table 5.1 Brazilian trade with Japan and the United States, 1964–91 (annual averages, million dollars)

	1964–73	1974–79	1980–83	1984–90	1991*
Total Trade					
Exports	2,644.6	11,128.8	22,499.1	28,897.4	31,636.4
Imports	2,479.9	13,504.2	18,757.1	15,784.7	21,014.0
Balance	164.7	−2,375.4	3,742.0	13,112.7	10,622.4
Trade with USA					
Exports	683.9	2,080.8	4,019.3	7,599.0	6,284.7
Imports	745.5	2,759.3	3,072.8	3,254.4	4,853.0
Balance	−61.6	−678.5	946.5	4,344.6	1,431.7
Trade with Japan					
Exports	122.7	681.6	1,338.7	1,919.1	2,567.8
Imports	150.8	1,040.5	759.1	938.6	1,216.0
Balance	−28.1	−358.9	579.6	980.5	1,351.8

* Prelimiary data.
Source: Banco Central do Brasil.

imports) grew by over 60 percent between 1987 and 1991 to reach $3.8 billion in the latter year. Japanese–Brazilian commerce today accounts for 6.7 percent of total Brazilian foreign trade and 0.7 percent of total Japanese trade. Japan is Brazil's second largest trade partner, but Brazil ranks twenty-first on Japan's list. Among Latin American countries, however, Brazil remains Japan's largest trade partner.[18]

One specific characteristic of Brazilian trade relations with Japan is that Brazilian exports are still heavily skewed towards primary products or low value-added primary processed goods such as iron ore, steel, aluminum, pulp, soybeans, and orange juice. These items accounted for 76 percent of total Brazilian exports in 1989. Manufactured goods accounted for less than 10 percent of total exports to Japan–the same as the late 1960s and less than the peak of 15.9 percent in 1980–despite the increasing share of manufactured goods in total Japanese imports from 20.2 percent in 1968 to 37.5 percent in 1988. This is radically different from the general trend of Brazilian exports, even with most developed countries. From 1975 to 1989, for example, the share of manufactured goods in total Brazil exports to the United States increased from 40 percent to 80 percent; the comparable rise for West Germany was from 28 percent to 42 percent.[19]

As for Brazilian imports from Japan, the most important character-istic was the sharp decrease in total value of imports during the 1980s, a consequence of the recession of the domestic economy and the lack of credit lines from Japanese banks. In 1988, 91 percent of total imports from Japan were manufactured goods, mostly electrical products and general machinery. These figures show that despite enormous structur-al change in the Brazilian and Japanese economies, bilateral trade is still based on the traditional pattern of complementarity. Like other countries in Latin America, Brazil's primary or primary-processed goods are exchanged for high value-added manufactured products from Japan.[20]

JAPANESE DIRECT INVESTMENT IN BRAZIL

The first wave of Japanese direct investment in Brazil occurred in the late 1950s and early 1960s. At that time, the Brazilian economy was growing rapidly. Many foreign enterprises were investing in Brazil because the government pursued policies to protect the domestic market and to encourage greater involvement by foreign companies. For the Japanese, investment in Brazil offered two important benefits: access to natural resources and a large market, on the one hand, and the opportunity to display their increasing industrial prowess, on the other. The presence of a large Japanese ethnic population was also important in these early years, for the latter could act as intermediaries for prospective Japanese investors. By 1961, 45 Japanese companies were doing business in Brazil, mostly in trade, raw materials for textiles, and textile equipment.[21]

In addition, three large industrial projects were started in this period. One was Usinas Siderúgicas de Minas Gerais (Usiminas), a steel firm established in 1958. Brazil held 60 percent of the capital and Japan 40 percent. The Brazilian investors were the State of Minas Gerais and the Brazilian National Development Bank (BNDE, now BNDES). On the Japanese side was a consortium of 54 private firms (Nippon Usiminas), headed by Nippon Steel, and a government financial institution, OECF. The first blast furnace began operation in 1962, and the integrated facilities were completed in 1965. With a capacity of 500,000 tons, Usiminas was to be one of the main steel companies in Brazil, designed to produce steel for automobiles, shipbuilding, and other projects envisioned in the government's ambitious development plans. Nippon Steel provided the most modern technology available, and workers were trained in Japan as well as in Brazil. By 1965, Japan had supplied $567 million of loans and risk capital, equivalent to 21 percent of total investment costs.[22] As will be discussed below, although Usiminas was a technological success, it became embroiled in bitter political controversies that soured relations between the two countries.

A second project, Ishikawajima do Brasil (Ishibrás), was in shipbuilding. In this case, the majority partner was the Japanese shipbuilding company, Ishikawajima–Harima; the Brazilian government financed 30 percent of the plant and equipment costs and placed orders for the Brazilian navy. Established in 1959, Ishibrás remains the largest shipyard in Brazil and Latin America. It also has a machinery division that produces diesel engines, cranes, and steel structures.[23] A third project was in the auto industry. Toyota Motor Company set up a subsidiary, Toyota do Brasil, to produce the Land Cruiser. Unlike Usiminas and Ishibrás, Toyota was neither a joint venture nor a major player in the Brazilian context; US and German auto plants were much larger.[24]

After 1962, Japanese investment dropped off due to the first severe domestic and external crisis of the Brazilian economy during the postwar period. During the Goulart government (1961–64), inflation ran out of control, economic growth declined, external reserves vanished, and the political situation became very unstable. Foreign investment in general fell off, and the Japanese were no exception to the trend.

Only after the military government brought inflation under control and the Brazilian economy resumed growth did the second wave of Japanese investments start in the late 1960s and early 1970s. By 1970, Japan had invested $157 million in Brazil, 4 percent of total foreign capital registered at the Brazilian Central Bank. Most of this capital was in manufacturing industries – shipbuilding, iron, steel, and textiles. In addition, there were important industrial investments (especially in electronics) in the Manaus Free Zone, and most of the Japanese banks established some type of foothold in Brazil. Japanese investment was small compared to the $1.2 billion invested by the United States and the $600 million invested by West Germany; Switzerland, Canada and the United Kingdom had invested more than the Japanese as well. At this time, however, Japan was a comparatively marginal direct investor in the world market, and its investment in Brazil was large by Japanese standards.[25]

After 1972, Japanese direct investment in Brazil entered a period of rapid expansion. From 1972 to 1974, more than 400 projects were undertaken by Japanese companies, involving $800 million. In 1979, Brazil was Japan's third largest host country in the world after the United States and Indonesia. Brazil represented almost 8 percent of total Japanese investment overseas and half of all Japanese investment in Latin America.[26] By 1980, Japanese investment had reached $1.9 billion according to Brazilian government statistics ($2.9 billion according to Japanese figures); see Table 5.2.

The boom was a result of three factors. First, Brazil was considered a good investment opportunity for Japanese companies, which expected the Brazilian economy to maintain the high rates of growth it had shown–10 percent in some years–during the coming decades. Moreover, there was a welcoming attitude toward foreign investors and little

Table 5.2   Direct foreign investment in Brazil, 1971–91 (million dollars and percent)

Country	Before 1970	1971–80	1981–85	1986–88	1989–91	Total**
	TOTAL AMOUNTS ($ MILLION)*					
USA	1,201.3	4,321.0	2,776.9	610.4	595.8	9505.4
W. Germany	572.2	2,358.3	1,590.7	151.1	122.4	4794.7
Japan	156.9	1,767.1	749.4	285.2	310.6	3,269.2
Others	1,849.7	7,292.2	4,247.3	858.7	1,186.4	15,434.3
Total	3,780.1	15,653.6	9,364.3	1,905.4	2,215.2	32,918.6
	ANNUAL AVERAGES ($ MILLION)					
USA	n.a.	432.1	555.4	203.5	198.6	1,389.5
W. Germany	n.a.	235.8	318.1	50.4	40.8	645.1
Japan	n.a.	176.7	149.9	95.1	103.5	525.2
Others	n.a.	729.2	849.5	286.2	395.5	2,251.9
Total	n.a.	1,565.3	1,872.9	635.1	738.4	4,811.8
	STRUCTURE (%)					
USA	31.8	27.6	29.7	32.0	26.9	28.9
W. Germany	19.2	15.1	17.0	7.9	5.5	14.6
Japan	4.1	11.3	8.0	15.0	14.0	9.9
Others	48.9	46.6	45.3	45.1	53.6	46.6
Total	100.0	100.0	100.0	100.0	100.0	100.0

* Data as of September 30 of each year.
** Cumulative total.
Source: Banco Central do Brasil, *Boletim Mensal*, March and September 1991.

prejudice against the Japanese as compared to Asian countries and even other countries in the Americas.

The other two factors arose from the oil crisis. On the Japanese side, the high price of oil led to cuts in the production capacity in some intermediate goods sectors and the resulting need to increase imports. Since Brazil had unexploited mineral and hydro-electric resources, it was chosen to become a direct exporter of mineral and agricultural products and an indirect exporter of energy to Japan.

The third factor was also related to the international energy crisis; in this case it was on the Brazilian side. Brazil, too, was severely hit by the high price of oil. The Brazilian government wanted to reduce import dependency by means of a new industrial policy based on promoting heavy industry and chemicals in order to catch up with the more industrialized countries. Because Japan was one of the most successful examples of catching up after World War II, Brazilian policy-makers were very much influenced by Japan's past experience and followed its lead.[27] The Second National Development Plan of Brazil (1974–79) called for investments to be speeded up for import substitution of intermediate and capital goods. The Brazilian government was also eager to promote investments on a joint-venture basis to export primary-processed goods and attract modern technology from abroad.

Many of the large projects of the 1970s were joint ventures with Brazilian state-owned enterprises – Companhia Vale do Rio Doce (CVRD) and Siderbrás – which had been engaged in business with Japanese companies for a long time. The key set of projects was agreed on during President Geisel's visit to Tokyo in September 1976. In addition to the Cerrado agricultural project already discussed, they included Cenibra (cellulose), Tubarão (steel), and Albrás–Alunorte (aluminum).

Cenibra, the cellulose project, involved 18 Japanese paper and pulp companies, a trading firm (C.Itoh), and the OECF; they combined into an investment company called JPB. JPB, in turn, contributed 49.4 percent of the capital for a joint venture with CVRD. The plant began operations in 1977, with a capacity of 255 million tons of pulp; inputs came from an associated eucalyptus project. Half of the output was to be exported to Japan.[28]

Tubarão was a three-way joint venture of Brazilian, Italian, and Japanese partners. The Japanese side consisted of Kawasaki Steel, Ishikawajima–Harima Heavy Industries, and 12 trading companies. They controlled 24.5 percent of the capital, and the Japanese government provided a $100 million soft loan for construction of harbor facilities adjacent to the plant. Unlike Usiminas, Tubarão was seen as a purely commercial venture. The company was to produce semi-finished steel products, with most of the output going to the partners for use in their own operations. Although the Tubarão operation was more positive than Usiminas, neither the Japanese nor the Italian consortia participated in capital expansions, so their share dropped.[29]

For the aluminum project, the Nippon Amazon Aluminum Corporation (NAAC) was established by 33 Japanese associates, under the leadership of OECF. As part of an agreement between the governments of Brazil and Japan, NAAC and CVRD established two joint ventures in 1978: Alunorte was to produce alumina, which Albrás would use as an input to make aluminum. The project has been funded mainly by loans from a syndicate of Japanese banks, headed by the Export–Import Bank of Japan. Albrás–Alunorte encountered substantial delays and then ran into trouble when the international price of alumina declined in the early 1980s, and the Japanese consortium lost interest. More recently, however, the price trends have changed, and OECF has decided to inject new capital into the project to revive it.[30]

In the 1980s, there was a radical change in Japanese–Brazilian relations. Japanese overseas investment increased from $6.5 billion in 1985 to $43.8 billion in 1989, but Brazil became a marginal host country for new Japanese foreign investment with less than $100 million a year, or 60 percent of the level reached during much of the 1970s (Table 5.2). For Japan, it became less important to invest in order to secure a supply of strategic raw materials as international prices started to fall and supplies became abundant. At the same time, Japan had to face new challenges in the international market. With the rapid appreciation of the yen, low value-added industries were relocated overseas, especially in Asia's Newly Industrialized Economies or NIEs (South Korea, Taiwan, Hong Kong and Singapore) and in ASEAN nations (Thailand, Indonesia, Malaysia and the Philippines). Japanese companies started assembling their products in these markets as a result of US and European restrictions on imports from Japan.[31]

Brazil has played only a limited role in the new Japanese strategy for the globalization of the production process. The most obvious reason is the distance between the two countries. Even in the era of large container ships, distance poses an important obstacle for trade between Japan and Brazil. The distance factor is especially significant if the products are inputs into the Japanese manufacturing process, given the "just-in-time" inventory system that characterizes Japanese industry. A second reason is that Brazilian industry has always oriented its production towards the domestic market behind high tariff barriers. As a consequence, Brazilian firms have not had to face international competition, thus remaining both inefficient and of lower quality than the Japanese demand. Brazil's international competitiveness in manufacturing relies mostly on low wages and abundant natural resources, not on dynamic factors such as technology.[32]

In the 1980s, Japanese investors already established in Brazil became frustrated because the domestic market stagnated. Because of chronically high inflation rates and unstable foreign exchange policies, non-operational profits in industry (those deriving from financial activities) became more important than operational profits (deriving from traditional production activities). Japanese subsidiaries were not prepared to face this new environment because they lacked the autonomy and flexibility to adapt their procedures rapidly.

Moreover, the head offices in Tokyo were frustrated by the situation where their Brazilian subsidiaries accumulated huge capital losses in yen despite being profitable in Brazilian currency (cruzeiros). This phenomenon was mostly a consequence of the appreciation of the yen–dollar exchange rate. As a consequence of the sharp devaluation of the dollar after 1985, the Japanese exchange rate reached almost 120 yen per dollar, while the rate until 1971 was 360 yen. Thus, all Japanese direct investment registered before 1971 was reduced to a third of its original value in yen. There were also some losses due to the real devaluation of the cruzeiro against the dollar and to the Brazilian indexed accounting system.

In addition, Japanese companies expressed complaints about the behavior of the Brazilian government, their partner in several joint ventures. Japanese investors, as opposed to other foreign investors in Brazil, have always preferred to have the national government directly or indirectly involved in their large investments. Due to the fiscal and financial crisis of the 1980s, the Brazilian government was unable to fulfill some of its commitments, and the Japanese felt they were being discriminated against.

An important example is the Usiminas project, which has been a technological success but a financial and diplomatic failure. Usiminas produces the cheapest and best quality steel in Brazil but, due to government price controls aimed at subsidizing exports of manufactured goods, the company has generally lost money. Moreover, the Brazilian government's steel holding company (Siderbrás), which took over the State of Minas Gerais' share of the investment, began to maneuver to increase its share at the expense of Nippon Usiminas (and BNDES). Nippon Usiminas' share had already fallen from 40 percent of its original value to less than 20 percent by 1970 as a result of new capital injections, but by 1987 it was down to 4.7 percent. Japanese shareholders, including the Japanese government, became quite bitter about their situation, and Usiminas became the most important Japanese–Brazilian conflict since World War II. Besides Usiminas there were also frictions between the Brazilian government and two other Japanese companies: Kawasaki Steel and Ishikawajima–Harima. Kawasaki was a minor shareholder in Tubarão (steel) and had the same complaints against Siderbrás as Nippon Usiminas. The problems with Ishibrás were due to government debts with the company.

As a consequence of these frictions, the relations of the Japanese and Brazilian governments became increasingly tense during the 1980s. The situation began to change in May 1991, when Nippon Usiminas, Siderbrás and BNDES reached an agreement that made possible the successful privatization of the company six months later. The Brazilian government decided to give an option to Nippon Usiminas to buy an additional 19 percent of the shares of Usiminas at historical values. At the same time, the Japanese renounced all their claims and preference rights in the company.

In the case of Tubarão, a previous agreement had guaranteed Kawasaki (as well as the Italian partner, Finsider) the right to buy the shares of Siderbrás in case the Brazilian government decided to sell its holdings. This agreement came into conflict with the new Brazilian privatization law, which requires a public auction to sell government shares and limits foreign participation in privatized companies to 40 percent of capital. A new shareholders' agreement was reached with foreign partners in February 1992. Kawasaki and Finsider agreed to limit their right to buy new shares to the legal ceiling of 40 percent and to purchase them at the auction price. With this agreement in hand, the Brazilian government privatized Tubarão in July 1992. Although it had been expected that Usiminas would take control of its sister company, conflicts arose among the Japanese stockholders, and the majority of shares were bought by CVRD and two Brazilian banks.[33]

With the privatization process now well underway, the government-to-government approach of Japanese investors in Brazil will probably have to change in the near future. The Brazilian government wants to privatize many important state-owned enterprises and drastically reduce state intervention in the economy. Thus, in order to increase their operations in Brazil, Japanese companies will have to either invest in their own projects or find new partners in the private sector.

FINANCIAL RELATIONS

During the 1970s and early 1980s, Brazil accumulated a large external debt. As of the end of 1972, this debt was $9.2 billion; 10 years later, it had reached $90.5 billion, most of it in the hands of private banks. The rapid build-up was due to the Brazilian strategy of growth-cum-debt during the 1970s. After the first oil crisis, Brazil's terms of trade deteriorated sharply, but the government attempted to maintain a high rate of economic growth. In order to finance its large trade deficits, Brazil decided to increase public investments financed by the international capital market. Until 1976, the trade deficit was the main component of the current account deficit, but after 1978, owing to the sharp increase in international interest rates, debt service became the most important component. From then on, Brazil needed more and more loans simply to finance its debt service.

Japanese banks were late in entering the international financial market. When they started to expand their overseas operations in the late 1970s, Brazil was regarded as a profitable and promising market. At first, they merely participated in syndicated loans managed by US and European banks. A few years later, however, they had taken charge of their own syndicates. By 1982, Japanese banks held 10 percent of all Brazilian medium and long-term external debt with private banks. In Latin America, only Mexico surpassed Brazil in the size of its debt to Japanese banks.[34]

After Mexico's near-default in 1982, Japanese as well as other foreign banks halted new loans to Brazil. The result was that Brazil also ran into problems in servicing its debt and had to request a rescheduling of payments falling due. In order to negotiate a rescheduling arrangement with the Brazilian government, the banks organized themselves into a creditor committee, under the leadership of Citicorp. Among the Japanese banks, the Bank of Tokyo was chosen to represent Japan on the so-called Bank Advisory Committee. The reason was that Bank of Tokyo had the largest exposure in Brazil, and elsewhere in Latin America, and was the only Japanese bank with long-term international experience in the region.[35] In 1989, Mitsubishi was added to the committee as Brazil's second largest Japanese creditor.

The Bank of Tokyo not only supported the strategy of US banks for the renegotiation of the Brazilian debt; it adopted an even tougher policy for faster repayment of the debt service. As a consequence, the opinion of the Brazilian team involved in the 1986 negotiations with the private banking committee was that Japanese banks have been more inflexible than US institutions.[36] Despite their official hard line, however, Japanese banks were the only ones to increase their share of Brazilian debt. By the end of 1990, Japan was Brazil's second largest creditor, holding 16 percent of the total Brazilian debt with private banks (Table 5.3).

The Japanese policy of merely following the US strategy started to change in the late 1980s. Despite the debt crisis, some of the Japanese banks became interested in strengthening their position in the Brazilian market as part of their world-wide strategy.[37] At the same time, the Japanese government proposed a different course to cope with the debt crisis. The Miyazawa Plan was presented at the 1988 annual meeting of the World Bank and the International Monetary Fund (IMF). Partly encouraged by the new ideas of the Japanese government, then Brazilian finance minister, Luiz Carlos Bresser Pereira, tried to persuade the US government to change its debt negotiating approach. Bresser was openly criticized for his proposals and resigned soon after.[38] The Miyazawa Plan was also rejected, but a few months later, the US government adopted most of the Japanese ideas under the Brady Plan.

Despite the US and Japanese initiatives, Brazil's debt problem changed little for several years. A debt moratorium, which had been decreed shortly before Bresser took office and maintained by him, was

Table 5.3   Brazilian external debt with private banks, 1985–90 (billion dollar)

| Bank home country | 1985 | | | | 1989 | | | | 1990 | |
| | Long term | Short term | Total | | Long term | Short term | Total | | Total | |
			Value	Share			Value	Share	Value	Share
USA	18.6	5.6	24.2	31.4	17.0	8.2	25.2	32.1	24.1	30.5
Japan	8.8	1.5	10.3	13.4	9.9	2.0	11.9	15.1	12.4	15.7
UK	8.5	0.8	9.3	12.1	7.8	1.0	8.8	11.2	5.6	7.1
Brazil*	7.6	0.6	8.2	10.6	6.5	0.1	6.6	8.4	6.9	8.7
Others	23.5	1.5	25.0	32.5	22.0	4.2	26.1	33.2	29.9	37.9
Total	67.0	10.0	77.0	100.0	63.2	15.5	78.6	100.0	78.9	100.0

* Branches of Brazilian banks overseas
Source: Banco Central do Brasil, *Annual Report*, 1985, 1989, and 1990.

cancelled by his successor and a rescheduling program negotiated, but Brazil soon began quietly to accumulate arrears again. In 1990, Fernando Collor de Mello was inaugurated president of Brazil under a program stressing an open economy and a smaller economic role for the state, including the privatization of many public-sector firms. Bankers, including the Japanese, assumed that Collor would quickly resolve the outstanding debt problems, but a nationalist stand on debt was used to try to build support for other reforms. As a result, Brazil became increasingly isolated from the international economy, unable to get new money from any source. Finally, in spring 1991, under the leadership of Finance Minister Marcílio Marques Moreira, the government changed its defiant stance and began to negotiate seriously with the banks and the IMF, in hopes of reducing its debt via Brady Plan mechanisms and getting new money. An agreement with the IMF was signed in January 1992 and with the Paris Club in February. With these agreements in hand, Brazilian officials intensified their negotiations with the private banks and reached an agreement in July to reschedule almost $45 billion in debts.

One of the primary reasons for the more accommodating debt policy was Brazil's eagerness to obtain new funds from the Japanese. Although the private banks are unlikely to offer new money, especially if they have to take big losses on their Brazilian portfolios, public-sector lenders are a different story. Brazil has a long history of loans from Japan's Export–Import Bank (JEXIM) and the soft-loan agency (OECF). Both were important participants in the big national resource projects discussed above.

In the 1980s, disbursements through JEXIM or OECF loans were very low compared to the needs and possibilities of Brazil (Table 5.4). This was mainly due to the Brazilian external debt crisis but also to the frictions between the two countries. The Japanese government insisted on finding a solution for Usiminas, Tubarão and Ishibrás, as well as clearing Brazil's arrears, before lending any large amount of new money. Meanwhile, since the late 1980s, JEXIM and OECF had been discussing new projects with the Brazilian government for the total amount of $1.5 billion, in areas such as electricity, port facilities, transportation, and irrigation. Once the arrears with Japanese entities were settled and the agreements with the IMF and Paris Club signed, the Japanese government announced new loans to Brazil for the first time in almost ten years. The announcement took place during the United Nations Conference on the Environment and Development (UNCED) in Rio de Janeiro in June 1992. The loans included a

Table 5.4   Japanese government assistance to Brazil, 1960–90 (disbursements in million dollars)

Years	Eximbank Loans	ODA			Total
		Loans	Grants	Technical coop.	
1960–80	n.a.	89.3	2.0	48.4	139.6
1981	45.0	15.3	–	16.1	76.4
1982	38.0	35.8	–	14.6	85.5
1983	60.0	12.5	–	14.6	87.1
1984	30.0	19.9	–	15.8	65.6
1985	25.0	24.9	–	15.7	65.6
1986	60.0	8.4	–	23.9	82.3
1987	48.0	55.0	–	27.1	130.1
1988	33.0	31.6	0.2	34.6	99.4
1989	24.0	87.0	–	37.2	148.2
1990	22.0	26.7	–	38.0	86.7

Source: Banco Central do Brasil, *Annual Report*, 1989 and 1990 (for Eximbank loans); Ministry of Foreign Affairs of Japan, *Japan's ODA*, various years (for Official Development Assistance).

JEXIM credit for $300 million to BNDES to fund untied imports of machinery and equipment, and $600 million from OECF to control water pollution in Rio's Guanabara Bay and São Paulo's Tiete River. Moreover, Japan is likely to provide financial support for Brazil's new debt agreement.[39]

PERSPECTIVES FOR THE 1990s AND IMPLICATIONS FOR THE UNITED STATES

The Japanese economy grew steadily during the 1980s, and Japan is now the world's largest creditor. Japanese banks have become the largest in the world, and Japan is seeking to play an increasingly important role in multilateral agencies, including regional agencies such as the Interamerican Development Bank (IDB). Japanese enterprises are the leaders in various important industrial sectors and have accelerated their expansion in the international market through globalization of their production. This increased Japanese economic power will likely continue in the present decade, since Japan will probably keep growing faster than other OECD economies. Japan will also increase its ratio of imports to total production in the manufacturing sector in line with its globalization strategy.

Almost 80 percent of all Japanese investment will be earmarked for the United States, Europe and Asia. Until now, Brazil and other Latin American countries have not been regarded as important host countries in the Japanese globalization process. A recent survey conducted by MITI, for example, indicated that only 2 percent of the companies consulted had chosen Latin America as a priority region for foreign investment in manufacturing in the near future.[40]

Nevertheless, it is still possible for this pessimistic scenario to change because Japanese investors are facing problems in some of their overseas markets. In particular, Americans are uneasy with the increasing Japanese presence in their country. The United States has become dependent on Japanese technology even for some defense-related programs, not to mention savings to fund its external and fiscal deficits. Europeans are even more afraid of Japanese competition, especially in high-tech industries. In Asia, some of Japan's neighbors, who still resent that country for historical reasons, fear increasing Japanese hegemony in the Pacific Basin.[41]

None of these obstacles exist in relations between Japan and Brazil. Although this is a strong point, it is not enough to change Brazil's position in Japanese strategy. Any significant change in the bilateral relationship will require a special effort and a new approach by the Brazilian government and private sector in regard to Japan. Macroeconomic stabilization and an agreement with foreign banks on the external debt are necessary but not sufficient steps. What is most important is to rebuild credibility by means of a comprehensive long-term set of policies that clearly provides a new context for doing business and for deepening bilateral economic relations. Furthermore, Brazil's initiative to accelerate economic integration with other Latin American countries would improve the possibilities of future negotiations with Japan. Brazil is the only country in a position to promote the economic integration of the region and is already actively doing so with Argentina and other countries of the Southern Cone. A final crucial step is to re-ignite economic growth in Brazil itself and its Southern Cone partners. As Kotaro Horisaka indicates (see Chapter 2 in this volume), high growth will attract Japanese firms regardless of the intentions of host governments. Good intentions without growth, he says, will not produce investment.

In terms of Brazilian external trade, Japan and the rest of Asia represent a market of growing importance. In 1991, Asia became almost as significant as the US market for Brazilian goods: $5.7 billion in sales to Asia (including $2.6 billion to Japan) compared to $6.2 billion to the United States. The European Community was still the largest market with $9.7 billion of export sales.[42] Since Japanese imports of manufactured goods are rapidly increasing, it will be vital for Brazil to gain a larger share of that market–especially in light of increasing protectionism in the United States and Europe. In order to achieve this goal, Brazilian entrepreneurs will have to take part in the industrial network that is currently being built through the process of globalization of Japanese companies. This means that the Brazilian government and private sector, including Japanese subsidiaries, will have to work hard to change present Japanese expectations regarding Brazil.[43]

In addition to trying to attract more Japanese investment and gain a larger share of the Japanese market, Brazil will have to deal with the impact of such a strategy on relations with the United States. As discussed in the Introduction to this volume, Brazil has become the center of a debate in the literature on Japan and Latin America about whether Japan poses a threat to the United States. Professor Leon Hollerman has written a book, entitled *Japan's Economic Strategy in Brazil: Challenge for the United States*, in which he argues that Japan will help Brazil build up its economic capacity as part of a "headquarters strategy." In essence, Brazil would become part of an integrated world-wide network, producing raw materials and low, medium-technology goods while Japan retained the high value-added industries. Japan would eliminate its trade surplus with the United States because a large volume of the exports would come from Brazil (and similar countries). Rather than openly confronting the United States, Japan would "outflank" it.[44]

It is the view of this author that Hollerman is mistaken in his analysis. There is no reason to expect that a closer economic relationship between Brazil and Japan will result in harm to US interests. The United States has always been Brazil's most important partner in the world economy, and US businesses have established a close personal network with the Brazilian power structure. Furthermore, there are indications that Japan is trying to avoid heightened tensions with the United States in Brazil. This means that Japan will not readily take new initiatives in Brazil that can be interpreted as a challenge to the United States. An example is the US veto of the transamazonic highway to the Pacific Ocean that Brazil had planned to build using Japanese funds.[45]

Moreover, Brazil itself is not in a position to take advantage of the open rivalry between these two big powers as it has in the past, because it is no longer of great strategic importance to either the United States or to Japan. This is one of the main reasons why the Collor government, since it took office in March 1990, has placed a high priority on resolving bilateral disagreements with the United States. Those initiatives were intensified after the appointment in May 1991 of Marcílio Marques Moreira, former ambassador in Washington, as the new minister of finance. While working to reach an agreement with the IMF and the private banks, Moreira also developed a quiet and successful strategy of approximation with Tokyo.

In a short period of time, all disagreements with Japanese enterprises in Brazil were solved, negotiations with OECF and JEXIM were stepped up, and contacts with Keidanren – Japan's powerful private industrial organization – were renewed. The Brazilian government also gave an important sign of the new importance of Japan with the nomination of Eliezer Batista as Minister of Strategic Affairs. As president of the Brazilian state firm, Companhia Vale do Rio Doce, Batista had been responsible in the 1970s for the implementation of the most successful partnerships between Brazil and Japan. He has very good connections with the Japanese government as well as private companies. His first official meeting was to host a high-level mission of Keidanren, headed by Hiroshi Saito, president of Nippon Steel. Indirectly, the Brazilian government was providing an answer to Saito's earlier public complaint that Brazilian government officials 'have no time available to worry about Japanese problems [in Brazil].'[46] During his stay in Brazil, Saito had a personal meeting with President Collor.

Nonetheless, this rapprochement with Japan should not be regarded as a challenge to the United States. Marcílio Moreira is a man with very close relations with Washington. Brazil's strategy seems thus to be precisely the trilateral one discussed in the Introduction to this volume. It is seeking to diversify its international economic relations, and Japan is regarded as a very important partner that will complement–rather than challenge–the American position. Although there are clear strategic limits on the Brazilian–Japanese partnership in sensitive areas such as the external debt, strategic investments (for example, the transamazonic road to Peru) and military technology, it can be expected that economic relations between Brazil and Japan will increase in the coming years.

Notes

1. This statement pertains to Latin America excluding the tax-haven investments in the Caribbean and the flag-of-convenience operations in Panama.
2. There are no official data on the total population of the Japanese community in Brazil. The Centro de Estudos Nipo–Brasileiros (Center of Japanese–Brazilian Studies), a non-governmental organization based in São Paulo, conducted a survey in 1988 and reached the figure of 1,228,000 people.
3. For a more detailed account of Japanese migration to Brazil and elsewhere in Latin America, see Iyo Kunimoto, "Japanese Migration to Latin America" (ch. 4 this volume).
4. Mitsuhiro Kagami, "Japanese Business Activities in Brazil" (Santiago: ECLAC, 1989).
5. Wellington Amorim, "Contraste e Contato: Aspectos do Relacionamento Econômico entre o Brasil e o Japão," M.Sc. thesis, Universidade de Brasilia, 1991.
6. Kunimoto, "Japanese Migration," Table 4.4.
7. The *dekasegi* have become an important source of foreign currency to Brazil, usually sending home most of their savings. This amount reached $1.4 billion in 1991. See "US$ 1,5 bilhão de poupanca japonesa," *Gazeta Mercantil*, April 8, 1992.
8. On the trading companies, see Terutomo Ozawa, *Multinationalism, Japanese Style* (Princeton, NJ: Princeton University Press, 1979).
9. Banco do Brasil (CACEX–DEPEC), "Intercambio Brasil-Japão: Participação no Comércio Exterior Brasileiro," unpublished paper, May 1990.
10. Leon Hollerman, *Japan's Economic Strategy in Brazil: Challenge for the United States* (Lexington, MA: Lexington Books, 1988).
11. According to Hollerman, Pierre Rinfret, a Nixon economic adviser, on a tour sponsored by the US State Department, told the Tokyo Foreign Correspondents Club in October of 1973 that the soybean embargo was initiated "strictly with malice . . . [in order to] show something to the people who thought our economic strength was low. Frankly, the Japanese have been increasingly cooperative since then" (Ibid., p. 225).
12. Interview with Yutaka Hongo, JICA representative in Brazil, Brasilia, September 1990.
13. See Mario Carvalho, "Exportações de Frango Congelado," *Revista Brasileira de Comércio Exterior* (July 1988).
14. Interview with Brazilian diplomats at the Brazilian Embassy in Tokyo, September 1989.

15. See Kotaro Horisaka, "Japanese Economic Relations with Latin America" (ch. 2 this volume).

16. On the interest in independence from the United States, see Roberto Abdenur, *O Marco Econômico e Global das Relações Brasil–Estados Unidos na Transição Democrática* (Rio de Janeiro: Paz e Terra, 1985). On Geisel's stance, see Ministério das Relações Exteriores do Brasil, "Presidente Reafirma ao Congresso o Pragmatismo Responsável," *Resenha de Política Exterior do Brasil* (1975) and Maria Regina Lima and Gerson Moura, "A Trajetória do Pragmatismo," *Revista Dados* 25 (1982).

17. Banco Central do Brasil, *Annual Report*, 1983–86.

18. Tsuneta Yano Memorial Society, *Nippon: a Charted Survey of Japan (1989/90)*, 1989.

19. See Amorim, "Contraste e Contato."

20. Ibid.

21. Banco Nacional do Desenvolvimento Econômico e Social (BNDES), *Investimento Direto Japonês no Exterior*, 1990.

22. Ozawa, *Multinationalism*; Kagami, "Japanese Business Activities;" Gilson Schwartz, (ed.), *Japanese Economic Cooperation with Brazil: Progress Report* (Tokyo: Institute of Developing Economies, 1990).

23. Ozawa, *Multinationalism*; Kagami, "Japanese Business Activities."

24. Ibid.

25. Banco Nacional do Desenvolvimento Econômico e Social (BNDES), *Investimento Direto Japonês no Exterior*, 1990.

26. Kagami, "Japanese Business Activities" and Imai Kamara, "Trends in Japan's Direct Investment Abroad in Fiscal Year 1979," *Exim Review* (May 1981).

27. According to Zysman, "Catch-up allows the government to identify both the importance of a sector and the appropriate technologies; the maps to the future are available in the industrial histories of one's competitor." See John Zysman, *Governments, Markets and Growth: Financial Systems and the Politics of Industrial Change* (Ithaca: Cornell University Press, 1983) p. 43. According to Cooper, "With the exception of France . . . the main criterion of other countries [for selecting the sector to be favored by the industrial policy] is to look at the economic evolution of the United States and identify as leading sectors those which seem to have been the cutting edge of the US economy. In recent years, such countries as Korea and Brazil now look increasingly to Japan for guidance on what sectors to emphasize." See Richard Cooper, "Some Reflections on Industrial Policy for the United States," paper prepared for the Conference Industrial Policy: Past, Present and Future, MITI, Tokyo, 1989, p. 3.

28. Kagami, "Japanese Business Activities."

29. Kagami, "Japanese Business Activities;" Schwartz, (ed.), *Japanese Economic Cooperation*.

30. Kagami, "Japanese Business Activities;" Oliver Bomsel *et al.*, *Mining and Metallurgy Investment in the Third World: The End of Large Projects?* (Paris: OECD, 1990). Also interviews with OECF and Eximbank representatives in Rio de Janeiro, August 1990.

31. See Ernani Torres, "O Novo Ciclo do Investimento Direto Japonês e os NIC Latino–Americanos," paper prepared for the Seminar on the Brazilian Position in the International Economy in the 1990s, CORE-CON-SP, March 1990. See also Industrial Bank of Japan, "Factors Behind Japanese Direct Investment Abroad," *Quarterly Review*, 80 (1989).

32. Banco Central do Brasil, *Annual Report*, 1990; Long Term Credit Bank of Japan and Instituto de Planejamento Econômico e Social, "Current Brazilian Economy and Business Opportunities," IPLAN/IPEA, Brasilia, 1988.

33. On the Usiminas privatization process, see Ministério da Infra Estrutura, "Informação ao Público," Estado de Minas Gerais, May 24, 1991. On Tubarão, see "Tubarão Privatizada," *Gazeta Mercantil*, July 17, 1992. The Japanese conflict arose because Nippon Steel (leading Japanese company in Usiminas) did not want to share control with rival Kawasaki Steel (leading Japanese firm in Tubarão).

34. Kotaro Horisaka, "Japanese Banks and the Latin American Debt Problem," *Revista de Economia Política* 10, No. 3 (1990).

35. See Barbara Stallings, "The Reluctant Giant: Japan and the Latin American Debt Crisis," *Journal of Latin American Studies*, 22, 1 (February 1990); interviews with Japanese bankers and officials in Tokyo, September 1989, and in Rio, August 1990.

36. Interview with Professor Paulo Nogueira Batista Junior, adviser to former Minister of Finance, Dilson Funaro, São Paulo, March 1990.

37. Interview with Brazilian government bank officials, Rio, June 1989.

38. Interview with Professor Yoshiaki Nakano, adviser to former Minister of Finance, Luiz Carlos Bresser Pereira, São Paulo, May 1990.

39. Interviews with officials of the Export–Import Bank of Japan, Rio, October 1990 and Tokyo, July 1992.

40. Interview with MITI officials, Tokyo, September 1989.

41. On the United States, see *Newsweek*, October 9, 1989; on Europe, see Masaru Yoshitomi, "Perspectivas para o Comércio Internacional nos Anos 1990: Desequilíbrios, Competição em Tecnologia Avancada e Liberalização," *Japão Informativo Econômico*, Fundação Getúlio Vargas (April 1991); on Asia, information is from interview with Professor Yuji Suzuki, from Hosei University, Japan, a specialist on Japan–Asian Countries relations, Rio, September 1990.

42. "Basil Vende mais a Asia," *Gazeta Mercantil*, May 19, 1992.

43. Interviews with Japanese enterprise managers, Tokyo, August and September 1989.

44. Hollerman, *Japan's Economic Strategy*.

45. Toshiro Kobayashi, Vice-President of the Bank of Tokyo in Brazil, confirmed that the Japanese government was pressured by the US State Department not to fund the transamazonic road to the Pacific; interview in Rio, December 1990.

46. See the interview of Hiroshi Saito in the Brazilian newspaper, *Folha de São Paulo*, December 5, 1990.

6 Mexico's International Strategy: Looking East and North

Gabriel Székely

Mexico represents the most compelling case of how trilateralism might work in Latin America as we approach the end of the twentieth century. Japan has become Mexico's second largest international economic partner, although the dollar value of Mexican–Japanese trade and the flow of investment and loans pale in contrast to Mexico's economic relations with the United States. Yet seldom has Japan committed itself so strongly to a developing country outside Asia. From the perspective of the economic superpower that Japan has become, the value of these transactions is still limited, but they are increasingly salient for Mexico. Indeed, the emerging trilateral relationship involving Mexico, Japan, and the United States is a prime example of Mexico's strategy to reduce its economic dependence on the United States and benefit from growing integration into the world economy.

Before discussing Mexico's current economic relations with Japan and their implications for the United States, a brief analysis is necessary of Mexican–Japanese contacts over a longer historical period. In addition to hosting immigrant workers from Japan, Mexico takes pride in having been one of the first nations in the world to extend full diplomatic recognition to the new Japanese regime back in 1888. Japan gratefully acknowledges Mexico's move for it furthered the Japanese goal of earning the respect and recognition of the large and important nations of the time.

Following the historical introduction, the chapter goes on to the evolution of trade, investment, and financial relations between Mexico and Japan during two main periods. First, from the 1950s through the early 1970s, these relations evolved rather gradually. They were strengthened substantially during the second stage, after Mexico's petroleum development program took off in the mid-1970s. Oil became the core of the bilateral relationship because Mexico, while providing only 5 percent of Japanese oil imports, became that country's largest

149

non-OPEC supplier. Even now, the Japanese government, specifically the Ministry of International Trade and Industry (MITI), argues that supplies from countries like Mexico will help strengthen national security and expects that Mexico will play an even more prominent role in meeting Japan's oil needs.

Hovering over the growing but still fragile ties between Mexico and Japan is the pervasive presence and influence of the United States. In some instances, such as in the aftermath of the Mexican debt crisis, Japanese resources have been provided with strong encouragement on the part of the United States. Investments, by contrast, have been initiated by the Japanese themselves. Now that Mexico and the United States have completed negotiations to establish a North American Free Trade Area (NAFTA) that includes Canada as well, the Japanese are worried. They do not want to be left out of their most important market and the preferred location for their manufacturing and financial investments.

If the Japanese are accommodated rather than excluded after the NAFTA agreement is ratified by the legislatures of the three countries, we might be on the threshold of a third period in the evolving economic relations between Mexico and Japan that would not be the subject of apprehension and criticism in the United States. A trilateral relationship of this sort is what Mexico wants. This Mexican foreign policy objective coincides with Japan's, but there are powerful interest groups in the United States that would like to prevent this course of events. There is no certainty that Mexico's aspiration toward trilateralism will succeed, since its strategy hinges on smooth relations between the US and Japanese governments. The novelty here is Mexico's active role to try to bring about the success of the trilateral model.

HISTORICAL BACKGROUND

Although Japan and the kingdom of New Spain had some trade relations as early as the sixteenth century, the roots of contemporary bilateral relations can be traced to the last decades of the nineteenth century.[1] Two prominent public figures of the newly-independent Mexican nation played an important role in the exploration of economic opportunities for Mexico in the Far East. Historians have reported that Minister of the Economy Lucas Alamán sought to open a trade route linking Tokyo with Acapulco and Mexico City. Further, the astronomer Francisco Díaz Covarrubias is credited with preparing the groundwork, during a scientific visit to Tokyo in 1874, for the negotiations that led to the Treaty of Friendship, Commerce, and Navigation signed in 1888 and the opening of diplomatic offices three years later in the capital cities of the two countries.[2]

There were extensive contacts with Japanese cultural organizations and business interests during the prolonged administration of Mexican dictator, General Porfirio Díaz, from 1876 to 1911. In particular, the first contracts to promote the immigration of Japanese workers for Mexican agriculture in the state of Chiapas were signed by the Díaz government in 1897. The fate of this first group of Japanese migrants was not a successful one, as they found local infrastructure and the resources needed for production to be wanting. Subsequently, the flow of Japanese immigrants to Mexico dwindled to only a few after the United States banned these migrants from its own territory, and later signed a Gentlemen's Agreement with Japan where the latter restricted this migration voluntarily.[3]

Although Díaz held a generally sympathetic view of Japan, he established a commission to study and help him determine whether Mexico would benefit from immigrant workers who were arriving on Mexico's western coast from China and Japan. The commission's findings were embarrassing, given their discriminatory tone and the main recommendation that came out of the study: to bar aliens "who constitute a negative element, who are from the lower classes and have repugnant habits."[4] Moreover, during these years Chinese settlers in northwest Mexico were the subject of continuous harassment by local populations.[5] It is in this kind of attitude toward foreigners, and not just repeated invasions by foreign powers, that we find the roots of several quite restrictive Mexican immigration laws during the present century.

The Mexican government decided to maintain a neutral stand when Japan went to war with Russia in 1904, although historian Enrique Cortés argues that the Mexican press expressed a discreet but clearly pro-Japanese position through the duration of the conflict.[6] As Mexico itself exploded in revolution in 1910, and subsequently dedicated itself to rebuilding its social and economic systems, contact between the two countries was rather limited. In the three decades that ensued, there were some groups of immigrants that included professionals and farmers who established themselves primarily in Baja California. They planted the cotton fields and developed the local fishing industry that boomed in a later day, with exports surging to the United States. Elsewhere in the country, however, Mexican peasants were the main beneficiaries of agrarian reform programs, with the result that the few Japanese immigrants who had remained in rural areas slowly moved toward urban centers. This process was completed when returnees from concentration camps after World War II opened their own shops in several cities.[7]

Acting in solidarity with the United States, Mexico broke diplomatic relations with Japan in December of 1941 and, when two of its ships were sunk and its demands for compensation went without response, Mexico joined the allied effort and declared war on Japan and the other Axis powers on May 22, 1942. Many Japanese were placed in concentration camps in Baja California, Guadalajara, and Mexico City; they were freed only after global hostilities came to an end in 1945.[8]

Mexico was one of the first countries to ratify the peace treaty with Japan in San Francisco in 1952. Soon after, cultural exchange programs and a Mexican art exhibit in Tokyo were organized.[9] The first prominent Japanese investment in Mexico was the pharmaceutical firm, Laboratorios Takeda, in 1957. Leaders of the two countries exchanged state visits, particularly when their respective capital cities were chosen to host the two Olympic competitions during the decade of the 1960s. After two decades of hard work, both Japan and Mexico wanted to show the world their respective accomplishments in the social and economic arenas. It is ironic that there was a perception at the time that these two emerging industrial countries were at a comparable level of development.

Economics began to take a more prominent position in relations between the two nations when the first large Japanese multinational opened shop in Mexico. The Datsun Motor Company (later Nissan) opened a plant in 1966 in Cuernavaca, 40 miles south of Mexico City, and it was soon followed by some other companies like Panasonic (Matsushita) that were destined to become giants in their field during the 1980s.

TRADE AND INVESTMENT RELATIONS

As Chapter 5 indicates, in the aftermath of World War II Brazil was the Latin American country of greatest interest to Japan. Government-orchestrated emigration flows were one reason, but Japanese businesses also began to play a role in that country. It was imperative for the recovery of the Japanese economy to find profitable markets for

Japanese products as well as raw material inputs. Whereas Brazil offered good business prospects given its natural resources and the size of the domestic market, and it provided a hospitable environment as a result of the local Japanese population, Mexico's sound economic performance and the country's closed borders lured some Japanese investors to try their luck.

The first investments from Japan thus sought to circumvent the protective barriers erected by Mexican authorities, who pursued the industrialization of their country through import substitution. The Mexican government offered a series of incentives and maintained a high level of protection to encourage the domestic production of goods that were previously imported. This included sophisticated industries such as petrochemicals, automobiles, steel, and telecommunications. In return for providing a protected market, the Mexican government expected that foreign companies would not only create jobs and provide capital, but also transfer technology and managerial skills, help to develop local suppliers, and assist in reducing pressure on the balance of payments.

A survey of all Japanese manufacturing facilities in Mexico has found that, before 1970, only 10 Japanese firms were doing business in Mexico.[10] This is consistent with the fact that few Japanese manufacturing firms had ventured to move outside their country at that time. One reason is that the government of Japan, concerned with the availability of foreign exchange, regulated foreign direct investment flows. In 1990, by contrast, Japanese investment world-wide is enormous, equivalent to 72 percent of US direct overseas investment.[11] What explains the phenomenal growth of Japanese foreign direct investment from $1 billion in 1966 to close to $300 billion a quarter-century later?

In the 1970s, the first expansion of Japanese investments abroad resulted from factors such as Japan's own economic success, which drove domestic wage rates to high levels and hurt the competitive position of many Japanese firms; the rising costs of imported raw materials, especially oil; and government incentives for industries with a high energy consumption and those that produced basic materials to expand overseas. A large proportion of these investments went to secure a stable supply of natural resources that Japan generally lacks. Mining, particularly iron and steel, was a priority target of Japanese investment. Within manufacturing, textiles, metal products, and chemicals received a large infusion of Japanese capital. Many of these Japanese companies were of medium size and received significant support from their government to expand overseas. They also had a strong export orientation which, together with the other features just described, made them attractive to the governments of developing countries. By the end of the 1970s, Japanese businesses had assets worth $32 billion world-wide.[12]

Yet the real investment explosion occurred during the 1980s when, as discussed in the Introduction to this volume, Japan accumulated huge annual trade surpluses approaching $100 billion. It is not coincidental that the bulk of these Japanese investments are found in industrialized nations – particularly in the current environment of growing protectionism and widespread resentment of Japan's economic success. Having captured a major share of industrial country markets through exports, the strategy of Japanese businesses to preserve and even expand their access to these markets has been to open production facilities in industrial countries. For example, the United States had received a full one third ($22 billion) of Japanese world-wide investment in manufacturing by 1990.[13]

Given that the assets held by Japanese businesses in the manufacturing sector in Mexico have a comparatively low value, $1.1 billion out of a total stock of $1.7 billion of Japanese direct investment in Mexico through 1990, what is the significance of discussing these investments in the context of the trilateral relationship? To answer this question, we must distinguish between two periods during which the bulk of Japanese capital came to Mexico. The first took place in the midst of the oil boom during the late 1970s and early 1980s. It was focused on a series of government-sponsored projects involving joint ventures with several Japanese multinationals, and it had the objective of gaining a foothold in the domestic market. More recent investments can be explained as a result of Mexico's geographical location and some structural features of the local economy, which have turned Mexico into an important asset for the strategy of Japanese businesses seeking to penetrate the US market.

Investments for the Domestic Market

In 1970, the level of Japanese investment in Mexico was as low as $22 million, with Nissan representing half of this total and 75 percent of investment in manufacturing (Table 6.1). While 36 new Japanese manufacturing plants began operations during the 1970s, total investment from Japan rose only to the modest sum of $152 million by 1978; but this changed rapidly once Japan decided to pursue a deal to turn Mexico into a key supplier of petroleum. A total of $180 million was

Table 6.1 Stock of Japanese investment in Mexico, 1970–90 (million dollars)

	1970		1980		1990	
	Value	%	Value	%	Value	%
Total	22.0	100.0	818	100.0	1,707	100.0
Manufacturing	16.2	74.0	275	33.6	1,001	58.6
Metals	–	–	47	5.7	117	6.9
Chemicals	2.0	9.0	38	4.6	48	2.8
Electronics	1.0	4.5	17	2.1	38	2.2
Textiles	–	–	4	0.5	8	0.5
Transport Equipment	12.0	54.5	132	16.1	699	40.9
Foodstuffs	0.3	1.3	15	1.8	41	2.4
Machinery	0.3	1.3	18	2.2	44	2.6
Other	0.6	3.4	5	0.6	6	0.4
Commerce and Services	5.6	25.4	32	4.1	191	11.2
Resources Development	–	–	510	62.3	514	30.1
Mining	–	–	500	61.1	502	29.4
Agriculture/Forestry	–	–	2	0.2	4	0.2
Fisheries	–	–	8	1.0	8	0.5
Other	0.2	0.1	1	0.1	1	0.1

Sources: Banco de México, *Información Económica* (for 1970) and the Export–Import Bank of Japan (for 1980 and 1990).

added to Japan's capital stock in Mexico in 1979 alone and, more importantly, two large contracts that were the subject of tough negotiations since 1978, involving the Mexican government, Kobe Steel, and a conglomerate of Japanese firms, were signed in 1980.[14]

In accordance with Mexican legislation, which until recently reserved mining activities for firms with majority control by domestic capital, the Mitsubishi Corporation had established a successful precedent by purchasing 49 percent of the stock of a salt-mining company in the state of Baja California in 1972. This firm has been operating successfully to the present date. Over 60 percent of annual output is exported to Japan, where this input satisfies over half of demand in that country; the balance is exported to the United States leaving a handsome profit to both Mitsubishi and the Mexican government. Salt is used as a basic input for the petrochemical industry, especially to manufacture plastics.[15]

Japanese investors hoped that the other two joint ventures would follow in the footsteps of this successful project, but their experience has been marred by a number of problems.[16] The investment in an iron and steel plant/foundry complex responded to the perceived need on the part of the Mexican government to develop a domestic capital goods sector. The latter had been lagging far behind in comparison to other Third World countries at a similar stage of development. In particular, the objective was to develop the capability to supply equipment for other government-owned firms in energy, mining, railroads, and petrochemicals. While in this case the Japanese company provided a minimum amount of capital, it played the key role in supplying engineering services, technology, and specialized equipment and parts.

On the production side, most objectives were accomplished. The project was severely hurt, however, first by the demise of Mexico's state-owned companies, following the prolonged economic austerity that set in with the 1982 debt crisis, and then by delays associated with the devastating earthquake of 1985. Construction of the plant was started with the economy growing at 8 percent annually, but when it was completed in the mid-1980s, the economy was not growing at all. Efforts were made to restructure the plant and adapt it to the new economic reality, but in 1989 the government gave up and has been trying to sell the plant to Japanese investors. The latter have been cautious and, to this date, no deal has materialized.

The second project was specifically designed to supply the massive amounts of pipeline that most analysts anticipated would be needed for the expansion of the state oil monopoly, Petróleos Mexicanos (Pemex). The pipelines would carry petroleum and natural gas through Mexico's distribution system. In this case, the dramatic fall in oil prices both in 1981 and 1985 dealt a devastating blow to the firm that included 15 percent Japanese capital. Inputs for this plant were to be supplied by the other joint venture that produced steel products. In 1989, surprised Japanese managers found one morning that the government had decided to close the plant.

According to an investigation conducted by Wilson Peres, in both these cases changes in domestic and international economic conditions helped to seal the fate of the joint ventures. More importantly, however, Japanese managers complained about poor communication with the government, the lack of continuity in industrial policy, and the decision to build the plants in a region that did not have the urban infrastructure needed for a successful operation.[17]

The Japanese government played an important role in encouraging some of the country's multinationals to pursue these investment projects. The goal was to strengthen economic relations with a producer that had the potential to supply a strategic raw material, oil. Mexico has provided the oil, though not without certain complications. But the experience for some Japanese firms was negative and, as discussed later in this chapter, these firms would join Japanese commercial banks in the late 1980s in complaining about doing business with Mexico.

The Central Role of Oil in Trade Relations

In 1980, during a visit by Prime Minister Masayoshi Ohira to Mexico City, a 10-year oil contract to supply 100,000 barrels per day (bpd) was signed between Pemex and a syndicate of Japanese refineries, banks, and trading companies (MEP). While the deal appeared to be successful, Mexico actually missed an opportunity at a time when Japan was bent on establishing a special relationship. Mexican officials assumed that the financial and technical assistance they had requested for modernizing the steel industry, and for an ambitious port development program, would be provided. The Japanese expected in return a Mexican commitment to increase oil export sales three-fold (up to 300,000 bpd), but Ohira returned to Tokyo empty-handed.

One reason was that the peak of Mexico's oil output was reached only in 1982, when a larger volume of oil became available for export. More importantly, Mexico had in place an oil policy that emphasized a diversified profile of national customers, which sought to prevent what was viewed as a dangerous overdependence on one market for its foreign sales. The main target of this policy was the United States, a market to which no more than 50 percent of total exports were to be sold. But the Mexican government refused to consider reallocating deliveries to many smaller clients to satisfy Japan's request for more oil. Mexico paid the price since it did not receive the loan it sought till several years later.[18]

Partial increases in the petroleum deliveries Japan had expected were negotiated in 1983 (up to 160,000 bpd), and again in 1986 (180,000 bpd). This was accomplished in connection with a large loan of $1 billion extended by the Japanese Export–Import Bank (JEXIM) and the Overseas Economic Cooperation Fund (OECF) in 1986. Half of these monies were used for expanding Mexico's oil export facilities on the Pacific coast (Port of Salina Cruz, in Oaxaca state), together with an investment of $250 million by Pemex. A pipeline to carry oil from the Gulf of Mexico's wealthy oil zone to the Pacific was constructed, and off-shore storage tanks and inland caverns were built, while a refinery was expanded. The project was completed in 1991. An additional $250 million were lent for the steel industry, and a similar amount of money was lent for Japanese trading companies to help Mexican non-oil exports gain access to international markets.

Not surprisingly, oil has been at the core of Mexico's trade with Japan for over a decade. Japanese sources report higher trade figures than Mexico does, allegedly because some trade is diverted or "triangulated" through the United States. Table 6.2, which is based on Mexican sources, shows the growth of Mexico's exports and imports, as well as trade relations with Japan and the United States over the last two decades. In 1970, trade with Japan represented 4.6 percent of the sum of Mexico's total exports and imports. Mexico sent to Japan primarily raw materials (cotton, salt, and precious stones), and food-stuffs (shrimp and coffee). It purchased from Japan mostly manufac-tured goods (autoparts, large transformers, and other machinery).[19]

The share represented by Japan in Mexico's total trade rose only slightly to 5.2 percent in 1989. Through much of the 1980s, close to half of this total trade was accounted for by Mexican oil exports ranging from $1 to $1.5 billion annually. The sectoral composition of trade in

Table 6.2 Mexico's trade with Japan and the United States, 1970–90 (million dollars)

Year	Total exports*	Exports to US*	Exports to Japan	Total imports*	Imports from US*	Imports from Japan
1970	1,281	876	82	2,327	1,431	86
1976	3,655	1,873	103	6,300	3,370	307
1979	8,555	5,902	239	11,997	7,570	779
1980	15,570	10,072	671	18,533	10,890	899
1986	16,237	11,163	1,065	12,320	8,272	771
1990**	20,260	13,450	1,887	24,900	16,300	1,938

* Figures exclude trade of *maguiladoras*; for 1990, inclusion of *maguiladora* trade would increase Mexican exports by about $10 billion and imports by $8 billion (all to the United States).
** Estimates.
Sources: SECOFI, *México en el Comercio Internacional*, 1990; International Monetary Fund, *Direction of Trade Statistics*, various issues.

the late 1980s, however, experienced some change. The Japan External Trade Organization (JETRO) reports that the share of manufactures in total Japanese imports from Mexico doubled, from 10 percent in 1986 to 20 percent in 1989. At the same time, Mexican imports of Japanese electronics are now twice as large as imports for the automobile industry.[20]

Overall, however, even though Japan is Mexico's second largest trading partner, trade is not an area that has particularly strengthened Mexico's economic relations with Japan. Table 6.2 indicates that in 1990 the sum of exports to and imports from Japan represented only $3.8 billion, 13 percent of Mexico's trade with the United States ($30 billion). The proportion is even lower if we take into account the *maquiladora* sector, whose trade operations are reported separately by the Mexican authorities. In 1990, total trade with the United States, including the *maquiladoras*, reached $48 billion. At the same time, it is noteworthy that Japanese-owned companies are a leading participant within this sector of the Mexican economy, which is bent on exporting to the US market.

Investment for the International Market

Although the Mexican economy suffered a severe and prolonged depression beginning in mid-1982, a full half of the 179 Japanese manufacturing plants doing business in Mexico in 1990 started their operations during the 1980s. Close to 60 of the 70 existing *maquiladora* plants were established during this period.[21]

Several factors account for the more than three-fold increase during the last decade of Japanese manufacturing investment in Mexico as reported in Table 6.1. Some factors are related to the strategy that Japanese firms such as Nissan, which were already established in Mexico, have followed to survive the contraction of the domestic market. Others, such as Sanyo in electronics and Yasaki in the auto sector, are associated with the globalization strategy of Japanese firms that went to Mexico to support their broader operations within the North American market.

As far as Nissan is concerned, it went to Mexico initially in the mid-1960s to gain market share and to earn the high profits guaranteed by strong protectionism. In return, it provided what Mexican authorities expected (technology and managerial skills), and it helped to create a powerful local network of suppliers. When the domestic crisis set in in the 1980s, Nissan expanded its capital assets significantly, to about $600 million in 1990.

Nissan's strategy has paid off handsomely. Beginning in 1988, it became the single largest automobile producer and the top-selling auto firm in Mexico as well as a key exporter–surpassing the "big three" from the United States and even the popular Volkswagen. It is interesting to note, however, that while Nissan was one of many firms contributing to the success of Mexico's auto industry, unlike other auto firms it does not own *maquiladora* plants. Mexico's success in the auto industry is also in no small measure the result of an industrial policy that pressured all foreign firms to become internationally competitive since the late 1960s. Mexico's exports of auto parts, engines, and automobiles totalled only $132 million in 1976; they then grew at high rates to exceed $3 billion in 1989. Most of these exports are sold in the United States.[22]

Already in 1981, Japanese auto producers had captured such a large share of the US market that they were pressured by the US government to accept voluntary quotas on their exports to the United States. The Japanese response was to begin to invest directly in the United States. With the advent of massive Japanese production of automobiles in the United States, Mexico has emerged as an ideal site for production of parts and components as well as finished automobiles. Thus, for example, Honda owns a plant in the state of Jalisco that produces motorcycles and some auto parts; it may become an auto plant in the future. Opened in the mid-1980s through an initial $41 million investment, this plant has been exporting goods worth $100 million annually.[23]

Nissan's success in Mexico led the firm to announce in 1990 a dramatic expansion for the next 5 years, worth an additional $1 billion, in order to strengthen its new international orientation. While the older plant in Cuernavaca mostly produces low-priced vehicles for the Mexican and Latin American markets, the newer plant in Aguascalientes will produce more expensive and technologically complex automobiles and auto parts to be sold in the United States and even Japan, thus strengthening Mexico's position within the increasingly sophisticated world auto market.[24]

Although import substitution in Mexico and the recent restructuring of some older plants toward export have proved appealing to Japanese investors, they do not weigh as heavily in their decisions as either Mexico's proximity to the United States or its low labor and other production costs. Particularly within the *maquiladora* sector, lower wages associated with Mexico's economic crisis, a stronger Japanese yen resulting from that country's spectacular economic boom, and sustained US demand for imported goods are the principal factors that drove Japanese investment in this sector of the Mexican economy in the 1980s. The *maquiladora* program allows plants to import raw materials, components, and capital equipment into Mexico duty-free. Assembled products exported back to the United States are subject only to duties on value added (i.e., Mexican labor, inputs, and services provided in Mexico).

The Japanese joined investors from the United States, Mexico, and a few other nations to take advantage of these conditions. While in 1980 the *maquiladora* sector employed about 120,000 workers and registered a value added of $886 million, by 1991 over 500,000 workers generated close to $3.5 billion in value added.[25] Indeed, for this type of investment the United States has replaced the Mexican market as the chief target for Japanese producers expanding their business in Mexico. These Japanese *maquiladora* plants have maintained their independence from other plants set up by the same parent company to meet the needs of the Mexican market. Rather, their decisions are closely coordinated with those of Japanese-owned firms in the United States–just as American affiliates that operate facilities in Mexico receive directives from their parent companies across the border. Yet, the Japanese are highly visible because their plants are heavily concentrated in the electronics (56 percent) and auto (24 percent) industries, and because their success in gaining a larger share of the US market has occurred at the expense of US producers through exports and new investment.[26]

In a recent study, a Japanese analyst contends that beyond the factors already mentioned, the long-term dynamic of international competition, especially competition between the United States and Japan, has been the driving force for the aggressive growth of Japanese *maquiladoras*. He argues that exports from this sector are no longer limited to labor-intensive products. The production of goods that require more sophisticated technology is evident in several products, such as color television sets.[27] Mexico has become the largest supplier of parts and complete color television sets to the United States.

In addition to huge plants owned by the United States' Zenith, France's Thomson, and Holland's Philips, many Japanese producers (especially Sanyo and Matsushita) export their products to the United States. Sanyo has six and Matsushita has two large plants based in Tijuana, across the border from San Diego. Sony owns twin plants in these two border cities. And Toshiba operates a plant in Ciudad Juárez, across the border from El Paso, which relocated there from Singapore.

Certain groups in the United States complain about the failure of Japanese firms to establish linkages in the US and Mexican economies, especially since their output is sold in the US market. In particular, organized labor and some manufacturers in the United States, who fear being displaced by Japanese firms based in Mexico, favor restrictions on the latter's activities. In all fairness, with regard to their purchasing patterns within Mexico, the problem is not limited to the Japanese; none of the *maquiladoras* buy on average more than 3 percent of their inputs within Mexico. Nonetheless, the complaints by US groups are focused on the large volume of imports from East Asia that the Japanese firms make rather than buying from US-based suppliers. It is also noteworthy that some of the Japanese plants have become so profitable and have come to dominate the market in such an overwhelming manner that they can afford to use non-US components and parts in their products, even if this bars them from special US tariff allowances. While it is difficult to imagine the circumstances under which either the US or Mexican governments would pursue a policy that specifically discriminates against the Japanese, this issue is discussed in the concluding section of the chapter.

FINANCIAL RELATIONS

Oil was also a key factor accounting for the expansion of the business activities of Japanese commercial banks in Mexico. Even before Mexico's oil boom started, these banks were eager to lend in order to recycle petro-dollars, similar to the activities of their counterparts in other industrial countries. Moreover, through the state oil company (Pemex), the government of Mexico itself used oil as a guarantee for a good share of the borrowing spree in which it engaged during the late 1970s and early 1980s. The problem for the banks was that the worst possible scenario materialized: interest rates rose sharply while oil prices collapsed. Consequently, Mexico announced in August 1982 that it would not be able to meet its debt payments, which was a precursor of the devastating crisis that would afflict an overwhelming majority of developing countries during the rest of the decade.

News of Mexico's inability to continue servicing its foreign debt sent shock waves through Tokyo–and world–financial markets. The exposure of Japanese commercial banks in Mexico was quite high; short and long-term loans totalled $27 billion (Table 6.3). About a

Table 6.3   Japanese loans to Mexico, 1982–91 (million dollars)

Year	Commercial bank claims (short and long-term)		
	Public sector	Private sector	Total
1982	8,103	19,107	27,210
1985	10,704	16,719	27,423
1988*	15,312	7,028	22,340
1990	13,410	5,483	18,893

* As of 1988, reductions in principal owed are the result of debt restructuring under the Brady Plan, and the Mexican Government's FICORCA program.

Year	Government loans*
1986	1,100
1988	300
1989	2,050
1991	1,000

* Export–Import Bank of Japan and OECF.
Source: Mexico, Ministry of Finance.

third of these loans had been extended to the public sector and the balance to private business through 1982.[28]

After the debt crisis began, Japanese banks responded to pressures from Washington to help debtor countries weather the crisis. The US government expected that Japan would fulfill its growing international responsibilities as a major economic power. In Mexico's case, a substantial rescue effort was put in place in 1986 in association with the Baker Plan, leading to "new money" by banks from industrial countries including the Japanese.[29] But by the end of the decade, Japanese banks had joined their US counterparts in reducing their exposure. They purchased principal-reduction bonds sold by the Mexican government in the context of the Brady Plan, and they began to sell Mexican debt in the secondary market. Table 6.3 shows that by 1990 their loans to Mexico had been reduced to $18.9 billion, with the public sector now accounting for two thirds of this total.[30]

Private business's foreign debt was lowered significantly through a support program (FICORCA) offered by the Mexican government.

Japanese commercial banks, unlike most manufacturers and trading companies that waited for a turn-around in the local economy's performance, became bitterly disenchanted with their experience in Mexico. Several banks closed their offices and others scaled back their operations. More important from Mexico's perspective is the obtrusive role that some of these banks are playing in advising potential new investors from Japan to go elsewhere. Interestingly, since many of these investors also seek the advice of Japanese trading companies, many of which have been operating in Mexico for the last three decades, these two important actors within the Japanese business community are pitted against one another.

The assessment of the trading companies is that risks in Mexico are not as high as a decade ago as a result of the sustained effort to turn around the fortunes of the domestic economy. The basis for a shock program was laid under President Miguel de la Madrid, and subsequently carried out by his successor Carlos Salinas de Gortari. Trade liberalization, the privatization of banks and most public enterprises, an ambitious tax reform, and across-the-board government deregulation measures restored economic growth to a healthy 4 percent annual rate in the early 1990s – although the social costs of this program have been staggering.

Just as the commercial banks became cautious, the Japanese government filled the gap and became a key source of new loans to Mexico. First, there was a loan of an undetermined amount to help with reconstruction following the 1985 earthquakes in Mexico. This was followed by the $1 billion loan package in 1986 for oil, steel, and export promotion projects that were already discussed, and by an additional Eximbank loan of $300 million in 1988 for the national telephone company, Telmex, which has since been privatized. Many more loans were also to come.

Carlos Salinas and Prime Minister Sosuke Uno met in Paris on the occasion of the bicentennial celebration of the French Revolution. Later in the year Salinas hosted Uno's successor, Toshiki Kaifu, and subsequently he visited Tokyo in June 1990. It is noteworthy that the government leaders of these two nations met, during the course of one year, as many times as their predecessors had met in the previous 10 years.

Kaifu agreed to disburse a $1.4 billion loan ahead of time to bolster Mexico's foreign debt renegotiation strategy. These monies were part of a $2 billion package comitted by Japanese officials through 1992, along with financial assistance extended by the US government, the World Bank, and the International Monetary Fund (IMF) worth a total $7 billion. Mexico had been made the test case of the Brady Plan. Moreover, an additional loan of close to $1 billion was negotiated to fund an ambitious program to clean up air and water pollution in the Mexico City metropolitan area. This amount represents a full 25 percent of the environment-related loans that Japan will make available to developing countries over the next few years.[31]

On the occasion of these meetings, Mexican officials agreed on their side to renew the oil contract for an additional period of 5 years, though deliveries will no longer be through the MEP in order to encourage Mexico to offer more competitive prices to interested Japanese buyers. Salinas also promised to be attentive to the proposals of trading companies like Mitsui, which want to establish petrochemical facilities in Mexico.[32] The importance and timeliness of the Japanese government loans cannot be overemphasized. The economic rebound has been possible to an important degree thanks to the successful debt restructuring package put together by Finance Minister Pedro Aspe, with the initial strong support received from Japan. And Salinas' popular measures to enhance the quality of the environment in Mexico City, such as closing an old refinery, helped his party to bounce back from an embarrassing defeat at the polls in 1988 in the capital city, winning first place during the 1991 mid-term federal elections. In the public's mind, actual loan disbursements by the Japanese have been quite significant compared to US government's refusal to do more than provide loan guarantees.

PROSPECTS FOR THE 1990s

The United States government has been content with Japan providing resources to help Mexico get back on its feet, as long as US economic interests are not affected. In this regard, the single most contentious issue in the trilateral relationship involves Japanese ownership of *maquiladora* plants. This is especially important in the context of the free trade negotiations encompassing all of continental North America, a critical region for Japanese economic interests.[33]

Examples of the complaints that are more often heard include the following. For US manufacturers, the Japanese do not provide a comparable access to their market that America offers to Japanese affiliates within Mexico's *maquiladora* sector. For organized labor, the effect of increased exports from Mexico is to expand the US trade deficit, a problem that is growing worse because Japanese *maquiladoras* import a large proportion of parts and components from East Asia instead of purchasing them in the United States. The question is whether pressures from some interest groups in the United States might conceivably result in unilateral decisions to restrict Japanese investment in the United States, Mexico, or both. In theory, as discussed in the Introduction to this volume, such an outcome might result if one of the scenarios stressing conflict between the US and Japanese governments were to materialize. But such a course of action would constitute a self-inflicted wound for the United States.

For one thing, the interdependence of the Japanese and US economies, the two largest economies in the world, has increased substantially. The United States would face hard times if Japanese direct investment, which averaged $17 billion each year from 1988 to 1990, or Japanese purchases of US securities in much higher figures, came to a halt. For Japan these investments in North America, which grew from $11 billion in 1982 to $76 billion in 1989, are a priority.[34] In addition, the combined markets of continental North America account on average for 38 percent of Japan's exports and 28 percent of its imports every year.

Moreover, by depriving Mexico of a key source of capital, the United States would be working at cross-purposes. Under conditions prevailing through the years of economic austerity, Mexico has had no incentive or even the power to place restrictions on foreign investment because the latter has been critical to help restore growth. It is in Mexico's interest, however, to coordinate its efforts with the United States (and Canada) in certain cases in order to enhance its negotiating position with Japan. For example, Mexico is in principle as interested as the United States in increasing purchases of local inputs by foreign firms, setting export diversification goals so that Japanese firms raise the volume of sales to Japan itself, defining common standards regarding rules of origin for providing tariff exemptions within regional markets, and enhancing access to the relatively closed Japanese market for many of their products. The North American Free Trade Area (NAFTA) might provide the institutional framework needed to discuss these common concerns and to implement a strategy toward firms from third countries that benefit, to this date with few restrictions, from the factors of production found within the North American economy.[35]

Although the effects of the NAFTA cannot be known precisely until the agreement is ratified and implemented, some general comments are possible. The three participating countries share the goal of attracting investment on a massive scale to North America, which would take advantage of economies of scale. They also want to attract quality investment in cutting-edge industries, rationalize production within individual sectors, and boost productivity. As regards the *maquiladora* sector, its status would necessarily change over time. Special provisions regulating this program will have to be phased out eventually, as free trade will be extended to cover the regional economy in full. Any changes deemed necessary by any of these parties would no longer be considered part of the domestic debate within each country alone. Rather, they would become the subject of legitimate discussions among the three nations within a larger framework for consultation and policy coordination.

This is the approach that Mexico would like the United States to share. With Western Europe's attention focused on the political and economic transformations within Russia and Central Europe, the importance of Japan in the eyes of Mexican leaders has greatly increased. At the same time, because Japan and the United States are economic rivals in the world arena, Mexican leaders know that they must develop a strategy to deal effectively with two partners they do not want to alienate. Moreover, the existing record indicates that Japan will become more responsive if and when it faces a united North America. The latter will be a formidable partner in negotiations on tough economic issues such as those discussed here.

At the core of Mexico's international strategy is the realization that its emergence as an industrial nation requires it to pursue two paths simultaneously: full economic integration with the United States and Canada and expanded ties with Japan. The NAFTA will turn Mexico into a much more attractive investment site and lead to expanded trade relations. Most important, Mexico will gain the leverage necessary to negotiate more forcefully with Japan. This assumes a scenario of cooperation between the US and Japanese governments. Should the tensions between the United States and Japan escalate, Mexico will face a no-win situation. Japan is a key source of financial resources that Mexico cannot afford to alienate. Neither can Mexico turn and look the other way if the United States demands unqualified support in the event of a showdown with Japan. This is a dilemma that Mexican leaders would rather not face, since it would deal a devastating blow to their country's current international strategy. Mexico wants a strengthened relationship with the United States within a North American framework, but it also needs space to pursue a healthy degree of diversified economic relations with the rest of the world—especially a trilateral relationship that includes Japan.[36]

Notes

1. Mexico, Secretaría de Relaciones Exteriores, *México y Japón en el siglo XIX: la política exterior de México y la consolidación de la soberanía japonesa* (Mexico City: 1976).

2. Mutsuo Yamada, "Perfil histórico: visión retrospectiva, alcances y perspectivas de las relaciones entre México y Japón," in Omar Martínez Legorreta and Akio Hosono, (eds.), *Relaciones México–Japón: nuevas dimensiones y perspectivas* (Mexico City: El Colegio de México, 1985) pp. 51–84.

3. María Elena Ota, *Siete migraciones japonesas en México, 1890–1978* (Mexico City: El Colegio de México, 1982) pp. 17, 39.

4. Ibid, p. 20.

5. Evelyn Hu-Dehart, "Popular Protest and Nationalism in Sonora," paper presented at the Workshop on Rural Revolts in Mexico, Center for US–Mexican Studies, University of California, San Diego, 1987.

6. Enrique Cortés, *Relaciones entre México y Japón durante el Porfiriato* (Mexico City: Secretaría de Relaciones Exteriores, 1980) p. 108.

7. Ota, *Siete migraciones*, pp. 86–89.

8. Ibid, pp. 97–101.

9. Alfredo Romero C., "Perfil histórico: visión retrospectiva, alcances y perspectivas de las relaciones entre México y Japón," in Martínez Legorreta and Hosono, (eds.), *Relaciones México–Japón*, p. 40.

10. Gabriel Székely, (ed.), *Manufacturing across Borders and Oceans: Japan, the United States, and Mexico*, Monograph Series 36 (La Jolla, CA: Center for US–Mexican Studies, University of California, San Diego, 1991) p. 119.

11. JETRO, *1990 JETRO White Paper on Foreign Direct Investment: Summary* (Tokyo: JETRO, 1990) and *Survey of Current Business*, June 1991.

12. JETRO, *1990 JETRO White Paper*.

13. Székely, (ed.), *Manufacturing across Borders*, pp. 116, 118.

14. Miguel Wionczek and Miyokei Shinohara, (eds.), *Las relaciones económicas entre México y Japón: influencia del desarrollo petrolero mexicano* (Mexico City: El Colegio de México, 1982) pp. 70–78.

15. Project on Japanese Investment in Manufacturing in the United States and Mexico, Center for US–Mexican Studies, University of California, San Diego.

16. Wilson Peres, "Japanese Joint Ventures with the Mexican State: The Limits of Forced Cooperation," in Székely (ed.), *Manufacturing across Borders*, pp. 77–92. See also María Amparo Casar and Wilson Peres, *El estado empresario en México: ¿Agotamiento o renovación?* (Mexico City: Siglo XXI, 1988).

17. Peres, "Japanese Joint Ventures," p. 89.

18. For a detailed analysis of this issue, see Gabriel Székely and Donald Wyman, "Japan's Ascendance in US Economic Relations with Mexico," *SAIS Review* 8, 1 (Winter–Spring 1988), pp. 171–88.

19. Wionczek and Shinohara (eds.), *Las relaciones económicas*, pp. 64–65.

20. Toru Yanagihara, "Japanese Perspectives on Expanding Trade and Investment in Mexico," in *Opportunities for Trilateral Cooperation: Mexico, the United States, and Japan* (Washington, D.C: The Citizens Network for Foreign Affairs, 1991), pp. 54–55.

21. Székely, (ed.), *Manufacturing across Borders*, p. xi.

22. United States Department of Commerce, *Foreign Trade Highlights* (Washington, DC: 1989).

23. Drew Winter, "Still Cheap but No Longer Third Rate, Mexico Nears Automotive Bigtime," *WARD'S Auto World*, August 1984, p. 24.

24. Harley Shaiken, *Mexico in the Global Economy: High Technology and Work Organization in Export Industries*, Monograph Series 33 (La Jolla, CA: Center for US–Mexican Studies, University of California, San Diego, 1990); and Harley Shaiken and Harry Browne, "Japanese Work Organization in Mexico," in Székely (ed.), *Manufacturing across Borders*, pp. 25–50.

25. Mexico, Instituto Nacional de Estadística, Geografía e Informática, *Estadísticas sobre la industria maquiladora de exportación* (Mexico City: 1991).

26. Székely (ed.), *Manufacturing across Borders*, p. 122.

27. Akihiro Koido, "The Color Television Industry: Japanese–US Competition and Mexico's Maquiladoras," in Székely (ed.), *Manufacturing across Borders*, pp. 51–76.

28. Frances Rosenbluth and Kim Suehiro, "Japanese Banks in Mexico: The Role of Government in Private Decisions," chapter of a manuscript in progress, prepared for the Project on Japanese Investment in Manufacturing in the United States and Mexico (La Jolla, CA: Center for US–Mexican Studies, University of California, San Diego).

29. Barbara Stallings, "The Reluctant Giant: Japan and the Latin American Debt Crisis," *Journal of Latin American Studies* 22, 1 (February 1990), pp. 1–30.

30. According to the Federal Financial Institutions Examination Council's *Country Exposure Lending Survey*, US long and short-term loans outstanding to Mexico, as of the same date shown in Table 6.3, were only $15.2 billion. This would imply that Japan had surpassed the United States as a creditor to Mexico, but the different sources raise questions about the comparability of the data.

31. Interviews conducted by the author for the Project on Japanese Investment in Manufacturing in the United States and Mexico (La Jolla, CA: Center for US–Mexican Studies, University of California, San Diego) during 1990 and 1991.

32. Interviews with Japanese officials, Mexico City.
33. Gabriel Székely and Oscar Vera, "What Mexico Brings to the Table: Negotiating Free Trade with the United States," *Columbia Journal of World Business*, 26, 2 (Summer 1991).
34. Written communication from Japan's Ministry of Finance.
35. See Richard A. Matthew and K. Lorne Brownsey, (eds.), *Japan's Relations with North America: The New Pacific Interface* (Santa Fé, New Mexico: The North American Institute, 1990).
36. A recent analysis that agrees with many of the points made here is Luis Rubio's "Japan in Mexico: A Changing Pattern," in Susan Kaufman Purcell and Robert M. Immerman, (eds.), *Japan and Latin America in the New Global Order* (Boulder, CO: Lynne Rienner Publishers, 1992).

7 Peruvian–Japanese Relations: The Frustration of Resource Diplomacy

Pablo de la Flor

The surprising election of Alberto Fujimori as President of Peru has brought to public attention the special nature of Peruvian–Japanese relations. Peru was the first Latin American country to establish official contacts with Japan and to receive a large contingent of Japanese immigrants during the early part of this century. Today, the 80,000-strong community of Japanese descendants in Peru is one of the largest in the world.

Although immigration was the only salient feature of Peruvian–Japanese relations until the 1940s, it was displaced by trade, investment, and aid shortly after World War II. In the 1970s, Peru's efforts to diversify its foreign dependency and Japan's aggressive "resource diplomacy," aimed at securing new supplies of minerals and other primary goods, resulted in the strengthening of ties between the two countries. While the 1980s witnessed a reversal of these trends, it seems likely that the 1990s will again see a flourishing of Peruvian–Japanese relations, as Japan assumes a more active role in Latin America and its interest in Peru is boosted by the presence of President Fujimori.

In this chapter, I trace the evolution of Peru's relations with Japan from the ambitious designs of the 1970s to the disappointments of the 1980s.[1] I start with a brief historical account of Japanese immigration, then turn to an analysis of bilateral relations during the last two decades, emphasizing the role of trade, investment, loans, and official aid. I place this discussion within the broader context of Japan's resource diplomacy. I concentrate almost exclusively on economic interactions, since (for reasons explained in Chapter 3) formal "politics" have been noticeably absent from the relationship.

171

JAPANESE IMMIGRATION

The accelerated growth of export agriculture in the coastal areas of Peru during the mid-nineteenth century generated a dramatic increase in the demand for labor and a shortage of agricultural laborers. In order to overcome the resulting problems, the large plantation owners decided to promote the importation of foreign workers, primarily Chinese. In the 1840–73 period, nearly 90,000 "coolies" arrived at the Peruvian plantations, but the harsh working environment and the inhuman conditions of the coolie traffic triggered widespread discontent and uprisings among the new immigrants.[2]

Two of these incidents were instrumental in the establishment of official contacts between Peru and Japan. In January of 1868, the boat *Cayaltí* was taken over by its coolie passengers and forced back to China; 8 months later, the ship reached the port city of Hakodate, and the mutiny case was put in the hands of the Japanese judiciary. In 1872, further complications attended a second Peruvian coolie ship, the *María Luz*, which had stopped in Yokohama in route from Portuguese Macão after boarding 230 Chinese workers. One of the passengers escaped and complained about the ill-treatment given to his countrymen aboard the Peruvian ship. Japanese authorities took action in the matter and, after long and tedious negotiations, submitted the case to the arbitration of the Czar of Russia.[3]

The *María Luz* affair and the growing difficulties of the coolie trade convinced the Peruvian government of the need to establish friendly relations with China and Japan. Thus, in 1873, an official Peruvian envoy, Captain Aurelio García y García, was sent to both countries. His main mission was to secure a treaty that would give the Peruvians the same prerogatives granted by the Japanese to the major European powers. Captain García negotiated a 10-point accord that included a most-favored-nation clause.[4]

The reconstruction of Peru after the war against Chile (1879) and the renewed expansion of plantation agriculture produced another surge in the demand for labor. The closure of the port of Macão had brought an end to the coolie trade, however, thus prompting the local plantation owners to bring Japanese workers. By 1923, close to 18,000 Japanese immigrants had arrived at the Peruvian plantations under the aegis of the Morioka Immigration Company.[5] In the early 1900s, a majority of the immigrants moved to Lima, where they came to own a large number of small commercial establishments.

The rapid concentration of Japanese immigrants in the capital city and their expanding economic prowess produced suspicion and resentment among some segments of the local population. When the recession of the 1930s came around, the immigrants became easy scapegoats for the country's problems and the target of hostile attacks. Through the publication of slanderous and racist articles, several of Peru's main newspapers and magazines – in conjunction with one of the local retailers' associations – fueled the growing anti-Japanese sentiments. The news of Japan's imperialist expansion in the Far East only contributed to heightened local prejudices and fears.

Bowing to pressures from local manufacturers, in 1935 the Peruvian government suspended the Navigation and Commerce Agreement ratified by both countries the previous year, and imposed an informal quota on the import of cotton garments from Japan. More important, fearing that the anti-immigration legislation passed by Brazil and the United States would bring about a sustained upsurge in the arrival of new Japanese immigrants, President Benavides proposed his own restrictive legislation. Although general in its scope, the new law was specially aimed at the Japanese and imposed strict limits on their admission and naturalization. Likewise a cap was imposed on the number of non-Peruvian workers employed in commercial establishments – a particularly strong blow to the small family-operated Japanese businesses.

These anti-Japanese feelings flourished against the backdrop of increasing US–Japanese tensions. During the 1930s, officials in Washington expressed their concern about the expanding trade contacts between Japan and the region, and Japanese officials denounced alleged US efforts to undermine their country's position in the continent. Moreover, the Federal Bureau of Investigation (FBI) posted agents in Lima to keep track of the local Japanese community and gather information on particular Japanese citizens.[6]

The culminating event of this period occurred in May of 1939, when a group of agitators instigated an anti-Japanese riot that resulted in the killing of several immigrants and considerable loss of property. Shortly after the onset of the US–Japanese hostilities in World War II, the Peruvian government broke off relations with Japan, confiscated the property of the immigrants and deported close to 1,800 Japanese and their families to internment camps in the United States. After the end of the hostilities, the Peruvian government refused to re-admit the large majority of the deportees – despite efforts from the Red Cross and pressures from the US government.[7]

Relations between Peru and Japan were normalized in the 1950s, and Peruvian diplomats gave their full support to Japan's admission into the United Nations. President Prado became the first Peruvian president to visit Japan in 1961, and Prince Akihito reciprocated that visit 6 years later. Those gestures notwithstanding, Japanese immigration to Peru had virtually ceased, discouraged by memories of the poor treatment received by the immigrants during the war and the unattractive economic conditions that prevailed in Peru at the time. Nevertheless, the following decade saw the strengthening of commercial contacts between the two countries, as Japan turned toward resource diplomacy and Peru sought to diversify its foreign dependency.

A NEW BEGINNING

In 1968, General Juan Velasco Alvarado's military government launched a nationalistic program of social and economic reforms in Peru. The nationalization of US corporations and the new regime's close ties with Cuba, the Soviet Union and other countries of the Eastern bloc produced a deterioration in relations with the United States. Faced with threats of an American financial and commercial blockade and the need to diversify the country's foreign dependency, the Peruvian government tried to bolster relations with Japan.[8]

Japan, in turn, developed a strong interest in Peru's natural resources during the 1970s. Unlike the United States and some of the other western powers, Japan lacked a rich endowment of fuels and minerals and depended almost exclusively on overseas supplies. Rapid postwar economic recovery increased Japan's imports of raw materials. Thus Japanese reliance on imported copper and iron ore, to cite only two examples, jumped from 74 percent and 92 percent in 1960, to 85 percent and 99 percent in 1970, to 96 percent and 100 percent in 1979. Toward the end of the 1970s, Japan was the world's largest importer of minerals, absorbing close to 75 percent and 40 percent of world exports of copper and iron ore, respectively.[9]

The availability of natural resources in the 1960s had sheltered Japan from its resource dependency. The oil shock of 1973 and the US soybean embargo, however, demonstrated the extreme vulnerability of the Japanese economy, and produced an almost obsessive concern with resource security.[10] Those traumatic events triggered efforts to diversify and develop new supply sources, which would provide safe and stable flows of the needed primary goods at reasonable prices. To that end, the Japanese government and private-sector firms arranged inexpensive loans and technical assistance programs to expand the supply of natural resources abroad. The Japanese firms used this leverage to obtain long-term purchasing agreements; a less preferred strategy was Japanese direct investment.

As part of this resource diplomacy, Japanese government officials began exploring the possibility of holding regular governmental talks with nations that possessed natural resources.[11] Although this initiative did not crystalize in the signing of specific agreements, it did lead to the enhancement of economic relations with resource-producing nations. In the case of Peru, the strengthening of relations was helped by Japan's pragmatic foreign policy stance – the well-known separation of economics and politics in the pursuit of national security goals (see Chapter 3 in this volume). The US–Peruvian rift and the military's close ties to Soviet bloc countries did not hinder Japanese interests in Peru. Indeed, the Japanese exhibited a great flexibility in adapting to the new arrangements imposed by Peru's nationalist dictatorship.

After the initial Japanese reservations subsided, contacts between the two countries experienced a dramatic expansion. The presentation of a Peruvian traditional art exhibit at the 1970 Osaka fair was warmly received by the Japanese public, which also contributed generously to aid the victims of an earthquake in Peru that year. Official trade delegations met in Tokyo and Lima, and in 1971 the two countries signed their first mining cooperation agreement. Likewise, a delegation of Japanese financiers and industrialists gathered with President Velasco to discuss the prospects of expanding trade and investments.[12]

TRADE RELATIONS

Trade between Peru and Japan soared during the 1970s, showing a consistently positive balance in favor of Peru (see Table 7.1). This surplus contrasts with the negative balance that has typically characterized US–Peruvian trade. In 1972 Japan became the second largest market for Peruvian exports and the third largest supplier of imports after the United States and Germany. Over the last two decades, Japan has consistently purchased 15–22 percent of Peru's exports and supplied 10–15 percent of its imports.

Peruvian exports to Japan are highly skewed towards minerals, especially iron ore and non-ferrous metals (copper, lead and zinc). Indeed, minerals on average represent close to 80 percent of Peruvian

Table 7.1 Peruvian trade with Japan, 1971–90 (annual averages, million dollars)

	1971–75	1976–80	1981–85	1986–90
Exports	219.9	364.2	474.0	426.4
Foodstuffs	8.7	38.2	27.0	46.9
Raw materials	163.5	179.1	296.0	192.3
Textiles	(2.7)	(5.7)	(12.4)	(13.0)
Metal products	(160.5)	(173.1)	(184.7)	(176.6)
Petroleum	(0)	(0)	(97.4)	(0)
Manufactured goods	47.3	144.8	150.4	186.9
Textiles	(0.2)	(0.9)	(5.2)	(16.1)
Metal products	(45.8)	(143.8)	(144.3)	(169.8)
Others	(0.3)	(0.2)	(0.6)	(1.4)
Re-exports/others	0.3	0.3	0.5	0.3
Imports	134.3	161.5	231.1	142.6
Food/raw materials	9.3	16.5	13.8	5.6
Light industry	11.8	8.7	17.7	11.3
Heavy industry	113.0	135.1	198.3	124.9
Chemicals	(9.8)	(12.7)	(8.1)	(6.7)
Metal products	(41.6)	(50.0)	(41.9)	(23.0)
Machinery	(61.6)	(72.5)	(148.3)	(95.2)
Re-exports	0.1	1.2	1.3	0.8
Balance	+85.7	+202.7	+242.9	+283.8

Source: MITI, *White Paper on International Trade*, various issues.

exports to Japan – almost twice the percentage represented by metals in the country's total exports. Raw material exports to Japan declined, however, from a peak of 83 percent in 1970 to an average of around 40 percent during most of the 1980s. The falling share was captured by the expansion of exports of higher value-added refined copper and zinc. In the 1971–1973 period, Japanese corporations (Nippon Steel, Sumitomo Metal Industries, Nishen Steel Co. and Nippon Kokan) were the most important purchasers of Peruvian iron ore, absorbing close to 70 percent of total sales. Exports of zinc and lead also fueled the growth of trade with Japan in the mid-1970s. Most of those sales were made through long-term contracts.

Although Peruvian exports have tended to represent only a fraction of 1 percent of total Japanese imports, aggregate figures disguise the relative importance of some products. Starting in the 1970s, Peru became Japan's most important supplier of lead, zinc, raw copper, and (until recently) silver bars.[13] Accordingly, Peru played an important role in Japan's efforts to diversify its mineral dependency. Coffee, fish meal, and petroleum in the early 1980s were other primary products with an important but erratic presence in the basket of exports to Japan. In contrast, non-traditional goods have been marginal, accounting for less than 5 percent. The poor handling of the exchange rate policy, the difficulties of gaining access to the Japanese market, and the absence of a substantial and reliable exportable supply account for the failure of manufactured exports.

After reaching a peak in 1981, the value of Peruvian exports to Japan decreased or remained stagnant until 1987, when they experienced a rebound. Prices for Peru's major minerals suffered declining pressures in the first part of the 1980s and have regained their lost value only at the end of the decade. The government's exchange rate policy, the fiscal crisis, and prolonged labor strikes undermined the competitiveness of Peru's mining sector. As a result, Peru lost part of its share of the Japanese market to other competitors in the region (Chile) and elsewhere (Australia and the Philippines).

Capital goods make up the largest share of imports from Japan, followed by intermediate inputs. Their evolution, however, has been heavily influenced by tariffs, exchange rate policy, and non-tariff restrictions. In the 1971–74 period, the availability of hard currency facilitated the expansion of imports, while strict protectionist measures for consumer-goods industries produced a tilt in favor of capital goods. Imports contracted in 1975–78 as a result of the foreign exchange crisis, but expanded again with the resumption of economic growth and trade liberalization in 1979–81. The debt crisis of the early 1980s triggered a general reduction of imports. Although President Alan García's populist policies led to an expansion of imports in 1985–86, the lack of reserves and high tariffs triggered another contraction in 1987–90.

INVESTMENT

Japanese investments in Peru (total stock of $693 million at year-end 1990) rank fourth in Japan's total for Latin America. In terms of its importance for Peru, Japan remained in eighth place during the early 1970s, climbing to fourth place towards the end of the decade and staying there for most of the 1980s.[14] As can be seen in Table 7.2, the largest share of Japanese investment in Peru is concentrated in the

Table 7.2   Japanese direct investment in Peru by sectors, 1951–90 (thousand dollars)

	1951–80		1981–85		1986–90		1951–90	
	Cases	Amount	Cases	Amount	Cases	Amount	Cases	Amount
Industry	24	22,038	2	7,291	0	0	26	29,329
Food	6	9,359	1	436	0	0	7	9,795
Textiles	2	440	0	0	0	0	2	440
Chemicals	6	671	0	0	0	0	6	671
Metals	2	582	0	0	0	0	2	582
Electricity	2	3,143	1	724	0	0	3	3,867
Transportation equip.	6	7,841	0	6,131	0	0	6	13,972
Agriculture	1	4	0	0	0	0	1	4
Fishing	12	16,421	1	1,092	0	698	13	18,211
Mining	21	408,999	9	190,736	0	0	30	599,735
Construction	2	26,320	0	0	0	0	2	26,320
Commerce	5	1,349	3	1,210	0	0	8	2,559
Finance/insurance	1	3	0	2	0	0	3	5
Others	5	10,054	0	0	0	0	5	10,054
Subsidiaries	5	3,239	0	5,242	0	0	5	8,481
Property	5	1,600	0	0	0	0	5	1,600
Total	81	487,171	15	205,573	0	698	96	692,744

Source: Japanese Ministry of Finance.

mining sector ($600 million), which accounts for 25 percent of Japan's mining investment in Latin America.[15]

Japan's resource diplomacy placed little weight on asset ownership, since stable supplies at low costs could be secured through other means, such as the provision of funding for the development of mineral deposits and the subscription of long-term contracts with suppliers. The maintenance of a thin ownership position in foreign mines had the added advantage of sheltering the Japanese from the growing Third World resource nationalism of the 1970s.

Copper, however, was an exception to that tendency. Unlike other minerals whose prices are tightly linked to purchaser–seller negotiations, copper prices are influenced more heavily by market forces as manifested in the quotations posted at the London Metal Exchange. Thus the signing of long-term contracts did not secure lower purchasing prices for copper.[16] Accordingly, the Japanese developed from early on a special interest in establishing asset positions in overseas copper mines so as to minimize the negative effects of upward price swings. Japanese investment in Peru's medium-sized mines was meant to test the waters for a heavier involvement in the large-scale copper mining sector.

In 1973 Mitsui signed its first investment agreement ($4.6 million) with the Peruvian government. The Katanga mine was a wholly-owned subsidiary of Mitsui Mining and Smelting and Nippon Mining. All of its ouput was shipped to the Hebi and Tamano copper smelters in Japan.[17] The Santa Luisa poli-metallic mine is the most important Japanese investment in Peru and the fourth largest producer of zinc and lead in the country. Feasibility studies to gauge the productive potential of the deposits started in 1975. Santa Luisa is owned by a consortium of Mitsui and Nippon Mining, and all of its output is sold to the former's home company for smelting and refining.[18] The smaller Huanzala (copper), Condestable (copper), and Gran Bretaña (zinc and manganese) mines were abandoned or transferred to Peruvian interests during the late 1970s and early 1980s.

The Michiquillay project was the single most ambitious Japanese attempt to invest in large-scale copper mining. Asarco, a US corporation that had control of the deposit, lost its rights in 1973. That year a mission sponsored by the Japan Metal Mining Corporation (JMMC) conducted a feasibility study that proved a high volume of reserves. As a consequence, Mitsui Mining and Smelting, Nippon Mining, Mitsubishi Metal Corporation, Furukawa Corporation, Sumitomo Metal, and Dowa Mining formed the Michiquillay Copper Corporation (MCC) to negotiate a joint venture with Peruvian authorities.[19] In 1977, MCC presented a list of financing alternatives and proposed the creation of a special mining enterprise. It demanded a relaxation of capital remittance restrictions, lower taxes, flexibility in the use of foreign exchange, and freedom to sell the output of the mine. MCC also asked to be exempted from the "labor community" regulations, which required companies to share ownership with their workers. The Peruvian government refused to accept MCC's demands but could not find any willing bidders for the $1 billion project.[20]

Japanese participation in Peruvian mining has been negatively affected by a poor understanding of local regulations and practices.[21] Labor disputes at Japanese facilities are among the worst in the industry and facilities at the mines are regarded as inadequate. Until recently, there were few Peruvians in higher managerial positions – a situation that changed in the late 1980s when Japanese firms started evacuating their home personnel for fear of terrorist attacks. More importantly, with the exception of Santa Luisa, the contribution of

Japanese investment to the dissemination of modern mining technology in Peru has been negligible. Overall, the Japanese mining firms have promoted the sale of equipment from home companies to a larger extent than their US counterparts.[22]

Japan's efforts to diversify its heavy dependence on Middle Eastern petroleum also contributed to the strengthening of its interest in Peru. Not only did the Japanese try to secure long-term oil purchasing agreements through the usual provision of soft loans, but they engaged in prospecting activities. Thus in 1973, a consortium of Japanese firms created the Andes Petroleum Co. to explore the promising Madre de Dios fields.[23] Andes abandoned its operations three years later, after investing $32 million in dry wells.

In the 1980s the abundance of natural resources at low prices lessened the need for an active Japanese resource diplomacy. Furthermore, Japanese firms gave greater priority to the development of extractive activities closer to home (Australia and the Philippines), where transportation costs were lower and they could benefit from a better knowledge of local conditions. The Peruvian government's adverse treatment of foreign capital and the threat of terrorism also contributed to the downturn of Japanese investment in the country. Accordingly, in the 1980–90 period, new Japanese investment amounted to only $207 million (15 cases); 90 percent of it was concentrated in mining (see Table 7.2).

Investment in the automotive industry was significant during the early 1970s, as Nissan and Toyota positioned themselves to take advantage of the expanded market opportunities offered by the Andean Pact and the closed Peruvian market. But the failure of the integration efforts, deteriorating domestic demand, exchange rate risks, and high operating costs brought the whole industry to the verge of collapse in the 1980s.

FINANCIAL RELATIONS

Debt-creating financial flows have played a critical role in Japan's resource diplomacy in Peru. Japanese firms in tandem with government agencies facilitated the development of the Peruvian mining and petroleum sectors through the provision of subsidized financing. These actions assured the Japanese firms direct access to new sources of high-quality minerals and secured long-term purchasing agreements with suppliers. Lending was thus actively manipulated by the Japanese creditors to advance that country's mineral and petroleum procurement strategy.

In 1973, the Japan Petroleum Development Corporation (JPDC) and the Japan–Peru Oil Corporation (JAPECO) – a consortium formed by the trading companies Mitsui, Marubeni, and Mitsubishi – extended a $330 million loan to the government-owned oil company (Petroperú) and the state financial firm (Cofide) for the construction of a 900 km trans-Andean pipeline.[24] The terms of the loan were quite generous, including below market interest rates and maturity periods of 14 years (5 years grace). Had this operation been contracted at prevailing market conditions, the financial costs of the project could have doubled.

As a result of this loan, JPDC and JAPECO obtained a preferential option for the purchase of petroleum and other derivatives, once domestic demand had been met. The agreement explicitly allowed for repayments in oil at international prices. The contract contemplated the supply of 153.3 million barrels (mb) of crude and 102 mb of refined products.[25] In addition, Kawasaki Steel secured a contract to supply steel pipes, and other Japanese companies obtained contracts for the sale of pumps and various key pieces of equipment.

Japanese financing in mining started with the Ilo copper refinery, the first project of Mineroperú, the government mining firm. Peruvian demands for its construction stalled negotiations with the US Southern Peru Copper Corporation (SPCC) for the development of the latter's Cuajone mine. The US company – an integrated producer at home – adamantly refused the request, which would have meant losing part of the profits it made by refining the copper in its North American installations. While pressing their demands, the Peruvian officials secretly started exploring other alternatives for the construction of the refinery. In late 1973, the government accepted Mitsubishi and Furukawa Electric's offer for the supply and installation on a turnkey basis of a $40 million electrolytic templating plant. The offer was backed with a $23 million soft loan from the two parent companies.[26]

This project gave the Japanese corporations access to refined copper, which complemented blister shipments from the Mitsui-owned Huanzala mine and purchases from SPCC. In the latter case, a consortium consisting of Dowa, Furukawa, Mitsubishi, Mitsui, and Sumitomo had obtained long-term contracts for the purchase of blister copper (7 percent of the mine's expected output) in repayment of the Japanese banks' participation in the funding of the Cuajone mine.[27]

Marubeni's $50 million loan in 1983 was the most important Japanese financial commitment for an investment project in mining. Mineroperú used those funds as working capital for the construction of the Cajamarquilla zinc refinery and for the Cerro Verde I copper project. In exchange for this loan, Marubeni obtained commercialization rights in East Asia for copper from Cerro Verde I and zinc from the refinery. Negotiations with the Japanese Export–Import Bank and commercial banks for the $130 million funding of Cerro Verde II (copper) foundered in the early 1980s, when the Peruvian government refused Japanese demands for official loan guarantees. Mitsui and Marubeni were interested in the project but conditioned their collaboration on the prompt repayment of $15 million in arrears from two previous loans (including $7.5 million owed from the Ilo refinery).

The government's iron ore company, Hierroperú, attempted to attract Japanese financing but was unsuccessful. The declining quality of Hierroperú's iron ore and the refined output of its pelletizing plant had caused the parastatal to lose a significant share of the Japanese market to other producers. In order to reverse those trends, Hierroperú drew ambitious modernization plans that it tried without success to sell in Tokyo. The parastatal's offer was to link the full investment program (over $100 million) to Japanese suppliers in exchange for the needed loans.[28]

Japanese financing not only played a pivotal role in securing the procurement of key metals, but it also helped home-country companies gain important sales of equipment. The development of the Peruvian communications and electricity infrastructure offers cases in point. In 1968, Nippon Electric won a tender to construct the country's first earth satellite receiving station. The same company later won another tender to supply the equipment and technology for Entelperú's microwave network. Whereas the supplier provided funding for the first project, the second operation was financed through a $13 million credit line put together by the Export–Import Bank and a consortium of Japanese commercial banks. Both loans were subsidized.

In 1971, the Japanese Electric Power Development Corporation gained a tender to construct a 420Km transmission line to link the cities of Chimbote and Lima. The financial agreement signed that year included, in addition to the line, the construction of two sub-stations and the remodeling of a third one. The Japanese offer was so comprehensive, however, that it triggered the protest of local industrialists who wanted to supply part of the equipment. Japan's

Overseas Economic Cooperation Fund (OECF) extended a concessionary $20 million loan in support of that project.[29]

Peru's difficulties in servicing its debt with Japan preceded the eruption of the Latin American debt crisis. Indeed, as part of the Paris Club negotiations of 1979, the Peruvian government rescheduled the JPDC and JAPECO loans to Petroperú for the construction of the trans-Andean pipeline. The 1983–84 interest and principal payments were also rescheduled, but under more onerous terms (interest rates were increased to 9 percent). In March 1985, the Peruvian government attempted a third rescheduling. That time, JAPECO demanded full interest payment and rescheduled the payment of the principal for another 10 years; JPDC refused to enter a similar agreement. Both loans were contracted in yen and have to be repaid in dollars at the prevailing exchange rate, which has appreciated considerably over the last 15 years. Moreover, the contracts included a penalty clause that raised the interest rates on the unmet obligations to 14.5 percent or 1.5 points above Libor, whichever is higher. As a result, Petroperú's interest and principal arrears have climbed to over $500 million (the original loan was $330 million).

President García's decision to cap interest payments on the country's foreign debt after 1985 hampered ongoing efforts to reach an agreement on Petroperú's debt problem. The Japanese had accepted, in principle, a Peruvian proposal for partial payments in local currency. Negotiations came to a halt in 1987, however, when Peruvian representatives refused to consider penalty charges as part of the debt.[30] According to informed sources, JAPECO has been trying to persuade officials at home to condition new aid disbursements on a satisfactory Peruvian handling of the contentious debt issue.

Peru's outstanding debt with Japan amounts to $969 million ($410.8 million from official sources, $544.4 million from suppliers, and $13.8 million from commercial banks), and arrears add up to $724 million. The Japanese made it clear during the García period that, if Peru wanted to gain access to new funding, it would have to abandon its confrontational attitudes on the debt front and respect outstanding contractual obligations. After Fujimori's election, government authorities in Tokyo expressed a willingness to help the new Peruvian government but insisted that the expansion of financial flows to Peru would be conditioned on the implementation of an adequate economic stabilization program and the regularization of relations with the International Monetary Fund (IMF) and the World Bank. After extending several small loans, Japan agreed in April 1991 to join a "support group" to help finance Peru's arrears to the international financial institutions so as to make the country eligible for new loans.

TECHNICAL ASSISTANCE

In 1970–71, Peru was the most important recipient in Latin America of Japanese Official Development Assistance (ODA); 10 years later, it had dropped to the fourth place in the ranking after Brazil, Bolivia, and Paraguay. Although Japanese economic assistance to Peru continued growing in dollar terms in the 1980s, Peru's share of Japan's total ODA contracted from 0.6 percent to 0.3 percent, removing Peru from the top-twenty list of recipients of aid by 1987–88. Those trends notwithstanding, Japan became the second most important provider of economic aid to Peru, with average disbursements of $20 million in 1981–90 (unofficial figures for 1989 and 1990 are $30 and $35 million respectively). Since 1970, 1,212 members of Japanese technical missions have visited Peru, 534 experts have been assigned to development projects, and some 1,540 Peruvians have gone to Japan on official training fellowships.[31]

Development assistance also played a role in the advancement of Japan's resource diplomacy in Peru. Japanese technical missions have been actively involved in the exploration and mapping of new mineral deposits and the elaboration of feasibility studies. Peru is the country with the largest number of Japanese assistance programs in mining. These are joint operations between the Metal Mining Agency of Japan (which has offices in Lima and Mexico) and the Japan International Cooperation Agency (JICA). The most recent feasibility study at Iscay Cruz was abandoned, however, as a result of guerrilla activities in the highlands of Cajamarca. Although mining still plays a very significant role, JICA's figures indicate an overall decline in this type of assistance with more aid being put into agriculture, housing, and fisheries (see Table 7.3).

THE REVIVAL OF CONTACTS

As mentioned earlier, the election of Alberto Fujimori – the son of Japanese immigrants – as President of Peru in July 1990, opened new possibilities for the enhancement of contacts with Japan. It is interesting to note, in that regard, that Fujimori's ethnic origin and

Table 7.3 Japanese technical assistance to Peru, 1980–88 (thousand dollars)

Sector	1980	1981	1982	1983	1984	1985	1986	1987	1988	Total
Agriculture	0	625	1,088	1,023	1,085	838	2,813	4,021	8,200	19,693
Education	28	505	526	274	0	1,643	1,689	4,805	3,301	12,771
Energy/mining	1,166	1,791	1,101	570	807	1,300	2,561	548	616	10,460
Industry	145	228	695	980	236	756	2,276	1,730	1,525	8,571
Fishing	1,201	927	676	1,650	597	300	231	8,986	4,029	18,597
Health	65	590	435	880	702	840	461	399	116	4,488
Communications	455	1,071	1,709	1,550	483	477	345	449	135	6,674
Construction	0	2,000	2,153	97	0	3,881	6,084	6,471	308	20,994
Others	1,150	896	892	9,730	4,882	3,539	3,521	3,037	4,561	32,208
Total	4,210	8,633	9,275	25,704	8,792	13,575	19,983	30,445	22,790	143,407

Source: JICA-Peru.

relative social and political marginality played a crucial role in attracting the vote of the poorest sectors of Peruvian society against the center-right coalition headed by novelist Mario Vargas Llosa.

Since his appearance on the political scene, Fujimori has suggested that his Japanese ascendency would assure Peru special treatment from Tokyo. Mindful of the problems that their high profile brought about in the 1930s, however, the local *nikkei* community – and the Japanese embassy – initially sought to distance themselves from Fujimori's candidacy. After the election, however, several Peruvians of Japanese origin occupied key positions in the new administration (including cabinet posts), and the Japanese ambassador became one of the most public figures in the diplomatic circuit.

Fujimori's victory generated a warm response among the Japanese public, but it presented some difficulties for the Tokyo government. The election of the first citizen of Japanese descent to the presidency of a country was an important source of pride for the Japanese population; hence the support, echoed in the Diet and the Ministry of Foreign Affairs, for the provision of special assistance to Peru. Government officials, however, especially in MITI and the Ministry of Finance, wanted to avoid the international image problem that might result if they appeared to grant preferential treatment to a fellow Japanese. This explains the mixed signals received by Fujimori during his two trips to Japan.

Finally, the Tokyo government decided that it would extend special support to Peru but only to the extent that the new president applied an adequate set of economic policies and abandoned the disruptive rhetoric of his predecessor, Alan García, on the debt front. President Fujimori – who soon after taking office started implementing the harshest economic adjustment program in the country's history – received a $60 million balance-of-payments grant, the first of its type extended by Japan to a Latin American government. Likewise, Tokyo sent a delegation of aid officials, headed by ex-Foreign Minister and development expert Saburo Okita, to explore prospects for an enhanced aid program.

Nontheless, the trend toward improved Peruvian–Japanese relations has not been easy. In 1990, the terrorist group Sendero Luminoso, in its efforts to undermine the new government, launched a campaign of violence against Peruvian *nikkeis*, the Japanese embassy and Japanese assistance projects, killing two Japanese citizens in one of its attacks. The Japanese embassy recalled its remaining aid personnel, but assured the Peruvians that it would continue with its assistance program.

President Fujimori's usurpation of dictatorial powers in April 1992 further troubled relations. Although Japan was more sympathetic than the United States to the problems leading to the suspension of the constitution and dissolving of congress, the government in Tokyo realized that Fujimori faced major international opposition to his moves. Therefore, it pushed him toward restoration of democracy through advice from its ambassador and a trip to Lima by a high official of the Ministry of Foreign Affairs, who carried a letter from Prime Minister Miyazawa. The Japanese thus take some credit for Fujimori's decision to attend a meeting of the Organization of American States to present a calendar for restoring democratic procedures.[32]

CONCLUSIONS AND IMPLICATIONS

During the 1970s, concerns about the vulnerabilities implicit in its position as a heavy importer of minerals and other primary goods moved Japan to expand its base of suppliers in order to minimize the risks of disruptions in the inflow of imports. Peru, with its rich endowment of minerals and promising oil fields, offered interesting opportunities to the Japanese. At the same time, Japan could provide the capital goods and financial resources needed to sustain Peru's ambitious industrialization program. Furthermore, it offered the opportunity to diversify Peru's foreign dependency, one of the government's top priorities during most of that decade.

Japan's resource diplomacy, its procurement strategy for the provision of primary goods, relied on a multi-pronged approach in the Peruvian case. One of its components was to build up stable relationships with producers through the signing of long-term contracts that guaranteed lower purchasing prices. Second, the Japanese firms sought a limited equity position in the development of medium-sized reserves (lead and zinc), with the aim of moving into larger-scale (copper) projects. Resource diplomacy's strongest tool, however, was the extension of soft loans. This last approach allowed the Japanese companies to secure long-term contracts or exclusive marketing rights, while promoting the sale of technology and equipment. Japan's overseas development assistance, and its emphasis on mining surveys, further complemented the procurement strategy.

The financial and economic crises of the 1980s negatively affected Peruvian–Japanese relations. Downward price pressures and bad domestic macro-economic management undermined Peru's exports to

Japan. More important, the easy availability of natural resources during the 1980s lessened the need for maintaining an active resource diplomacy and limited Japan's interest in Peruvian primary products. The accumulation of arrears with Japanese official creditors also crippled the relationship. New Japanese investments and credit fell to a trickle.

The 1990s, by contrast, are likely to witness a strengthening of contacts between the two nations. Technical missions have been visiting Peru, and official assistance is expected to increase significantly. Likewise, if Peruvian policy makers liberalize the treatment of foreign capital, Japanese investors might engage in large-scale mining investment, on which conversations are already in progress. In addition, there is the possibility of investments in the establishment of mineral-processing industries, since such activities are becoming unprofitable in Japan. Thus, although resource diplomacy in the 1990s has become less important as an overall strategy for Japan, its commercial relationship with Peru will continue to revolve around the Peruvian mining sector.

This renewed Japanese interest in Peru has some interesting features in terms of the trilateral model discussed in the Introduction to this volume. One of the reasons for the Japanese government's reluctance to extend assistance to the Fujimori government, despite popular pressure in favor of doing so, was a fear of being perceived as giving special treatment to a fellow Japanese. Thus, Japan waited for the United States to take the lead. At issue in the short term was the formation of the support group of donor nations to cancel Peru's arrears with the multilateral agencies. Only during the Interamerican Development Bank (IDB) annual meeting, held in Japan in April 1991, was an agreement reached on the support group; meanwhile Peru's economy continued to decline.

Since then, the Japanese government has yielded to Peruvian requests for more funding. In his second official visit to Japan in March 1992, Fujimori received an additional $100 million from the Japanese government for the co-financing of a $321 million structural adjustment loan from the IDB. President Fujimori also obtained the renewal of a $200 million Export–Import Bank insurance scheme, which had been suspended by Japan in 1984, and initiated negotiations for the subscription of an investment guarantee agreement along the lines of the United States' OPIC program and the World Bank's MIGA.

So far, the Peruvians have sought to maximize the attainment of official financing from the Japanese government by emphasizing President Fujimori's ethnicity and the importance of the country's *nikkei* community, not by building an active foreign economic policy that tries to take advantage of the potential for trilateralism as the Mexicans and Chileans have. From that perspective, the government's approach to the United States and Japan seems somewhat disjointed and uncoordinated. Fujimori's auto-coup has increased the difficulties because of the differing US and Japanese responses.

In order to analyze the potential for trilateralism in Peru, it is important to take into account that such a strategy can be pursued only in relation to foreign assistance issues, since the grave condition of the Peruvian economy and the country's political instability currently thwart any prospects for increased foreign investment or a significant diversification of trade in the near future. Official cooperation from the United States has expanded, but it is almost entirely dominated and conditioned by the American government's concern with drug trafficking and human rights violations in Peru. Thus, the possibility of designing a coordinated approach to the foreign aid establishments in both the United States and Japan is quite limited. Peruvian officials, however, have made some efforts to get the Japanese interested in financing the introduction of new crops in the coca growing regions of the Huallaga Valley – an issue they have pushed in Washington as well.

Despite the lack of a coordinated trilateral policy, Fujimori has successfully negotiated the expansion of official Japanese aid flows to Peru. If the most recent IDB co-financing is included, projected Japanese assistance could surpass US disbursements in 1992. The non-conflictive nature of foreign aid, and the US interest in getting the Japanese to step up its cooperation outside Asia, allowed the diversification of Peru's aid financing without generating frictions in the United States. It remains to be seen if such a success can be replicated in trade and investment once the conditions are ripe.

Notes

1. For a fuller analysis of Peruvian–Japanese relations, see Pablo de la Flor, *Japón en la escena internacional: sus relaciones con América Latina y el Perú* (Lima: Centro Peruano de Estudios Internacionales y COTECNA, 1992).
2. A more detailed account of Chinese immmgration to Peru is found in E. Rodríguez Pastor, "Los chinos en el Perú: balance de las fuentes e investigaciones," paper presented at the Primer Seminario sobre Poblaciones Inmigrantes, Lima, CONCYTEC, 1987.

3. C. Harvey Gardiner, *The Japanese and Peru, 1873–1973* (Albuquerque: University of New Mexico Press, 1975) p. 15. For a complete account of Japanese immigration, see also Amelia Morimoto, *Los inmigrantes japoneses en el Perú* (Lima: Universidad Nacional Agraria, 1979).

4. Manuel Roca Zela, "Base y perspectivas de las relaciones entre el Perú y Japón," *Revista de la Academia Diplomática del Perú* (January–June 1985).

5. Gardiner, *The Japanese and Peru*, p. 33.

6. C. Harvey Gardiner, *Pawns in a Triangle of Hatred: The Peruvian Japanese and the United States* (Seattle: University of Washington Press, 1981) p. 54.

7. See ibid. for a full account of the circumstances surrounding the deportation and life in the internment camps.

8. This strategy was suggested in a special document prepared by the Ministry of Foreign Affairs at the request of General Velasco (interview with Ambassador J. C. Mariatisui, March 1990).

9. Dani Rodrik, "Managing Resource Dependency: The United States and Japan in the Market for Copper, Iron Ore and Bauxite," *World Development*, 10, 7 (1982) p. 542.

10. Saburo Okita, *Japan and the World Economy* (Tokyo: The Japan Foundation, 1975).

11. *Japan Economic Journal*, July 18, 1972.

12. See *Bulletins* and *Annual Reports* from the Ministry of Foreign Affairs, 1969–73.

13. G. Castellanos and J. Cortez, "Relaciones comerciales Perú–Japón: 1971–1986," unpublished thesis, Universidad del Pacífico, 1988.

14. Consejo Nacional de Inversiones y Tecnología del Perú, *Annual Report*, 1980–88

15. Japanese Ministry of Finance, International Finance Bureau, *Annual Report*, 1989.

16. Rodrik, "Managing Resource Dependency," p. 589.

17. *The Lima Times*, June 28, 1974.

18. *Carta Minera*, March 1, 1983.

19. *The Lima Times*, February 2, 1973.

20. *Andean Report*, January and August 1978.

21. Interviews with various mining experts, 1991.

22. G. David Becker, *The New Bourgeoisie and the Limits of Dependency: Mining, Class, and Power in "Revolutionary" Peru* (Princeton, NJ: Princeton University Press, 1983) p. 191.

23. *Japan Economic Journal*, August 22, 1972.

24. *Ingeniero Andino*, June 1974.

25. *Japan Economic Journal*, March 17, 1973.

26. *The Lima Times*, October 19, 1973.

27. Becker, *The New Bourgeoisie*, p. 115.

28. *Carta Minera*, May 17, 1983.

29. Gardiner, *The Japanese and Peru*, p. 144.

30. Interviews with officials of Petroperú, Lima, 1991.

31. JICA annual reports, 1978–88.

32. *Nikkei Weekly*, August 1, 1992.

8 Chile and Japan: Opening Doors Through Trade

Neantro Saavedra-Rivano

Chile is viewed by many Japanese businesspeople and government officials as the country offering the most favorable business climate in Latin America. Growth is relatively high, inflation is under control, and the budget is balanced. Tariffs have been reduced to a uniform 10 percent, most state-owned firms have been sold to the private sector, and foreign investment is strongly encouraged. Moreover, the transition from a military dictatorship to a democratic government has gone smoothly, and the new civilian administration has kept its campaign promise to maintain the liberal economic model introduced by its predecessor.

As a consequence, Chile is one of the few Latin American countries where Japanese companies are investing, and two Japanese banks participated in the $320 million bond issue that marked Chile's return to the "voluntary" capital markets in early 1991. Despite the widespread praise and flurry of foreign investment activity, however, Japan's presence as investor and financier remains low although rising. Much more important at this point is the growing Chilean access to Japanese markets, especially for non-traditional (non-mineral) exports.

Overall, Chile has taken an aggressive stance toward participation in the international economy. It has opened its own economy and sought entry into others. While most of its attention is currently focused on trying to secure entry into the North American Free Trade Area (NAFTA) being negotiated by the United States, Canada, and Mexico, Japan – and other Asian countries – remain an important concern. Together with Mexico, Chile is perhaps the only Latin American country with a serious strategy for its international activities. As suggested in the Introduction to this volume, that strategy can be seen as an example of trilateralism in its attempt to incorporate both North American and Asian participation in a complementary way.

This chapter examines the various components of Japanese–Chilean relations. After a brief historical sketch, it studies in detail the dynamic trade links between Chile and Japan. Investment and financial relations are also discussed. The conclusion returns to the issue of Chilean insertion in the world economy and the role of Japan.

HISTORICAL SKETCH

Of all Latin American countries, Chile has been the most explicit and consistent throughout its history in expressing its vocation as a Pacific nation and acting in accordance with this conception. There are good reasons: the depths of the Atacama desert to the north and the heights of the Andes to the east force the Chileans to look to the sea and try to take advantage of their thousands of miles of seacoast.

It was certainly this vision that led Bernardo O'Higgins to propose, after the end of the Independence War, to carry the Latin American emancipation struggle to the Philippines Islands.[1] Later, during the second half of the nineteenth century, as the Chilean economy expanded considerably, trade with other Pacific nations and regions (Australia, Polynesia, California) increased greatly. Between 1849 and 1864, for instance, there was a tripling in the tonnage of the Chilean merchant marine fleet, which concentrated much of the traffic between the American Pacific and the Far East. At the same time Chile increased its diplomatic presence, opening several consulates in Asia, Australia and Polynesia. Then, in 1888, Chile annexed Easter Island and established itself as a Polynesian country.[2]

This brief account illustrates that, from the point of view of Chile, its relations with Japan occupy a privileged position. Chile recognized the importance of Japan early, and it was there that its first embassy in the Asian Pacific was established in 1899. Nonetheless, these early trends did not develop into an important set of economic relations between the two nations during the postwar period, which has witnessed an explosive growth in world trade and investment. Even in Latin America, the record of Chilean relations with Japan is not impressive if compared with those of Brazil or Mexico, or even Peru in earlier years. Chile's small market, and perhaps its lack of a significant Japanese population, led to its being overlooked. These negative factors were accentuated by economic problems – low growth rates and sharp swings in economic policy. It is only in the last half dozen years that a successful path seems to have been found, with Japan and Asia playing a crucial role.

TRADE RELATIONS

Trade has been by far the most important and dynamic element of the Chilean–Japanese economic relationship. Chile has usually enjoyed a surplus in commercial exchanges. As it would be expected, Japanese exports to Chile are mainly composed of machinery, cars, and electronic products. Chilean exports to Japan, by contrast, have been heavily concentrated in mineral products, mainly copper and iron, although this situation has changed substantially in recent years.

Table 8.1 shows the evolution of bilateral trade from 1978 to 1991. Exports from Chile to Japan fluctuated around a modest annual value of $400 million until 1986. They then began a quick rise, soon crossing the billion-dollar threshold, to reach $1.6 billion in 1991. The average annual rate of growth for the 5-year period of 1986–91 was 30 percent. This performance has been exceptional within Latin America. The share of Chile in Japanese imports from the Latin American region went from 8.8 percent for 1985 to 20.7 percent for the first 6 months of 1991, displacing Mexico from the second place. To be sure, the share of the whole region in total Japanese imports during that period was only in the 4–5 percent range. Even so, the behavior of Chilean exports to Japan

Table 8.1 Chilean trade with Japan, 1978–91 (million dollars)

Year	Exports*	Imports**	Balance
1978	283.7	217.7	66.0
1979	415.8	318.6	97.2
1980	501.6	607.8	−106.3
1981	414.0	829.5	−415.5
1982	440.0	229.6	210.5
1983	348.1	161.2	186.8
1984	407.7	312.7	95.1
1985	392.5	188.5	203.9
1986	420.1	296.4	123.7
1987	561.3	387.2	174.1
1988	881.2	391.8	489.5
1989	1120.5	737.0	383.5
1990	1388.2	568.4	819.8
1991	1644.0	645.7	998.3

* Exports are calculated fob.   ** Imports are calculated cif.
Source: Central Bank of Chile.

was very dynamic and can be compared in this respect with some Southeast Asian countries.[3] In 1987 Japan displaced West Germany to become the second most important market for Chilean products, and in 1991 it took first place from the United States, albeit by a small margin. The share of exports to Japan among total Chilean exports went from 9.9 percent in 1986 to 18.2 percent in 1991. Thus, Chile is far and away the Latin American country most dependent on the Japanese market. Since Chile is also the most open Latin American economy, the relative value of its exports to Japan, at around $125 per inhabitant, is absolutely exceptional for the region.[4] Indeed, this value compares favorably with *per capita* exports from the European Community to Japan.

The behavior of Chilean imports from Japan has been much less dynamic (see Table 8.1). They increased markedly until 1981, when the Chilean peso was overvalued, crashed in 1982 together with the Chilean and other Latin American economies, and have fluctuated substantially since then. In 1991 imports from Japan amounted to $646 million, well below their 1981 peak and also below the second highest value in 1989. In the process, Chile's trade surplus with Japan reached almost $1 billion in 1991, 63 percent of its total trade surplus in that year. In general, Chilean and Latin American imports have been low since 1982 and very sensitive to adverse macroeconomic conditions in the region. Thus, in spite of the modest values just presented, Japan has maintained its position as second largest supplier of goods to Chile throughout most of this period. In addition, Chile's importance as a market for Japanese goods within Latin America has increased, with the country's share going from 2.3 percent in 1985 to 4.7 percent in the first 6 months of 1991.[5]

The sectoral composition of Chilean exports to Japan has traditionally been overwhelmingly oriented toward mineral and chemical products, which represented 86.5 percent of total value in 1978 and 82.5 percent in 1984. Chile produces many other goods potentially of interest to Japanese consumers, especially fishing, agricultural, agroindustrial and forestry products, and some of these have started to make relatively large inroads in Japanese markets. In the last few years, Chilean exports to Japan have shifted markedly toward these sectors. Two factors have contributed to this important change in the pattern of Chilean exports to Japan in the 1980s. In the first place, Chilean economic policy defined as one of its explicit goals the increase of so-called "non-traditional" exports (as opposed to "traditional" or mineral exports). This policy provided incentives for production and exports in the agricultural, fishing, and forestry sectors, since it was thought that these sectors (in addition to mining) constituted Chile's comparative advantage and that their development would provide a much needed diversification of exports. The export push was intensified after 1982 as Chile, like other Latin American countries, could no longer rely on the international capital markets to finance its current account deficits. Chile once again looked to the Asian Pacific, and offices of ProChile (the government's trade promotion agency) were established in Tokyo, Hong Kong, Bangkok, and Singapore.

The second factor contributing to the change in export composition is more widely known, and originated in Japan. The extraordinary export-led growth of Japan and the consequent prosperity of its population provoked great pressures for Japan to open its markets to foreign products. At the same time, new demands by ever more sophisticated Japanese consumers resulted in a new commercial environment that is stimulating and propitious to enterprising traders.[6]

The effects of these factors were felt especially after 1986. As Table 8.2 shows, there has been a continuous decrease in the share corresponding to traditional exports, which shrank from 82.5 percent in 1984 to 58.4 percent in 1991. Indeed, the loss of their share would have been much more pronounced had it not been for large increases in the price of copper in 1988 and 1990. In other words, the increase in volume of non-traditional exports to Japan was much higher than the figures in Table 8.2 indicate. In addition to the increase in value, the

Table 8.2   Sectoral composition of Chilean exports to Japan, 1984–91 (percent)

Sector	1984	1985	1986	1987	1988	1989	1990	1991
Mineral and chemical products	82.5	78.8	72.3	70.8	66.8	65.2	61.3	58.4
Fishing products	7.3	10.0	12.8	14.0	13.9	11.3	14.3	15.9
Forestry products	6.0	7.9	10.7	10.8	14.4	18.3	19.9	21.7
Agricultural and agroindustrial products	4.0	3.2	4.1	4.2	4.9	4.9	4.4	3.9
Other	9.2	9.1	9.1	9.2	9.0	9.1	9.2	9.2
Total	100.0	100.0	100.0	100.0	100.0	100.0	100.0	100.0

Source: Elaborated from data provided by Tokyo office of ProChile and JETRO.

diversification of Chilean exports to Japan must be noted. Thus, according to the classification of products used by ProChile, trade from Chile to Japan was composed of 73 products in 1982, 113 products in 1986, 138 in 1987, and 234 in 1991.[7]

For fishing products, substantial diversification started in 1987. In that year 24 products belonging to that group were exported, while by 1991 the number had more than doubled to 56. A new product is salmon, whose production is very recent in Chile. Exports of fresh and frozen salmon to Japan started in 1986 and until 1987 stayed modestly below $200,000; in 1988, they increased to $7.6 million and reached $83 million in 1991. In all, exports of fish (fresh and frozen) jumped from $8.9 million in 1984 to more than $140 million in 1991. A more traditional product, fishmeal, also experienced large increases in volume and value. Exports of fishmeal have progressed steadily from $6.3 million in 1984 to $120 million in 1991, thus being the largest export product in this category.[8]

Forestry products is the group whose exports have grown at the fastest rate. As can be seen from Table 8.2, their share in total exports increased from 6 percent in 1984 to 21.7 percent in 1991. For the period 1984–91, their value increased at an average annual rate of 40.4 percent, and this rate was 57.7 percent between 1987 and 1991. Such growth should not be surprising since Chile possesses extraordinary advantages for growing pine woods. The yearly growth rate of pines in Chile is 20–30 cubic meters, as compared with 2–7 cubic meters in North America and the Soviet Union. This makes Chile the most competitive country in the world for the production of wood pulp of this extraction.[9] Exports of cellulose from Chile to Japan have increased at a yearly average rate of 28.9 percent in the 1984–91 period, reaching a value of $48.5 million in 1991. Other important products in this group are serrated wood, wood chips, and logs. It is noteworthy that logs, which were the leading product in this category until 1985, are now down to a distant fourth place, indicating that Chile has succeeded in increasing the value-added of its exports to Japan. It is also managing to sell some non-traditional products in this group too, as witness the increase in Chilean exports of chopsticks to Japan!

Agricultural and agroindustrial products have been been less dynamic than the last two groups, and their share in total exports has slightly decreased from 4.0 to 3.9 percent during the period 1984–91, but it is here that some of the most promising developments are taking place. In the first place, there has been a large increase in the variety of products traded in this group, whose number went from 30 in

1986 to 60 in 1991. Second, some of these new products have quickly established themselves as important items, and may open the way to other similar products.

A particularly interesting case is that of table grapes, which started to be exported in 1988, having a value of $2.4 million that year and of $6.9 million in 1991. Chile is a large exporter of table grapes to the world markets, and Japan is a significant and appreciative consumer of this fruit, especially black grapes of the Ribier variety. For years, Chilean producers tried to penetrate the Japanese market, to comply with the exacting requirements of the Japanese authorities, and to convince them that the Chilean product could satisfy the standards of Japanese consumers. The whole process involved many trips by trade missions in both directions and trial shipments over some 10 years. But in the end exports of table grapes were approved and they have been a success with Japanese customers. It is telling that, instead of being annoyed by the obstinacy of Chilean producers, the Japanese acquired a sense of admiration for what they perceived as perseverance and determination to succeed.[10]

This example is frequently raised by Japanese familiar with economic relations with Latin America to illustrate that other Latin American countries can also increase their sales to Japan, provided they try hard enough. Since the episode has enhanced Chile's reputation in Japan, exporters of other fresh fruits, such as kiwi and berries whose production is rapidly expanding in Chile, can expect to encounter less difficulty in penetrating the Japanese markets. Indeed, the negotiations on the access of Chilean kiwi to Japan were recently concluded and the first shipments arrived in 1992. Other dynamic products are beet pulp (a product that started to be exported in 1988 and attained in 1991 a value of $16.7 million), tomato paste ($9.2 million in 1991), broiler chickens ($9.4 million), and wine ($3.0 million).[11]

JAPANESE DIRECT INVESTMENT IN CHILE

Although Latin America was a favorite early destination of Japanese investment abroad, the deteriorating economic environment of most countries in the region in the 1980s, as well as the emergence of other investment opportunities (Southeast Asia) or priorities (United States and Europe), have relegated Latin America to a less prominent position. Indeed, if we ignore the investment in the finance and shipping sectors in Panama, the Bahamas, and the Cayman Islands, the amount of

Japanese direct investment in Latin America since 1987 has been only around 2 percent of their direct investment in the world.[12]

In the case of Chile it must be added that, in contrast to trade, Japan has historically been a relatively minor foreign investor. Until 1990 Japan ranked sixth among foreign investors, well behind not only the United States but also Australia and the United Kingdom among others. The single major investment up to then had been the participation (around $110 million) in the La Escondida copper mining project in 1988. Indeed, before that investment, Japan was not even among the 10 largest foreign investors in Chile. The year 1991 was very significant as it witnessed the commitment of Japanese firms to several projects, the largest of which is the participation of Sumitomo in the La Candelaria copper mining project. In all, in 1991 the Central Bank of Chile authorized Japanese direct investment for $423 million, effectively tripling the total value of authorized

Table 8.3a Japanese direct investment in Chile according to Japanese sources, 1951–90 (million dollars)

Fiscal year	Investment*		Relative to Latin American total	Relative to world total
	No. of cases	Value		
1951–76	28	91	2.76	0.47
1977	1	0	0.0	0.0
1978	5	13	2.11	0.28
1979	5	12	0.99	0.24
1980	4	9	1.53	0.19
1981	1	3	0.25	0.03
1982	6	13	0.86	0.17
1983	2	3	0.16	0.04
1984	5	36	1.57	0.35
1985	1	0	0.0	0.0
1986	2	2	0.04	0.01
1987	5	7	0.15	0.02
1988	13	46	0.72	0.10
1989	10	47	0.90	0.07
1990	11	30	0.83	0.05
1951–90	99	311	0.77	0.10

* Intentions to invest as reported to Ministry of Finance.
Source: Japanese Ministry of Finance.

Table 8.3b Japanese direct investment in Chile according to Chilean sources, 1982–91 (million dollars)

Calendar year	Investment*		Relative to world total
	No. of projects	Value	
1982	1	1.4	0.26
1983	2	7.6	2.30
1984	0	0.4	0.44
1985	0	0.03	0.01
1986	2	2.3	0.88
1987	1	2.2	0.39
1988	6	123.0	6.30
1989	13	37.2	1.26
1990	n.a.	45.5	3.14
1991	n.a.	423.8	12.48
1982–91	n.a.	643.1	5.40

* Authorized investment under Decree Law 600 (i.e., excluding debt conversion operations).
Source: Chilean Foreign Investment Committee.

foreign direct investment by Japanese firms and taking Japan to the fourth place among foreign investors. Tables 8.3a and 8.3b give an account of the figures authorized by the Japanese and Chilean authorities; they also illustrate their wide discrepancy.

It is worthwhile to note that, in relation to other Latin American countries, Chile has offered a very attractive institutional environment for foreign investment during the last decade. Most important among the legal instruments to regulate, attract, and protect foreign investment are the Foreign Investment Statute (established in 1974 and revised in 1985) and Chapters XVIII and XIX of the Compendium of Rules on International Exchange.[13] With the help of these mechanisms, foreign investment projects corresponding to an authorized total amount of almost $12 billion were initiated between 1982 and the end of 1991. An important element in this environment, and one that certainly contributed to the acceleration of the pace of foreign investment in Chile, has been the wide-ranging privatization process taking place, particularly since 1982. Included were firms in various key sectors of the Chilean economy–steel, utilities, telecommunications, air transportation and chemicals – which had been in the hands of the state. Some important firms partly or totally privatized were LAN Chile (airline), Compañía Aceros del Pacífico (steel), Intel (telecommunications), Chilectra (electric utility), and Soquimich (chemicals). Thie environment was maintained by the civilian government that assumed control in March 1990 and supplemented by the prospects of lasting political stability in the context of normally functioning democratic institutions.

In addition to this institutional environment, the country has several sectors offering exceptional potential. Investment in fishing has produced excellent results, explained by the privileged location of Chile in the South Pacific. Another important sector where Chile has strong comparative advantages, as already discussed, is forestry. Besides these, there are mining (with large reserves of copper, lithium, and molybdenum among others) and agroindustry and agriculture (fresh and canned fruit among other products).[14] These opportunities have attracted investors from many countries and, although until very recently the Japanese did not seem particularly impressed, the events of 1991 may signal a new responsiveness.

If this really happens, it will be due in no small measure to persistent efforts by Chilean and Japanese institutions to maintain open channels in spite of the deteriorated image of Latin America in the 1980s. The work of the Japan External Trade Organization (JETRO) representatives in Santiago is noteworthy in this regard, as they were keen to prod Childean agencies (such as the Foreign Investment Committee) to increase their promotion efforts and send regular missions to Japan.[15] Another important forum for bilateral contacts is the regular Joint Meetings of the Chile–Japan Business Committee, which have taken place every year since 1979, alternating in Santiago and Tokyo. They are organized by Chile's Industrial Society (Sociedad de Fomento Fabril) and the Japan Chamber of Commerce and Industry. The thirteenth such meeting took place in Tokyo in October–November 1991 and attracted some 170 businessmen from both countries. Although trade is the most important topic in these meetings, discussions of investment opportunities are starting to take a larger share of their time. Indeed, the most promising efforts to stimulate Japanese direct investment in Chile are those that link investment and trade.

A good example is the proposed $600 million investment of the Daio Paper Company in reforestation and production of forestry derivatives. Daio Paper set up a Chilean subsidary (Forestal Anchile Ltda.) in July 1989, which by 1991 had reforested 3,600 hectares. Reforestation activities will continue at an accelerating pace with a planned target of 52,000 hectares by the year 2000. The firm also envisions setting up several plants using the new trees as input, the most significant of which, for the production of paper pulp, will be established after 1995. In spite of the large distance from the prospective markets in Asia and the United States, Daio Paper reckons that the products will be competitive. Indeed, Chile was selected for this investment after a study involving several other possible locations.[16] A second significant example is provided by Nippon Suisan, which invested $10 million to acquire the largest salmon plant in Chile, Salmones Antártica SA. Annual sales of combined Nippon Suisan subsidiaries amount to over $80 million, a large fraction being exported to Japan.[17] One might also consider in this regard the recent investment of $10 million by Kawasaki, taking a participation in the Southern port of Puchoco.[18]

It is interesting to note the especially prominent role played by the trading companies (*sogo shosha*) in Chilean trade-cum-investment activities. In the Daio Paper project, for instance, C.Itoh is a 16 percent partner and played a key role in introducing Daio to the Chilean market. Other examples include Sumitomo's experimental plyboard project and Kanematsu's paper mill. The most prominent trading company in Chile, however, is the Mitsubishi Corporation, generally acknowledged to be the leading Japanese firm in the country.[19]

Mitsubishi and its affiliates are leading Japanese players in the largest mining investment in Chile in recent years, the $1.1 billion La Escondida copper mine, which will export 50 percent of its output to Japan. Mitsubishi Corporation provided $40 million in equity plus a $100 million loan. Japanese commercial banks supplied a loan of $105 million, and the Export–Import Bank added another $245 million. In addition, Mitsubishi is currently the largest Japanese participant in the forestry sector. It began by purchasing wood chips for export to the Mitsubishi Paper Mills in Japan, but in 1987 it set up its own affiliate, Astex, in Concepción. Astex produces 400,000 metric tons per year of wood chips for export to Japan. In 1990, Mitsubishi Corporation and Mitsubishi Paper Mills set up another affiliate, Forestal Tierra Chilena, to engage in a large-scale reforestation project. Finally, Mitsubishi is active in the fishing sector, both in off-shore fishing and in the cultivation of salmon in the south of Chile.[20]

It will be noticed that Japanese investment activities in Chile are almost exclusively located in the natural resource sector. One reason is Japan's own lack of raw materials, which has been amply discussed in other chapters of this volume. In addition, however, during the late 1970s and 1980s, Chile went against the grain in Latin America by allowing foreign exploitation of its natural resources with few restrictions. During the last several years, such a policy has become more common in other nations; at the same time, Chile is reconsidering the need for regulation, thus producing a convergence of sorts with its neighbors.

Japanese firms have been especially criticized in Chile for their contribution to environmental problems. Two sectors are of major concern: forestry and fishing. A problem particularly related to the Japanese in forestry is the native or virgin forests. While other foreign investors stay away from native forests, planting or purchasing "man-made" plantations, the Japanese have frequently chosen the easier, more lucrative path. In theory, cutting native woods requires permission of Chile's Forestry Corporation, but the lack of manpower to police violation means that over one third of the wood shipped to sawmills is felled illegally, according to a Forestry Corporation official.[21] As indicated above, however, some Japanese firms are now beginning to follow their US and European counterparts into reforestation. In fishing, the main issue concerns the so-called factory boats, which fish off-shore and process the catch on the boats for sale in Japan. Japan's activities have become extremely controversial because they fish with large nets that sweep up all marine life. The Chilean congress is considering a new law to restrict net fishing, and two of the three Japanese companies engaged in the activity have therefore decided to withdraw from Chile.[22]

In spite of these sources of friction, the prospects for largely expanded Japanese investment look much more favorable now than any time in the past. Besides the considerable increase observed during 1991, some other huge projects are being talked about. One is for an aluminum smelting plant in the south of Chile, which would tap the ample hydro-electric potential of that region. The investment would be in excess of $1 billion, and the Marubeni Corporation is said to be actively exploring this possibility together with the Chilean power utility company, Endesa, and other firms from Australia and the United States. Interestingly, in spite of the obvious disadvantages of Chile as compared, for instance, to Venezuela (which is closer to the markets and rich in the necessary mineral resources that Chile lacks), Chile is preferred because of its political stability and its deregulated environment. A second important example is for a tri-national project involving Argentina, Bolivia and Chile, which would exploit Bolivian natural gas, transport it across Argentina, and ship it to Japan through the Northern Chilean port of Tocopilla. This project is said to require total investments in excess of $6.6 billion.[23]

FINANCE AND OFFICIAL DEVELOPMENT ASSISTANCE

As elsewhere in Latin America, Japanese banks lent aggressively to Chile until the financial crisis of August 1982. At that point, the dollar loans of Japanese private banks to Chile amounted to $692 million, as compared to an exposure of $3,172 million for US banks, making Japan the third largest Chilean creditor (the second largest was the United Kingdom).[24] The involvement was large enough to force Japanese banks to take an active role in the debt negotiations that took place after 1982, which frequently ended up with the banks providing new money to Latin American countries and increasing their exposure. In the case of Chile, the exposure of Japanese banks increased considerably, reaching $1.4 billion by 1985 and $1.6 billion by 1987 and amounting roughly to 10 percent of the external debt of the country.[25] In addition, Japanese banks have been very reluctant to participate in debt conversion operations, which has been another factor in increasing their share of Chilean debt. Chile's debt-conversion program, popularly known as Chapters XVIII and XIX of the Rules on Foreign Exchange, has processed a total of $9.2 billion since it began in 1985. The program was largely successful in reducing Chile's commercial bank debt, although much of it has been replaced by debt with public-sector agencies, especially the International Monetary Fund (IMF) and World Bank.[26]

Most people would agree that, within the Latin American environment of the 1980s, Chile has a good record of meeting its external obligations. Indeed, Chilean debt was being traded in secondary markets at 90 percent of its face value in April 1992 which, because of transaction costs, makes debt–equity swaps unprofitable. Traded volumes fell consistently from $2.9 billion in 1988 to $0.7 billion in 1991, according to rough estimates by market traders.[27] The Daio Paper investment is an interesting example of this phenomenon. In May 1991, Daio withdrew its request to convert $600 million of Chilean debt through Chapter XIX for its planned investment because the price of Chilean debt was so high. The investment will instead be channeled through the other legal mechanisms. Daio was said to be the last of the megaprojects scheduled to enter Chile via Chapter XIX.[28]

In January 1991, Chile marked its return to the voluntary credit markets by placing $320 million in Eurobonds with a group of twenty international banks. Among them were the Bank of Tokyo ($15 million) and Tokai Bank ($10 million). While this might appear to be a positive indication, the original estimates were that the Japanese would take a much higher participation. Despite the Bank of Tokyo's best efforts, however, it was able to line up only one additional bank. Generalized praise for Chile aside, the negative view held by Japanese banks about Latin America extends even to Chile. (See the similar discussion about Mexico in Chapter 6 of this volume.) It is significant that Chile remains on the Japanese list of high-risk countries although it has been eliminated from such lists in the United States and the international financial institutions. Being on this list, which is an unofficial but effective instrument of the Ministry of Finance, means that private banks lending to Chile are required to set aside reserves corresponding to 30 percent of disbursed funds, thus significantly lowering the profitability of such loans. The list is in principle composed of those countries that have renegotiated or shown other "irregular" behavior in dealing with their external debt, and indeed Chile proceeded in April 1990 to an ill-advised and largely unnecessary renegotiation of its $5 billion debt with private banks. The Ministry of Finance may remove countries from this list at its own discretion and it has done so for Turkey. Chilean officials in Tokyo have under-standably made a top priority of obtaining the removal of Chile from this list, and they seem to have the sympathy of some Japanese banks.[29]

Even though Japanese banks have been quite negative about Latin America in recent years, Japan has provided significant amounts of public-sector funds to help stabilize the financial situation there and in other developing countries. Thus the "Nakasone recycling fund" in 1987 committed $30 billion to be spent over 3 years, an amount supplemented in March 1989 by an additional $35 billion. These funds are channeled to developing countries in several ways, including assistance through the Japanese Export–Import Bank (JEXIM), both direct loans and co-financing with multilateral financial institutions. As of January 1991, JEXIM had committed $4.2 billion of these funds to 20 projects in nine countries of Latin America and the Caribbean. Mexico was the largest recipient with five projects and $2.2 billion, but Chile came in second place with three projects and $470 million.[30] In addition, JEXIM participated with $245 million in the financing for the La Escondida mining project in 1988. Table 8.4 details lending by JEXIM to Chile since 1987.

Table 8.4   Loans from the Japanese Export–Import Bank to Chile,
1987–90

Year	Purpose and amount
1987	Construction of hydro-electric unit at Pehuenche $120.6 million
1988	Syndicated loan for the Escondida mining project $245 milion Structural Adjustment Loan (SAL III) $200 million
1989	Credit line to Banco del Estado to finance imports of Japanese capital goods $35 million
1990	Road construction program for 1990–93 $150 million

Source: Central Bank of Chile, Tokyo office.

The $200 million structural adjustment loan of 1988 provides an interesting glimpse into how forthcoming JEXIM has been in collaborating with multilateral institutions. Chile had received from the World Bank two structural adjustment loans (SALs) for $250 million each in 1985 and 1986. As their name implies, these loans are tied to the attainment of "structural" targets, such as the savings rate and the rate of growth of exports. Chile performed well on both occasions and presented an unprecedented request for a third SAL complete with an economic program for additional structural reforms. While the World Bank programming did not contemplate so much structural reform lending, JEXIM came in with the funds, and the third program was administered by the Bank.[31]

Beyond JEXIM activities, Japan has become the largest provider of Official Development Assistance (ODA) among the member countries of the OECD Development Assistance Committee. The large majority of Japan's ODA is directed to Asia and more specifically to China and the ASEAN nations. Latin America's share of Japanese ODA is only about 8 percent, and Japan clearly targets the poorer countries (as measured by *per capita* GDP). Because of this criterion, and also its relatively small population, Chile ranks twelfth among Latin American beneficiaries of Japan's ODA. Nonetheless, Japan is the third largest provider of ODA to Chile, after West Germany and the United States.

Of the three main categories of ODA – loans, grants, and technical assistance–emphasis has rested on technical aid, which accounted for 47 percent of all ODA conceded up to March 1988.[32]

The Japanese have been especially eager to help the new civilian government in Chile and offered a large loan on soft terms shortly after the transfer of power in March 1990. In keeping with Japanese practice, the loan had to be linked to particular projects with the preference for a single large one. Because of lack of preparation of projects in the final years of the military government, however, none were ready. Moreover, the new Chilean government preferred smaller projects rather than large ones. Negotiations have not gone smoothly, in part because of the well-known Japanese policy of avoiding political entanglements. Thus, unlike the Americans and Europeans, the Japanese had virtually no contact with the opposition during the years of the military government. They were not well acquainted with the officials who came into office in March 1990, and they did not understand the new priorities. It may thus take some time for the Japanese to increase the effectiveness of their operations in Chile.[33]

CONCLUDING REMARKS

An important guiding principle of Chilean diplomatic and interna-tional economic policy has been its claim to membership and participation in the Pacific community. This principle has been restated by practically every Chilean government; it appeared expli-citly in the platform of the coalition of political parties that came to power in March 1990. The economic rationale for the principle, well sustained by Chile's geographical location, has been reinforced by the rapid development taking place in the Asian Pacific in the last decades.

It is natural to expect, then, that Chile will make every effort further to develop its economic relations with Japan and to project itself as a Pacific nation. Trade has proved so far to be the most important component of this relationship and, through it, Chile hopes to attract Japanese direct investment to expand its production further in the areas where it possesses a comparative advantage, namely agriculture, agroindustry, fishing, and forestry products. The relation between trade and investment is crucial and it goes both ways. Indeed, it can be argued that if Chile fails to attract Japanese direct investment, it will find it impossible to sustain the current high rates of growth of its exports to Japan. Moreover, one way of increasing Chilean exports to the United States and Europe will be through Japanese networks of direct investors and trading companies.

There are several indications that Chile is committing itself to the execution of an Asian strategy. Exports to Asia, at around 30 percent of total value, surpass those to either the United States or Latin America and are closing in on those to the European Community. Chile has applied for and been accepted as a member of the Pacific Economic Cooperation Conference (PECC). It also applied to join the Asian Pacific Economic Cooperation group (APEC), but the prospects for acceptance are uncertain. And in November 1992, President Patricio Aylwin paid an official visit to Japan, thus becoming the first Chilean president ever to visit Asia.

The strategic position of Chile in the South Pacific as a potential bridge between South America and the Asian Pacific, as well as its exemplary political and economic stability, seem to be recognized by Japan and the United States alike. The fact that Chile is clearly and openly seeking flexible and diversified relations with the rest of the world (witness its independent stance in relation to sub-regional integration agreements) does not give much credence to hypotheses about possible confrontation of Japan and the United States over their economic interests in Chile. On the contrary, there have been some signs that would instead support the trilateral cooperative model.

One good example is the envisioned aluminum smelting project mentioned earlier. In this case, Marubeni was reportedly introduced to the project by Bechtel, which had in turn got the idea from an old study done by the Japan International Cooperation Agency (JICA). A second example is the just agreed $96 million loan by the US Eximbank to Compañía Aceros del Pacífico (CAP) for the purchase of new equipment for its steel mill in Huachipato. The loan will be guaranteed by Japan's Ministry of International Trade and Industry (MITI) and the equipment will be purchased from Japanese and United States firms. The whole scheme is part of a joint program by the Export–Import Banks of Japan and the United States together with the Ministry of International Trade and Industry (MITI), which will provide finance for projects in five developing nations. In Latin America, Venezuela is included in addition to Chile. The program is considered to be a direct offspring of the Japan–US Global Partnership Action Plan launched in January 1992 during the official visit to Japan by President Bush.[34]

The new Chilean government has placed a high priority on developing an international economic strategy to take advantage of the sacrifices made over the previous 15 years in establishing an open economy. Within its plans, the United States and Asia occupy dominant positions. Like Mexico, Chile would like to increase relations with both in a trilateral framework. Although it lacks Mexico's overwhelming geographical advantage on the US border, Chile's strategy appears to be similar. It is hoping to follow Mexico into a free trade agreement with the United States, and it would like to encourage Japan to use Chile as a base for exporting to the United States as well as the rest of South America. Its striking break-through into the Japanese market, and its new access to Japanese direct investment, suggests a fair chance of success for its broader trade and investment plans in the future.

Notes

1. This proposal was not implemented, revolutionary energies being instead channeled into the liberation of Peru from Spanish rule.
2. For a good account of Chilean attitudes toward the Pacific, see J. Salazar-Sparks, *Chile y la Comunidad del Pacífico* (Santiago: Editorial Universitaria, 1984).
3. The definition of "Latin America" in this chapter is the IMF's "Western Hemisphere" category. See IMF, *Direction of Trade Statistics*, various issues.
4. Banco Central de Chile, *Boletín Mensual*, various issues.
5. IMF, *Direction of Trade Statistics*, various issues.
6. There are some indications that the first factor was more powerful than the second. According to one study analyzing the period 1985–88, if Chile had maintained its participation in each Japanese import sector as the structure of Japanese imports evolved, total Chilean exports to Japan would have diminished slightly instead of increasing as they did. This suggests that most of the growth observed is attributable to improvements in competitiveness of Chilean exports. See R.Z. Lawrence, *An Analysis of Japanese Trade with Developing Countries* (Geneva: UNCTAD, May 1990).
7. ProChile, *Análisis del comercio entre Chile y Japón*, Embassy of Chile, Tokyo, various issues.
8. Banco Central de Chile, *Boletín Mensual*, various issues.
9. T. Inoue, "Comercio de madera y productos de madera," paper presented at the 12th Joint Meeting of the Chile–Japan Business Committee, Santiago, October 1990.
10. Interviews with Japanese and Chilean officials.
11. The numbers in the last sentence come from JETRO-Tokyo and are not comparable to those from the Central Bank of Chile. In particular, the former are cif, while the latter are fob.

12. For more details on foreign direct investment in Latin America, see Neantro Saavedra-Rivano, *Recent History and Future Prospects of Economic Relations between Japan and Latin America* (Tokyo: Institute of Developing Economies, 1989) and Blake Friscia, "Japanese Economic Relations with Latin America: Structure and Policies," paper presented to the first session of the study group on Japanese Policies Towards Latin America, Americas Society, New York, March 1991.

13. The latter, established in 1985, refer to debt conversion operations; see R. Toso, "Macroeconomic Aspects of Debt Conversion Programs in Chile," Central Bank of Chile, New York Office, December 1987.

14. See J. Alé, "Sectores chilenos necesitados de inversión y cómo contactarlos con la oferta japonesa de inversión," paper presented to the 10th Joint Meeting of the Chile–Japan Business Committee, Santiago, September 1988.

15. Interviews with officials in Santiago and Tokyo.

16. See Inoue, "Comercio de madera," and T. Ikawa, "Condiciones chilenas para las inversiones japonesas," paper presented to the 13th Joint Meeting of the Chile–Japan Business Committee, Tokyo, October–November 1991.

17. See Y. Hoshino, "Sobre la pesca," paper presented to the 12th Joint Meeting of the Chile–Japan Business Committee, Santiago, October 1990.

18. Interviews with officials in Tokyo, April 1992.

19. Barbara Stallings and Kotaro Horisaka, "Japanese–Latin American Relations: New Patterns for the 1990s," in Abraham Lowenthal and Gregory Treverton, (eds.), *Latin America in the New World* (forthcoming).

20. Ibid.

21. Leslie Crawford, "Too Much of a Chips Feast," *Financial Times*, December 19, 1990. See also Charlotte Elton, *Japan's Natural Resource Strategies and their Environmental Impact in Latin America* (Tokyo: Institute of Developing Economies, 1991).

22. Stallings and Horisaka, "Japanese–Latin American Relations."

23. Interviews with officials in Tokyo, April 1992.

24. For a more detailed analysis of Japan's role in Latin American debt, see Barbara Stallings, "The Reluctant Giant: Japan and the Latin American Debt Crisis," *Journal of Latin American Studies*, 22, 1 (February 1990).

25. Saavedra-Rivano, *Recent History*, p. 18.

26. On shortcomings of the debt–equity swap program, see Ricardo Ffrench-Davis, "Debt–equity Swaps in Chile," *Notas Técnicas CIEPLAN* (Santiago) May 1989.

27. Interviews with officials in Tokyo, April 1992.

28. *Estrategia* (Santiago), May 8, 1991.

29. Interviews with officials in Tokyo, April 1992.

30. Friscia, "Japanese Economic Relations."

31. Interviews with officials in Tokyo, April 1992.

32. Ministry of Foreign Affairs, *Japan's ODA*, various years.

33. Barbara Stallings and Akio Hosono, *Dual Hegemony? The United States and Japan in Latin America* (forthcoming).

34. *Nihon Keizai Shimbun* March 17, 1992, and interviews with officials in Tokyo, April 1992.

9 Japan and Panama: the Role of the Panama Canal

Charlotte Elton

Panama is second only to the United States in this hemisphere as a host country for Japan's direct overseas investment. Japan is the second largest user of the Panama Canal. Moreover the Japanese government is participating in the Commission to Study Alternatives to the Panama Canal, together with the Panamanian government and the United States. Although evidently the United States has always been Panama's number one foreign policy concern, Japan is becoming an increasingly important country for Panama.

This raises some interesting questions about US–Japan relations, and the role Japan is playing in Panama. Whose interests are being served? Is Japan competing with the United States, or is its strategy complementary? What does this triangular relationship tell us about spheres of influence? What does it suggest about the possibilities of Panama's breaking away from dependence on the United States? In this chapter, I will examine these questions. I begin with an analysis of the historical background of Japanese–Panamanian relations. I then turn to the Panama Canal issue, the peculiar nature of Japanese trade and investment in Panama, political relations, and prospects for the future.

HISTORICAL BACKGROUND

Panama was the first area of Latin America to be visited by Japanese after their forced re-entry into contact with the outside world in 1853. The Panama railroad was the route chosen to cross the American continent for the official Japanese mission to the United States in 1860. This was their first encounter with a railway, "an electrical device made of wire, over which business may be transacted between Panama and Aspinwall [today's Colón], a distance of 57 miles, in the time it takes for a smoke . . . How it works I have not the faintest idea," confessed one of the members of the mission in his diary.[1]

This first contact was not promising, though prescient of things to come. Referring to the local population, the ambassador wrote: "The natives were brown and their hair very curly. They were naked and barefooted and their character was bad. Although the character of the natives worried the Americans they could do nothing to correct the conditions because this is Spanish territory."[2] The Panamanians, for their part, found their expectations disappointed by the long-awaited ambassadors from Japan. The newspaper of the day noted, "A great crowd gathered eagerly awaiting the Japanese. But they lost interest right away – no doubt they were expecting something different, instead of which they were disenchanted, as the Japanese are nothing but Chinamen, only they appear to be more civilized."[3] Forty years after this encounter, when Japanese contract labor was being used on a large scale in Peru and Mexico, conditions in Panama were considered too bad to send Japanese workers. Although the need for labor in the construction of the Panama Canal would have seemed an ideal opportunity for Japanese contractors, an inspection team from Japan, representing Japanese labor contractors, reported the isthmus was so unsafe that it might endanger the lives of their men.[4] Since Central America and Panama were not deemed attractive areas for organized emigration from Japan, the few Japanese immigrants came on their own.

Shipping was already a high priority sector in the Japanese economy, and the opening of the Panama Canal in 1914 increased the opportunities for expansion. Freight rates became cheaper, although the time taken for shipping goods between Asia and the east coast of the United States was longer than by the ship and rail route. Which route was used depended on the value of the commodity being shipped. For more expensive items, time was of the essence, and so the shorter route was chosen. New trade routes were also created as a result of the canal. In 1917, for example, the OSK line opened a route to carry goods and emigrants to Brazil. It took coal from Natal, South Africa, en route and, for lack of a direct return cargo for Japan, OSK carried Brazilian coffee from Santos to New Orleans, where it was replaced with raw cotton for Japan that went through the canal.[5]

World War II brought a break in the development of closer relations between Japan and Panama. After the bombing of Pearl Harbor, the United States was particularly nervous about the possibilities of an attack on the Panama Canal. Not only was a policy of internment of

Japanese nationals adopted in the United States, but Japanese residents of 12 Latin American countries were also sent to the United States for internment. Those from the five Central America nations and from Panama were transported to New Orleans in March 1942 for detention in Texas.[6]

The Panama Canal regained its importance for Japan after the war, as that country imported vast quantities of raw materials to feed its industrial development. By 1960, two thirds of all the seaborne transport in coal and iron in the world went to Japan. In 1972, 29 percent of all the cargo going through the canal was en route between Japan and the United States; likewise, nearly 11 percent of Japan's oceanborne commerce passed through the Panama Canal. The comparable figures for 1986 were 21 percent of total cargo on the US–Japan route and 5.3 percent of Japan's seaborne trade volume using the canal.[7]

The Panama Canal had traditionally been seen as a concern of the United States. In the 1960s, when the Atlantic–Pacific Interoceanic Canal Studies Commission was conducting studies for a sea-level canal across the isthmus between Mexico and Colombia, the Japanese were consulted and expressed interest in the United States building a new canal. But as the executive director of the commission, Colonel John P. Sheffey, later told Congress: "When we touched on construction money, the attitude was it's a United States problem. . . . Why should we Japanese get involved in this complicated problem of relations with Panama?"[8]

As it became clear that the United States and Panama were entering a new relationship with the Panama Canal Treaties of 1977, however, the Japanese realized that it was in their interest to get involved. They could no longer continue to rely on the United States to keep the canal open and operating efficiently. Soon it would be a Panamanian responsibility, and Japan was interested in promoting actions in Panama to help keep the operation flowing smoothly and to ensure that the canal capacity would meet the need for seaborne transport of goods.

Uninterrupted sea-lanes have always been of enormous concern to Japan, which considers itself a vulnerable country entirely dependent on the import of raw materials for survival. The critical straits from Japan's point of view are the Malacca and Singapore Straits, the Gulf of Hormuz, the Suez Canal, and the Panama Canal. In a 1983 Ministry of Transport study on the contribution of maritime transport policy to comprehensive security, the authors point to the availability of substitute routes as indispensable. If no alternative sea route is available, then a landbridge or pipelines should be developed. The study points out that the Panama and Suez Canals serve the function of providing an alternative route to the other, at least for some commodities.[9] During the time that the Suez Canal was closed, in the late 1960s, Japan-related trade using the Panama Canal increased noticeably. In early 1991, during the Gulf War, Panama Canal transits increased by 10 percent. Japanese cars bound for Europe took the longer Panama route, for example, as a precautionary measure.

In some cases, the study indicated, to secure safe passage it might be necessary to help countries neighboring on the straits to develop hydrographic surveys, charts, and navigation signals. Other means suggested to ensure safe passage included international cooperation with neighboring nations to deter military and political situations that might cause disruption. The general idea was to achieve this goal "through stabilization of the economy and the political situation through friendship with Japan and economic development."[10] Many of Japan's actions in Panama over the last decade or so fit into such a framework and represent an effort to cultivate closer relations, contribute to Panama's economic development, and work in concert with other industrial nations – in this case the United States – to take preventive measures.

THE PANAMA CANAL IN RECENT YEARS

Japan's initial interest in the Panama Canal in the 1970s was in a sea-level canal. This was a time of global trade expansion. It was also a time when Japanese demand for raw materials was still increasing, and the iron and steel industry was one of the hungriest consumers. Not surprisingly, then, Shigeo Nagano, former president of Nippon Steel, the largest steel company in the world, became a key actor in issues pertaining to the canal.

Brazil was always mentioned by Nagano as one of the places from which raw materials would be routed through a new sea-level canal in Panama.[11] Nippon Steel was involved in the huge Carajas iron ore project in Brazil, which has joint financing from Japan, the European Economic Community, and the World Bank. This project must have influenced Nagano's thinking on the need for cheaper transportation to Japan. Other new routes and cargoes mentioned by Nagano and other Japanese spokesmen as candidates to use a new sea-level canal in

Panama were grains from the Brazilian Cerrado project, which the Japanese government and private enterprise developed in an attempt to diversify food sources (particularly soya) away from the United States, and oil from Venezuela. At the end of the 1970s, the Japan International Development Center collaborated with the UN Economic Commission for Latin America on a study of possibilities for economic cooperation between Japan and Latin America, recommending among other things "joint efforts for the introduction of innovations in maritime transport of bulk cargoes, like new ocean transportation routes" and mentioning the second Panama Canal as part of that effort.[12]

One of the participants in the study, Professor Akio Hosono, was to recommend a packet of projects to alleviate geographical distance and fuel costs and to improve the efficiency of ocean and other modes of transport between Japan and Latin America. They included a second Panama Canal, a Pacific Coast port in Mexico, an export corridor project in Brazil, and Asiaport. This last project was to be a very large relay port in southern Japan that would receive large carrier ships from Brazil and transship their contents in smaller vessels to other destinations in Asia.[13]

These huge projects formed part of an elaborate plan developed in 1977 by the president of the Mitsubishi Research Institute, Masaki Nakajima, calling for a Global Infrastructure Fund (GIF). The super projects identified included a canal across the Kra Isthmus in Thailand, which would provide an alternative access route to the Indian Ocean; the construction of a second canal in Panama and one in Nicaragua; a global network of super ports; greening of the deserts; and electricity-generating projects using solar heat, sea currents, and hydro-power.[14]

Among the eminent persons whom Nakajima called on to form a GIF study group in 1981 were Toshio Doko and Saburo Okita, both of whom were important players in having the Panama Canal plan converted into a "national project." Another important player in getting the Panama Canal project off the ground in Japan was Kisaburo Ikeura, president of the Industrial Bank of Japan (IBJ). IBJ occupies a special role in Japanese banking and the economy. It was a government bank until 1950 and still maintains close links with and access to government bureaucrats. IBJ lists as its clients 180 of Japan's 200 largest corporations. From 1975 when Ikeura became president, the watchword in the bank was to push internationalization. IBJ had been active in Panama since 1980, when it participated with the World Bank in financing a multi-million dollar project for developing the Colón Free Zone at the Atlantic end of the canal. In February 1982, a representative office of IBJ was established in Panama – the only others in Latin America being located in Mexico City, São Paulo, and Rio de Janeiro.

By mid-1980 Kisaburo Ikeura was trying to obtain co-financing for the canal project from Japan's Export–Import Bank, the World Bank, and the US government, since the expected $12–13 billion cost was too much for Japanese banks to cover alone.[15] In 1986, when the tripartite Japan–United States–Panama Commission to Study Alternatives to the Panama Canal was finally installed, Ikeura was president of the Japan–Panama Friendship Association and, in that capacity, invited General Manuel Antonio Noriega to visit Tokyo and give a speech before the members of the association on Japan and Panama's mutual interests regarding future alternatives to the canal.

In addition to IBJ's interest in the project to study alternatives to the existing canal, the Japanese were also interested at the time in a project to widen the canal throughout the 9-mile narrow stretch known as Gaillard or Culebra Cut to allow two-way traffic along that stretch for the wide-beam ships that use the canal. In 1987, 20 percent of ships were over 100-foot beam, and it was projected that this would increase to 50 percent within 15–20 years. The fear was that costly waiting times would be incurred unless the widening project was carried out.

It was apparently to discuss this project that General Noriega was invited to Japan in 1986, since he noted in his speech "several sectors in Japan have made known their interest in contributing to the financing and execution of this work [the Cut Widening project]."[16] Panama's president, Eric Arturo Delvalle, later confirmed this to an American journalist, saying "Japan is more than willing to finance the whole thing 100 percent, both the Japanese government and the Industrial Bank, which is very keen on the idea."[17] The decision on this project, however, lay within the purview of the Panama Canal Commission, a US federal agency. Possible Japanese financing of the project seems to have been a sensitive subject. Despite the president's statement, no official overtures were made to Panama Canal Commission officials about Japanese financing of the project.[18]

Many reasons led Japan to favor participation in efforts to upgrade the canal. In addition to providing construction work for Japanese firms on a grand scale, it involved a developing country, which could help Japan gain favor in the Third World. It would help international trade and contribute to the western alliance by increasing the security value of the canal to the United States, a Japanese contribution to burden-sharing. And it was seen as a project that would help the United States and thus improve US–Japan relations. The second Panama Canal project was also used as an example of how Japan could become an economic superpower without substantial military might, through becoming an "aid great power."[19] These national prestige considerations carry considerable weight and should not be underestimated, particularly at a time when Japan was searching for a more active international role, an honored place in the world community, and escape from the characterization of being an "economic giant, political pygmy."[20]

After 3 years of meetings of a Preparatory Committee, from 1982 to 1985, the terms of reference for the Commission to Study Alternatives to the Panama Canal were finally agreed upon by the three governments involved, during a meeting of the United Nations General Assembly. The Study Commission itself was formally installed in Panama City in June 1986, but it advanced very slowly due to delays by the United States in appointing its delegates to the commission. In January 1988, the consortium in which the IBJ was participating was unofficially declared the winner on technical merit of the contract to carry out the feasibility study of the best alternative to the canal and to write the final report for the Study Commission. Other members included the Bechtel Corporation and Stone and Webster Engineering. The initiation of work under the contract was delayed until after US relations with Panama improved following the invasion in December 1989. The terms of reference were modified to allow completion of a first phase by September 1990, when the Commission was to complete its 5-year existence. In May 1990, the Commission was extended for 3 more years to allow for completion of the studies.

JAPANESE AID, TRADE, AND INVESTMENT IN PANAMA

Japan's recent involvement with Panama stems from the 1970s, when private-sector and official attention was drawn to the country as a result of the Canal Treaty negotiations. Japanese economic cooperation with the country shows all the characteristics of strategic aid, as Panama fits into the category of a country with which Japan has a relation of economic interdependence, because of the transit of raw materials and export products through the canal, and could be considered a place critical for world peace and stability. Although Panama could not qualify for Japanese assistance on humanitarian grounds, because its *per capita* income was over $2,000, the other criteria could outweigh that one in some cases.

Panama was one of the first Latin American countries to raise money on the Tokyo capital market, through a yen-bond issue in March 1978. At the end of 1987, Japanese financial institutions held $600 million of Panama's total foreign debt of $4.9 billion, just over 12 percent.[21] This proportion is similar to Japan's overall exposure to Latin American debt.

Technical assistance projects in Panama covered a variety of fields: from cartographic and fishing resource surveys to equipping the National Cancer Institute and upgrading the telecommunications system. Two integrated economic cooperation projects in which the Japan International Cooperation Agency (JICA) has been involved are the establishment of an educational television channel and a vocational training institute. The former gives local exposure to Japanese culture and programs made in Japan, while filling an important gap in the programming of commercial stations. At the Panamanian–Japanese Center, Japanese experts train their counterparts to improve labor skills in electronics, auto mechanics, bodywork, and painting.

The potential spinoffs for Japanese business are high. The vocational project could help Japan to resolve a serious handicap in its sales expansion to Latin America – the distance from service centers. A virtuous circle would be created as the graduates of the program go to work for local companies selling and servicing Japanese goods. In fact several Japanese companies, including Toyota and Sony, chose Panama as their marketing, distribution and service centers for South America. A Mitsui consultant, in a 1988 report to the Ministry of Planning and Economic Policy, suggested that former Albrook Air Field, which reverted to Panama under the Canal Treaties, could be used as a high-tech service center.

Another project in Panama important for Japan's commercial expansion in Latin America is the Colón Free Zone, a tax-free warehousing operation at the Atlantic entrance to the canal. With an annual turnover of goods peaking in 1982 at $4 billion, it claims to be the largest free zone in the world after Hong Kong. Of the goods traded there, 23 percent came from Japan, followed by Taiwan with 15 percent, the United States 11 percent, and Hong Kong 9 percent. Many of the Hong Kong origin goods are made by Japanese-owned companies, so possibly one third of all goods passing through the Colón Free Zone are related to Japanese companies.[22] One purpose of the IBJ–World Bank loan for the development of Colón was to carry out a landfill project to permit expansion of the Colón Free Zone. A Japanese company, Aoki, was awarded the $60 million contract in 1981.[23]

Japanese banks also became active in the international banking center in Panama at the end of the 1970s, coinciding with deregulation in Tokyo of international financial operations and expectations of greater trading links between Japan and North and South America. The Bank of Tokyo set up its Panama operation in 1973. It was followed by Sanwa Bank (1978), the Dai-Ichi Kangyo Bank (1979), the Sumitomo and Mitsui Banks (1980), the Mitsubishi Trust and Banking Corporation (1981), and the Mitsubishi Bank (1983).

There was a rapid build-up of Japanese banks' assets in Panama. By the end of 1984, they amounted to 17 percent of the $38 billion total reported to the National Banking Commission. At that time, Panama's banking center hosted 109 banks from 25 countries. Japanese assets were second only to those of the 12 US banks, whose assets that year amounted to 26 percent of the total (see Table 9.1). By March 1987, Bank of Tokyo assets had increased to $1.8 billion, the Sanwa Bank to $1.5 billion, and the Sumitomo Bank to $1.4 billion. A year later, however, their assets were reduced to a shadow of their former selves as a result of political and economic instability, culminating in a 9-week bank closure from March to May 1988. By early 1990, the only fully-functioning Japanese banks in Panama were the Bank of Tokyo and the Dai-Ichi Kangyo Bank.[24]

Seven of the nine largest Japanese general trading companies, the *sogo shosha*, have offices in Panama, all established since the Mitsubishi Corporation came in 1970. This was the year that Panama passed its modern banking law, which established the ground rules for the international banking center. Mitsui, Sumitomo and C. Itoh followed in 1972, Marubeni in 1973, Kanematsu-Gosho in 1975, and Nissho-Iwai in 1980. An office of the Japan External Trade Organization (JETRO) was also established in 1978 as a regional office to cover Panama and Central America. A director of that office declared that among the reasons Japanese businessmen liked doing business in Panama, in addition to stability and good living conditions, the use of the US dollar and the good airline connections and telecommunications, was that it was a free-flow information center, where it was easier for a Japanese banker to meet with his US counterpart than in New York.[25]

Extraordinary though it may seem, Japan's overseas direct investment in Panama has increased from a mere $112 million in 1977, when

Table 9.1   Assets of US and Japanese banks in the Panama International Banking Center, 1984 (million dollars)

Bank	Assets (12/31/84)
First National Bank of Chicago	$3,651
American Express Bank (Panama) SA	2,531
Chase Manhattan Bank	641
Bank of America NT and SA	632
Citibank NA	586
Citicorp International Bank, SA*	537
Merrill Lynch International Bank	487
Bankers Trust Co., Inc.	241
Republic National Bank of NY, Inc.*	195
Marine Midland Bank, NA	130
First National Bank of Boston	102
Banco de Credito Internacional, SA	4
Total assets in US banks	9,737
Bank of Tokyo, Ltd.	1,330
Sumitomo Bank, Ltd.	1,250
Sanwa Bank, Ltd.	1,043
Dai-Ichi Kangyo Bank	984
Bank of Tokyo (Panama) SA*	686
Mitsubishi Trust and Banking Corp.*	593
Mitsui Bank, Ltd.	380
Mitsubishi Bank (Panama) SA*	39
Total assets in Japanese banks	6,305
Total assets in all banks	37,985

* International license, i.e. for off-shore business only.
Source: Statistics Department, National Banking Commission, Panama.

it was behind Mexico ($171 million), Bermuda ($313 million), Peru ($457 million) and Brazil ($1.8 billion), to $16.2 billion in 1991, third only to Japanese investment in the United States and the United Kingdom. The explanation for this expansion becomes a little clearer by understanding Panama's tax-haven status, the ease of registry of corporations, and open registry for ships. According to the JETRO *White Paper on Foreign Direct Investment* in 1987, "Japanese subsidiaries in Panama are heavily concentrated in the service sector, such as information, finance and securities business, which operate either in free zones or the offshore markets in Panama. Though there are many Japanese paper companies, there is not a single Japanese subsidiary engaged in manufacturing business in Panama."[26] The law that controls Japanese investment abroad defines it as to include both acquisitions by the residents of shares issued by a corporation established under a foreign law, or loans to such corporations, provided such acquisition or loan is done with the objective of establishing a permanent economic relation with the corporation. The fact that overseas investment includes loans could explain why it appears (from Japanese statistics) that Panama does more trade with Japan than do any of the other Latin American countries except Brazil. Trade consists largely of ships, "exported" to Panamanian subsidiaries of Japanese corporations, presumably bought with loans from the parent company, which appear in the overseas investment statistics. Panamanian statistics show a very different pattern of trade (see Table 9.2). In 1990, Japan was Panama's second most important supplier of imports, after the United States, with $75 million, compared with $527 million from the United States. (To these should be added an estimated $30 million worth of Japanese products, imported to Panama through the Colón Free Zone.) Most of the direct imports from Japan were office equipment, vehicles, and car parts. On the other side of the coin, Japanese purchases from Panama in 1990 were worth a mere $2 million, mainly scrap metal. The peak value of Panamanian goods exported to Japan was in 1990; exports in the previous 5 years had averaged only $640,000.

Table 9.2   Two views of Japanese trade with Panama, 1984–90 (million dollars)

	1984	1985	1986	1987	1988	1989	1990
PANAMANIAN STATISTICS							
Exports to Japan	1.0	0.2	0.2	1.8	0.2	0.8	2.0
Imports from Japan	117.9	123.5	108.3	96.1	36.4	41.6	74.8
Balance	−116.9	−123.1	−108.1	−94.3	−36.2	−40.8	−72.8
JAPANESE STATISTICS							
Exports to Japan	166	84	86	71	137	84	113
Imports from Japan	3,453	3,357	3,224	2,440	2,660	2,511	2,902
Balance	−3,287	−3,273	−3,138	−2,369	−2,523	−2,427	−2,789

Source: International Monetary Fund, *Direction of Trade Statistics Yearbook,* 1991.

This dismal imbalance tells its own story of Panama–Japan relations. Between 1983 and 1987, Panama pursued a policy of structural adjustment aimed at increasing exports to help pay the foreign debt, in accordance with World Bank and International Monetary Fund (IMF) prescriptions. Despite the extensive nature of economic and financial links between Panama and Japan existing at the time, Panama was unable to exert any leverage to raise the paltry level of commodity exports to Japan. On the contrary, they declined.

The Panamanian ship registry has expanded greatly, and Japanese-owned ships were responsible for more than 20 percent of the increase between 1978 and 1984, when the total Panama-flag fleet tonnage increased from 27.6 million deadweight tons (dwt) to 62.1 million dwt.[27] Whereas in 1978 Japan had 30 percent of its total open registry under the Panamanian flag, by 1984 that percentage had increased to over 55 percent, indicating a marked preference for the Panama registry over the many competitors (Table 9.3). These data are confirmed by the growing importance of Panamanian consulates in Japan as sources of consular revenue for Panama. Whereas in 1979 they produced 12 percent of total consular revenue, by 1983 they produced 31 percent of the total. Total income to the Panama government from ship registry and other consular activities is around $45 million.[28] Business generated for private-sector lawyers and accountants could be at a similar level.

Table 9.3   Use of the Panamanian flag for shipping registry, 1978–1984 in Panama

	% in Panama	
	1978 (%)	*1984 (%)*
Total open registry tonnage	14	31
Total open registry ships	35	60
Japanese open registry tonnage	30	55
Japanese open registry ships	63	83
US open registry tonnage	10	15
US open registry ships	26	43

Source: Author's calculations from UNCTAD, *Review of Maritime Transport*, 1979 and 1986.

The ship registry business was one of the few areas of the economy not originally affected by the recent political and economic crisis in Panama. That changed in early December 1989, when the US government announced that Panama-flag ships would not be allowed to enter US ports after February 1, 1990. The order was rescinded, however, after the invasion of Panama by US troops on December 20, 1989. For other sectors, the panorama changed radically during the 1987–89 crisis. By February 1989, only two Japanese banks were offering complete services. An estimated half of the Japanese community had left, and all economic cooperation projects in the pipeline were on hold. Even the JETRO office was closed and moved to Costa Rica, indicating a lack of faith in a short to medium-term return to stability.

The Japanese reaction to the crisis gives some indication of the nature of Japan's interests in Panama. While Panama is a useful and convenient place to do business, it is by no means indispensable, as some Panamanians like to think. Nor does the Japanese reaction give much credence to the hypothesis that Japan is attempting to oust the United States in this part of the world. Japan's expectations of stability in Panama, compared with the rest of the Central American region, were related to the high US presence in the country. When, despite that presence, the United States was not able to take action to maintain that stability (it could be argued that its actions made the situation worse), the Japanese were in no position to challenge the United States, or to take independent action to guarantee their interests. As a Washington lobbyist for Japanese companies put it, "the United States gave the Japanese the signal that Noriega was the man to deal with; then they pulled the rug out from under him, and the Japanese were left stranded."[29] Thus, despite the efforts made to implement a comprehensive security policy in order to ensure Japanese interests independently, the crisis indicated that Japan has to follow the lead of the United States in Central America, even though it may not agree with US policy.

POLITICAL RELATIONS AND PROSPECTS FOR THE FUTURE

US policy towards Central and South America is dominated by security considerations, and Panama is no exception to that rule. Japan has not always shared the perceptions of its principal ally regarding the nature of threats to US security, whether directly from the former Soviet Union or in the Third World. In the Central American region and Panama, it should be pointed out that for the United States the complexities are uncomfortably close to home and full of historic intimacy, while for Japan they are physically remote and historically unfamiliar. The United States continues to be Japan's prime reference for policy in Latin America, so much so that personnel in the Japanese Embassy in Washington are assigned exclusively to the task of following US policy in the region. The Vice-Minister of Foreign Affairs of Japan told an audience in Boston, in February 1988, "we share the view that the economic stability and development of Latin American countries are crucial to the United States economy and security, and hence to the interest of Japan."[30]

Nevertheless, as discussed in Chapter 3 of this volume, Japan does not always conform without question to the dictates of US foreign policy. Japanese companies continued to trade with Sandinista Nicaragua and Castro's Cuba, despite commercial embargoes placed by the United States. When the Central American peace plan was signed in Guatemala (the Esquipulas Accords) in August 1987, Japan was among the first governments to hail this breakthrough as a hopeful indication for a negotiated peaceful settlement, whereas the United States was wary of the process.

For Japan, there was little problem in the area of political relations with Panama until the unrest that began to develop in the country in June 1987. Critical choices had to be made when President Eric Arturo Delvalle was ousted in March 1988 and Manuel Solís Palma became Minister-in-Charge of the Presidency. The United States continued to recognize Delvalle, referring to the Panamanian government as the Noriega/Solís Palma regime, and brought pressure to bear on several allied governments to prevent them from recognizing the new president.

There was considerable protest in Congress and the US administration at the news that Japan saw no problem in dealing with an administration headed by Solís Palma. The Japanese government backed off and formally recognized the Solís Palma government only in June 1988, after the Federal Republic of Germany had done so and once some bilateral trade negotiations with the United States had been resolved (see Chapter 3, in this volume). This does not mean that the Japanese government had a greater degree of moral approval of the Noriega/Solís Palma government than the United States, but Japanese government policy is to recognize those in effective control, considering the issue of who controls the government of a country to be an internal affair.

Another critical moment came in May 1989, after the opposition claimed victory in the elections, their leaders were defeated, and the elections declared null and void. The Japanese Foreign Ministry issued a communiqué that the Panamanian opposition distributed freely, though it was not published in its entirety in the government-controlled press. While the Ministry of Foreign Affairs attempted to move through this diplomatic minefield, private-sector interests voted with their feet, reducing further Japanese commercial activity in the country. Later that year, Japan's quick recognition of the new government, sworn in a few hours before the US invasion, was attributed to Japan's "global partnership" with the United States.

Under what conditions would Japanese private investment and funds be likely to return to Panama? As expressed by the manager of a Japanese bank in Panama in 1988, there would have to be an agreement between the United States and Panama. That agreement would have to be backed up by bilateral government aid, and the renewal of aid from multilateral institutions like the World Bank, the IMF and the Interamerican Development Bank (IDB). Only then would the climate be right for the return of the private sector.[31] Several months after the US invasion of Panama, and the electoral victory by the opposition in Nicaragua in February 1990, Japan began to send economic missions to those countries to see how it could help the so-called fledgling democracies. Also, in 1992, it made a substantial commitment to the economic reconstruction of El Salvador in accordance with the Global Partnership Plan of Action signed between the United States and Japan during President Bush's trip to Tokyo in 1992.

Japan's strategy with respect to Panama has evolved over the last few years. One declared Japanese vision of Panama, as the site of a sea-level canal linked with super ports in Brazil and Japan, has been overtaken by events: the economic/commercial rationale for such a combination does not appear to be present any more. With the trend in the Japanese economy to "the light, the thin, the short and the small," which expresses itself concretely in a decrease in raw materials input per unit of output, Japan's demand for raw materials will grow more slowly than the overall economy.

In the most recent studies of traffic demand for the Panama Canal, admittedly for the existing lock-limited canal, market research findings indicated that Brazil/Argentina to Japan/Far East grain is a future trade potential, but probably bypassing the canal; Brazil/Far East steel is a growing trade but mostly moves via South Africa; Japan will begin to take Colombian coal in large ships via South Africa; and Japanese automobile shipments to the east coast of the United States through the canal will decrease. Overall, cargo using the canal is not expected to grow at more than 1.6 percent per annum through the year 2010, and ship transits at 0.6 percent, as the average ship size will increase.[32]

A second vision linked Panama to Pacific Basin development. According to this view, Panama would play an important role in the Pacific era as the link of greatest importance between the Pacific and Atlantic Basins. This would require some adaptation, such as expansion and diversification of trade and greater sophistication in transport and financial services. These factors would require modernization of the physical infrastructure of the canal and related facilities, such as the Colón Free Zone, and of Panama's financial infrastructure.[33] Japanese commercial and economic interests in Panama certainly appeared to fit in with this scenario for Panama, but they received a rude shock with the development of the Panamanian political and economic crisis, culminating in the invasion and ensuing lack of national direction. The crisis disrupted the free flow of goods, money, people, and information for which Panama was famous.

A third interpretation of Japan's activities in Panama is as a hedging strategy. Though it is not clear how things will develop, the geographic location of the isthmus means it will continue to be an important crossroads, and it makes sense for Japan, with a domestic economy still dependent on foreign trade and long maritime transport links, to take part in the decision-making over future transport modes across this narrow neck of land between the Atlantic and Pacific Oceans. Moreover, Japan has assumed the position that it has an international responsibility regarding the Panama Canal. Japan is currently one of the main users of the canal and, while in the future the canal may be less important for Japan, it has to become a good international citizen and contribute to solutions, precisely because the canal provides an international public service.

Discussions of the prospects for a new canal in Panama cannot omit consideration of the joint Nicaragua–Japan studies for a canal, announced publicly in March 1989. While the Japanese government declared its commitment to the Panama studies, indicating that those involved in the Nicaragua project were from the private sector, this did not mean that the results would not be available to the government. Carrying out studies in Nicaragua was consistent with a risk-spreading and hedging strategy by Japan, promoting diversification of alternatives. This would not be the first time that canal alternatives in Nicaragua and Panama have been played off against one another by external actors, in an attempt by one to bring pressure on the other. It could also represent an attempt by Japan, using the private sector as the spearhead, to test the waters of taking action which, while not antagonistic to the United States, was unlikely to meet with its official approval.

It appeared that prospects for bilateral cooperation between Japan and the United States in providing strategic aid to Central America, or other countries in Latin America, might have been altered by the negative experience in Panama. At the same time, however, the crisis in Panama showed beyond a doubt that the Japanese government does not enjoy sufficient freedom of action in this part of the world to take an independent stance. The United States expects a certain amount of deference and receives it. It seems quite clear also that Japan is not seeking to usurp or replace the US role in the Central American region. Those people in Panama who view Japan as an alternative to the United States fail to see Japan's true intentions in this part of the world – to protect its commerce and to attempt to please the United States.

Notes

1. Masakiyo Yanagawa, *The First Japanese Mission to America* (1860). English translation reprint (Wilmington: Scholarly Resources, Inc. Wilmington, Delaware, 1973) p. 35.
2. Ibid., p. 34.
3. Juan Antonio Susto, "Los japoneses visitan al Istmo de Panamá por primera vez, en 1860," *Lotería*, 6, 66 (May 1961) p. 19.
4. David McCullough, *Path Between the Seas: The Creation of the Panama Canal 1870–1914* (New York: Simon & Schuster, 1977) p. 473.
5. William D. Wray, *Mitsubishi and the NYK 1870–1914: Business Strategy in the Japanese Shipping Industry* (Cambridge, MA: Harvard University Press, 1984).
6. C. Harvey Gardiner, "The Japanese and Central America," *Journal of Interamerican Studies and World Affairs*, 14, 1 (February 1972) p. 22.
7. The 29 percent figure was calculated from the Panama Canal Company, Canal Zone Government, *Annual Report*, fiscal year ending June 30, 1972, tables 21–22. The 11 percent figure is cited in Norman J. Padelford and Stephen R. Gibbs, *Maritime Commerce and the Future of the Panama Canal* (Cambridge, MA: Cornell Maritime Press, Inc., 1975) p. 72. The

1986 figures come from the Panama Canal Commission, *Annual Report 1987* and tables prepared by the Office of Executive Planning.

8. US Congress, House of Representatives, Committee on Merchant Marine and Fisheries, Subcommittee of the Panama Canal and Outer Continental Shelf, *Hearings on the Sea-level Canal Studies*, 95th Congress, 2nd Session, June 1978, p. 312.

9. Japan, Ministry of Transport, Transport Policy Council Subcommittee on Comprehensive Security, *Sōgō anzen hoshō ni kakawaru unyu seisaku no arikata: kokusai kyōchō no suishin to unyu no kakuho* (The Direction of Transportation Policy Relative to Comprehensive Security: Promotion of International Cooperation and Maintenance of Transport) (Tokyo: February 14, 1983) p. 23.

10. Ibid., p. 25.

11. Interview with Fernando Manfredo Jr., Deputy Administrator of the Panama Canal Commission, Panama, May 13, 1989.

12. UN Economic Comission for Latin America, *Towards New Forms of Economic Cooperation Between Latin America and Japan* (Santiago: CEPAL, 1980) pp. 57, 169.

13. Akio Hosono, "Japan and Latin America," in Robert S. Ozaki and Walter Arnold, (eds.), *Japan's Foreign Relations: A Global Search for Economic Security* (Boulder, CO: Westview Press, 1985) p. 222.

14. Masaki Nakajima, "Towards Globalism," *Research Review* (Mitsubishi Research Institute), 1, 1 (August 1986) pp. 4–5.

15. Stephen Bronte, "Ikeura's international way with IBJ," *Euromoney* (August 1980) p. 40.

16. General Manuel Antonio Noriega, "Los intereses mútuos de Panamá y Japón y las alternativas del futuro canalero," speech given before the Japan–Panama Friendship Association in Tokyo, December 12, 1986.

17. Allan Dodds Frank, "Everyone Wants Us," *Forbes*, February 23, 1987, p. 37.

18. Statement by Fernando Manfredo Jr., Deputy Administrator of the Panama Canal Commission, in response to questions in CADE 87, a business-sponsored conference on"The Canal in the Year 2000," Panama, April 27, 1987. In 1991, the Panama Canal Commission Board of Directors approved implementation of the Cut Widening project, to be completed after the year 2000, using internally-generated financial resources.

19. Dennis Yasutomo, *The Manner of Giving: Strategic Aid and Japanese Foreign Policy* (Lexington, MA: Lexington Books, 1986) p. 24.

20. Edwin O. Reischauer, "Can Japan Stay an Economic Giant but a Political Pygmy?," *Harvard International Review* X, No. 4 (April–May 1988) p. 27.

21. *Nihon Keizai Shimbun*, March 10, 1988.

22. Data provided by the Statistics Department, Colón Free Zone.

23. Aoki Corporation, *Annual Report*, 1982. The president of the Aoki Corporation, Hiryoshi Aoki, is the Director-General of the Japan–Panama Friendship Association. He invited General Noriega to be the guest of honor at his daughter's wedding during Noriega's trip to Japan in December 1986.

24. Data provided by the Statistics Department, National Banking Commission, Panama.
25. Interview with Hiroshi Yamada, Director JETRO-Panama, Panama City, June 1986.
26. JETRO, *Hakusho tōshihen 1987: sekai to Nihon no kaigai chokusetsu tōshi* (White Paper on Foreign Direct Investment, 1987) (Tokyo: JETRO, 1987) pp. 82–84
27. UNCTAD, *Review of Maritime Transport*, 1978 and 1984.
28. Figures from the annual reports of the Panama Contraloría General de la República, various years.
29. Personal communication, Washington, DC, May 1988.
30. Hiroshi Kitamura, Japan Deputy Minister of Foreign Affairs, "The Growing Role of Japan in the World," speech given before the Japan Society of Boston, February 24, 1988.
31. Interview, Panama City, August 1988. The banker's expectations were that such a recovery would be at least 3 to 5 years in the future. In March 1992, the Japanese representative of Citizen Corporation in Panama was kidnapped and assassinated, further delaying a return of private-sector confidence in the country.
32. Temple, Barker & Sloane, Inc., "Traffic Demand Forecast," study prepared for Panama Canal Commission, 1989.
33. Akio Hosono, "Planificación y desarrollo a la luz de la experiencia japonesa," *Suplemento Embajada del Japón* (Panama, April 29, 1986).

Index